Barrio Boy

Barrio Boy

40th Anniversary Edition

ERNESTO GALARZA

Introduction by Ilan Stavans

University of Notre Dame Press

Notre Dame, Indiana

This work was originally produced through the
United States–Mexico Border Studies Project at
the University of Notre Dame, under the direction
of Julian Samora, and sponsored by a grant from
the Ford Foundation.

Library of Congress Cataloging-in-Publication Data

Galarza, Ernesto, 1905–1984.
Barrio boy / Ernesto Galarza ; introduction by Ilan Stavans. —
40th anniversary ed.
p. cm.
ISBN-13: 978-0-268-02979-1 (paper : alk. paper)
ISBN-10: 0-268-02979-2 (paper : alk. paper)
1. Galarza, Ernesto, 1905–1984. 2. Galarza, Ernesto,
1905–1984—Childhood and youth. 3. Mexican Americans—
Biography. 4. Immigrants—United States—Biography.
5. Mexican Americans—Social life and customs—20th
century. 6. Mexican American neighborhoods—California—
Sacramento—History—20th century. 7. Sacramento (Calif.)—
Social life and customs—20th century. 8. Sacramento
(Calif.)—Biography. 9. Nayarit (Mexico)—Biography. I. Title.
E184.M5G3 2011
305.8968'72073—dc22
2010031797

∞ *The paper in this book meets the guidelines for permanence
and durability of the Committee on Production Guidelines
for Book Longevity of the Council on Library Resources*

In Memory of

DOÑA ESTHER

DOÑA HENRIQUETA

DON GUSTAVO

AND

DON JOSÉ

the caretakers of the barrio boy

Contents

Introduction to the 40th Anniversary Edition

ILAN STAVANS

*All sins have their origin in a sense of
inferiority otherwise called ambition.*
—CESARE PAVESE

AT THE OUTSET of *Barrio Boy*, Ernesto Galarza, sixty-six years old when the book was published, explains the volume's humble beginning. It started as a series of "thumbnail sketches" he repeatedly told his family about Jalcocotán (*aka* Jalco), the idyllic small village on the Sierra Madre, south of where the Gulf of California meets the Pacific Ocean, where he was born. For years those sketches enchanted those who listened. Then Galarza retold them in a gathering of scholars. The response was equally enthusiastic, to the point that he was encouraged to shape them into a book-length manuscript about his acculturation as a Mexican boy in California at the dawn of the twentieth century.

Passionate as he was about writing—although until then, most of what he had published was scholarly in nature—he nurtured some reservations. Throughout his life, Galarza had fought against economic individualism and for the improvement of labor relations, specifically among Mexican agricultural workers in the Southwest.

For a while he worked as the principal in a progressive school. He was a researcher for the Pan-American Union (the forerunner of the Organization of American States), a job that placed him at the center of more than one political storm in Washington, D.C. And he devoted his energy to building unions and establishing broader, more inclusive school curricula. In other words, the format of a memoir was a strategy to bring attention to himself, something he wasn't prone to do, at least not in front of a large public.

It is important to recognize that at the time, the genre of autobiography was beginning to have some traction in Latino intellectual circles. A number of memoirs had appeared by state governors, such as Miguel Antonio Otero, Jr. (*My Nine Years as Governor of the Territory of New Mexico, 1897–1906*), or outlaws such as Andrew García (*Tough Trip through Paradise, 1878–1879*). Later, Puerto Ricans, from the activists Jesús Colón (*A Puerto Rican in New York and Other Sketches*) and Bernardo Vega (*Memoirs of Bernardo Vega*) to doctor and poet William Carlos Williams (*Autobiography of William Carlos Williams*), delved into autobiography to explore their personal, social, ideological, and aesthetic loyalties. However, the Civil Rights era encouraged different viewpoints, and authors such as Piri Thomas (*Down These Mean Streets*), John Rechy (*City of Night*), and Oscar "Zeta" Acosta (*The Autobiography of a Brown Buffalo* and *The Revolt of the Cockroach People*) opened up the genre somewhat.

Galarza justified the endeavor, as he states at the beginning of the book, by coming up with a couple of clear-cut purposes he wanted to accomplish in *Barrio Boy*. The first, historical one is that he perceived his path not strictly in individual terms but as a Platonic universal, his odyssey a boilerplate that millions of other immigrants, Mexicans and otherwise, constantly replicated as they abandoned their places of origin somewhere in the so-called Third World in search of betterment. He was also conscious that, roughly until World War II, the majority of immigrants to the United States had come from Europe, and after the war they came from Mexico and other parts of the Spanish- and Portuguese-speaking Americas, the Caribbean, Africa, Oceania, and Asia. His story was theirs, too. By calling attention to his own plight, Galarza could amplify our understanding of the inner struggle a non-European newcomer faced upon arrival.

The second reason he describes—and, in my mind, the true force behind *Barrio Boy*—was psychological, and here Galarza's reservations about writing a memoir became incentives. He wanted to prove that *el complejo de inferioridad*, the inferiority complex from which Mexicans in the United States supposedly suffer, is nonsense. "The worst thing that has happened," he wrote, "is that some psychologists, psychiatrists, social anthropologists and other manner of 'shrinks' have spread the rumor that . . . Mexican immigrants and their offspring have lost their 'self-image.' By this, of course, they mean that a Mexican doesn't know what he is; and if by chance he is something, it isn't any good." Galarza quickly and forcefully responded to this allegation: "I, for one Mexican, never had any doubts on this score. I can't remember a time I didn't know who I was; and I have heard much testimony from my friends and other more detached persons to the effect that I thought too highly of what I thought I was." His complaint was not minor; nor was it targeted toward Anglo professionals with dubious knowledge of the Mexican psyche. Galarza was quietly referring to the Mexican intelligentsia who actively spread the notion of an inferiority complex.

The year in which *Barrio Boy* was released, 1971, is of the essence to understanding Galarza's reaction.

Roughly a decade before, a series of English translations of prominent sociohistorical and psychological studies of Mexicans at home and abroad had appeared, among them Samuel Ramos's *Profile of Man and Culture in Mexico*. Ramos offered a psychoanalytic interpretation of the nation's *Weltanschauung*, suggesting that since the time of the Spanish conquest a spirit of imitation of European modes had generated a feeling of unworthiness among Mexicans. Another was Octavio Paz's *The Labyrinth of Solitude*, which, in its first chapter, "The *Pachuco* and Other Extremes" (written after Paz spent time in Los Angeles on a Guggenheim Fellowship), discusses *pachuco* in particular, meaning the "variations" of Mexicanness filtered through the prism of acculturation to Anglo patterns of behavior. Knowing about the process of acculturation firsthand allowed Galarza to resist the easy categorization. His memoir was shaped accordingly. He added: "It seems to me unlikely that out of six or seven million Mexicans in the United States I was the only one who felt this way. In any event, those I knew and remember and tell about had an abundance of self-image and never doubted that it was a good one." Of course, the risk he was taking was large. He could have ended up producing not a wrenching narrative about the interior life of a boy but a programmatic treatise. Fortunately, Galarza's memoir still feels fresh four decades after the original publication.

Divided into five parts, it covers approximately thirteen years in Galarza's life. Roughly half of them take place in Jalco (he was born in 1905), and the other half, moving at a faster speed, cover his uprootedness in 1911, when some members of the family abandoned Jalco as a result of the Mexican Revolution, their northbound transit across the border, their arrival in Sacramento, California, their sink-or-swim transition into a culturally different environment, and his employment as a young farmhand. Coherently, only the first part of the book deals with Jalco, whereas the other four parts span a total of seven years, the span of time in which Galarza believes his transformation from a *mexicano* to a Mexican American took place.

Everything is seen from a child's perspective. Galarza portrays himself as a naïve yet curious child, passionate and full of humor, using the child's perspective as his unifying structure. The departure from his village is seen as banishment. "[It] was for the most part an easy place in which to live. The neighbors and *compadres* and *comadres* who scolded you for your bad manners or sent you on errands did not interfere much if you were respectful and stayed out of the way." There are enchanting scenes where he is taught how to roast *pinole*, brew *atole*, steam tamales, and barbecue bananas, which are used to show the passing of knowledge from mother to child in a rural setting. Or, the boy explains how people in Jalco speak in two languages, Spanish and with gestures, offering a catalogue of specific gestures used in the town ("if you bent one arm and tapped the elbow with the other hand, it meant "He is stingy") and describing the secret sign language that he and another child developed. *Barrio Boy* is imbued with this sort of enchanting detail.

But, again, it is the aftermath of the departure from Jalco that gives the narrative its traction. The child is made aware that peasants are up in arms against dictator Porfirio Díaz. In response, Díaz's special mounted police, *los rurales*, terrorize everyone. The boy doesn't know what kind of transformation is sweeping his family away as Mexico descends into a civil war. Galarza and his relatives seek refuge in nearby Tepic, the capital of the state of Nayarit. In Tepic he comes face to face with the real world as it is: unfair, anarchic, violent. Although he still appreciates the beautiful colors displayed on a *mercado*, for instance, all in all he is frightened; and fright gives way to disorientation as the boy slowly realizes that his village was an oasis. Among the things that most shake him is the abysmal division between the haves and have-nots. Galarza offers this description:

> Close about the plaza and the cathedral were the townhouses that intrigued me greatly. These were the homes of the rich, *los ricos*. The high front walls were neatly painted brown, grey, pink, or light cream. The street windows were even with the sidewalk with long iron bars that reached almost to the roof. Lace curtains, drapes, and wooden screens behind the bars kept people from looking in. Every townhouse had a *zaguán* and a driveway cutting across the sidewalk, ramped and grooved so that carriages could roll in and out. . . .
>
> By quick looks through the *zaguanes*, since my mother would not let me stop and stare, I began to have some idea of how *los ricos* lived. They rode in carriages directly into their houses. Servants opened and closed the grill and led the horses to the stable in a back patio. The *mandado* was always brought from the market by kitchen maids and cooks. The ladies and gentlemen had barbers and hairdressers come to their homes. Seamstresses and menders made deliveries to a servant at the *cancel*, not being allowed beyond that point. The bright patios, sometimes filled with the singing of canaries and warblers and the screeching of parakeets, settled in my mind another difference between people—those who lived in these *casas solariegas* and those who lived in *vecindades*. People who had townhouses and horses and carriages called themselves the *gente decente* of Tepic.

Ultimately, these impressions on class would play a major role in Galarza's career as activist and educator, defining his ideological stand in favor of workers on the international stage.

Like any other autobiography, *Barrio Boy* is about the self establishing its boundaries in the universe, finding its parameters. The narrative is packaged as a series of connected facts organized to persuade the reader that life is coherent, sequential, and meaningful. Obviously, life itself is anything but: it is messy, hectic, empty of any rationale. We, who live it, inject it with a purpose. Fittingly, Galarza opens with an epigraph from *The Education of Henry Adams:* "This was the journey he remembered. The actual journey may have been quite different. . . . The memory was all that mattered." Memory, indeed, is what makes the journey worth the effort.

The fourth part is called "Life in the Lower Part of Town," and it rotates around Galarza's view of the *barrio* as a new village. It is symbolic that the word *barrio* is constantly italicized: in his eyes the place itself, like the Spanish word for it, is Mexican, although little in it is actually *mexicano*. He comes across people of Italian, Portuguese, Filipino, Dutch, and other ethnic backgrounds, and Mexicans from Chihuahua, Sonora, Jalisco, and Durango. He makes the distinction between the physical place itself—the *barrio*—and the *colonia*, the community of Mexicans that live in it. In the *colonia* he first comes across the word for what he himself will one day become: a *chicano*. (Yes, he italicized this word as well.) Galarza uses the word to describe unskilled workers, who, like his family, were born in Mexico and just arrived in the United States:

> The *chicanos* were fond of identifying themselves by saying they had just arrived from *el macizo*, by

which they meant the solid Mexican homeland, the good native earth. Although they spoke of *el macizo* like homesick persons, they didn't go back. They remained, as they said of themselves, *pura raza*.

In the barrio, the boy's horizons expand. His family grows in number (he talks of two sisters and a brother). He witnesses a folk-healing scene of *curandería*, finds a job as a messenger at Western Union, then works in the field and gets his first try at negotiating with the *autoridades*, goes to dances, and is accepted into a music band at the Y.M.C.A.

In the concluding pages, the reader finds him working in agricultural camps. He loves music, books, and people. In fact, the last scene portrays Galarza on a bicycle headed for high school, inspired by a teacher, Mr. Everett. Might he make it to the debate team? he wonders. The story of his origins is thus complete, but the story after the story is just as compelling. Encouraged by a handful of adults he came across in high school, Galarza attended Occidental College on a scholarship. (His papers are archived at the College Library, where a room is named after him.) He spent his senior year in Mexico. After the armed struggle that forced his family to leave, Mexico sank into another war from 1926 to 1929, called *La Cristiada*, in which the government set out to persecute Catholic priests. (Graham Greene wrote about it in his novel *The Power and the Glory*.) Witnessing the debacle, Galarza researched the role of the Catholic Church in the nation's political and social fabric. This became the topic of his senior thesis, which was published in book form (*The Roman Catholic Church as a Factor in the Political and Social History of Mexico*) in 1928, shortly after his graduation.

He then received a master's degree from Stanford in history and political science and later completed his doctorate at Columbia in economics. His dissertation was released by Mexico's premier public publishing house, Fondo de Cultura Económica, as *La industria eléctrica en México*, in 1941. From 1932 to 1936, before he completed the doctorate, Galarza and his wife (Mae Taylor, whom he married in 1929 and with whom he had two daughters, Karla and Eli Lu) worked as principals, and subsequently as owners, of the Gardner School, an experimental private school in Jamaica, Long Island. Many of the pedagogical ideas he sought to implement later on started there. Then he was hired by the Pan-American Union as chief of the Division of Labor and Social Information. His task was to research labor disputes in Latin America. World War II was in progress. The fight against fascism was an imperative, followed closely by antagonism toward any form of communism. Galarza felt that good diplomatic relations between the United States and Latin America, although not a priority on the global map, were instrumental for a healthy future. The recruitment of millions of soldiers into the U.S. army led to a desperate need for cheap labor at home, which resulted in the creation, in August 1942, of the Bracero Program, designed to offer contracts to temporary Mexican workers employed in agricultural labor throughout the Southwest.

Convinced that it was unfair and exploitative, Galarza distrusted the program. An example of his stance and of the type of research in which he engaged at the Pan-American Union is the pamphlet *Labor in Latin America*, released in 1942 under the aegis of the American Council on Public Affairs. Here Galarza states that "the workers of Latin America have long been in the front line trenches of democracy. Their present solidarity with the workers of the United States, their support of the United Nations, their efforts on behalf of greater inter-American cooperation express long-held attitudes and convictions." In particular, he believed that maladjustment in Mexico impacted labor relations across the border. Thus, he argued, "The time has come for the creation of a joint international agency, composed of representatives of the United States and Mexico, to develop and carry out a long-term program of resettlement, rehabilitation and regulation of migration between the new republics." In other words, Galarza, based on his own experience in labor camps that are chronicled in *Barrio Boy*, wanted a replacement for the Bracero Program that was fair and egalitarian.

It was a Quixotic dream, yet it validated a lifetime of progressive thinking. As scholars Rudolfo Acuña and Richard Chabran have argued in their discussion of Galarza's achievements,* he often antagonized the U.S. State Department by proving that American companies were in cahoots with powerful business interests in the countries he studied, Bolivia among them, in order to keep their profit margins high. His report caused an uproar in Washington, D.C. He resigned but was asked to return to the Pan-American Union. *Harper's Magazine* offered him a contract to write a piece on the scandal. Once he submitted it, the piece was turned down. Yet Galarza did not give in to defeat. He spent the next two decades as an activist, as well as a relentless historian of Mexican labor in the Southwest. He was recruited by the National Farm Labor Union (later called the National Agricultural Workers Union, or NAWU), which prompted him

---

*See Rudolfo Acuña, *Occupied America: The Chicano's Struggle Toward Liberation* (San Francisco: Canfield Press, 1972); and Richard Chabran, "Activism and Intellectual Struggle in the Life of Ernesto Galarza (1905–1984)," *Hispanic Journal of Behavioral Sciences*, vol. 7, no. 2 (1985): 135–52.

to move to San Jose, and was involved in strikes against the Di Gregorio Fruit Corporation in Arvin, California, a tomato strike in Tracy, and a strike of cantaloupe pickers in Imperial City.

In 1974, Galarza was interviewed about a research project on which he had embarked in Alviso, a predominantly Mexican town on the southern tip of San Francisco Bay. The place was undergoing radical change as a result of the rapid growth of a nearby urban center, which made the site attractive to private and public interests and resulted in a gentrification that fractured the cohesion of the Mexican population. He witnessed how, in 1969, a health clinic started by the Ford Foundation expanded with a federal grant from the Office of Economic Opportunity. Soon the clinic was the town's major employer. The clinic concentrated power in a handful of people and decimated other employing entities. Galarza was asked what he could do to preserve the *barrio*. He responded, with pain evident in his words (included in the booklet *Action Research: In Defense of the Barrio*):

> Whenever you get into a study project of this sort you're in the presence of major forces, and you can't see what those forces are unless you're in action. But the preservation of a barrio is not the ultimate answer to anything. It's the same sort of thing you get when people talk about preserving a way of life. It's a pretty meaningless phrase. It doesn't tell you anything about what's going on in the present world today. Now there are always sentimental reasons for wanting to help people not lose their homes. These are powerful feelings but they don't give you much of an intellectual idea of what's going on.

His response is essential to understanding Galarza's character. He fought for the improvement of the conditions of Mexican labor. But he was a no-nonsense thinker, who realized the speed with which social mores are transformed. The picture he offers in *Barrio Boy* of the *barrio* as a place of encounter with other ethnic groups belongs to the past: the new American city is built as a galaxy of suburbs, and the immigrant's place of landing did not have the permanence in the 1970s that he had encountered in the 1920s.

During the 1950s, Galarza was a constant presence in congressional hearings, accusing the Bracero Program of bias. He even wrote another pamphlet, *Strangers in the Field* (1956), that became a cause célèbre and brought a grant of $25,000 to the NAWU to develop organizing strategies in order to help Mexican labor. Galarza's involvement led to three ground-breaking volumes: *Merchants of Labor: The Mexican Bracero Story* (1964), *Spiders in the House and Workers in the Field* (1970), and *Farm Workers and Agri-Business in California, 1947–1960* (1977). Anyone interested in the forces that led to the labor-organizing efforts of Cesar Chavez and other Chicano leaders of the United Farm Workers Union (a stepchild of NAWU) must start with these studies, produced during the years that Galarza was gradually moving from activism to college-level teaching and research as his *raison d'être*. He was on the faculty at various universities, including San Jose State University, the Universities of California at San Diego and Santa Cruz, and the University of Notre Dame.

The many black-and-white photographs he took of Mexican Americans, especially in his later years, are emblematic of Galarza's commitment to record Mexican-American culture in all its manifestations. The Chicano Movement, with figures such as Chavez, Dolores Huerta, Reies López Tijerina, Rodolfo "Corky" Gonzáles, Oscar "Zeta" Acosta, and Rubén Salazar, was a cathartic moment in the history of the United States. While the Civil Rights era was—and still is—perceived as an effort for equal opportunity for blacks, a fundamental role was also played by Mexican Americans, Puerto Ricans, and Filipinos. Although Galarza was older than most Chicanos active in *El Movimiento*, through his work at the Pan-American Union and NAWU he had been at the heart of the struggle for self-emancipation. In his writings he seldom uses terms like *Chicanismo*, but it is tangible in his tone that he regards himself simultaneously as a witness of, and a participant in, the dramatic changes the nation was undergoing. His photographs are the primary instrument for another pursuit that Galarza developed in his later years: the production of a series of children's books that he himself funded. Released in the early 1970s and published by Editorial Almadén, as a group these were called *Colección Mini-Libros*, including *Aquí y allá en California, Un poco de México,* and *Poems, pe-que, pe-que, pe-que-ñitos*. At a time when the children's book industry almost totally ignored Mexican Americans, these volumes were designed to promote literacy among young Spanish-speaking and bilingual readers.

At Notre Dame, Galarza met and forged a strong friendship with Julián Samora, a professor of sociology from 1959 to 1985 and a pioneer in Mexican-American Studies who specialized in immigration, civil rights, public health, and rural poverty among Latinos. Samora was the author of *Los Mojados: The Wetback Story* and co-author of *The History of the Mexican-American People* and *Gunpowder Justice: A Reassessment of the Texas Rangers,* among other works. (In 1990, Samora received the Águila Azteca medal from the Mexican government, along with Cesar Chavez.) Together with Samora and Hernán Gallegos, who was executive director of the Southwest Council of La Raza, Galarza published a history of Mexican

Americans in 1970 that includes scores of photographs; while he had always enjoying taking photographs, only in his last decade (he died in 1984) did he take the hobby seriously. In any case, it was his Notre Dame colleague who motivated him, in the scholarly conference I mentioned at the start of this introduction, to turn Galarza's family anecdotes about Jalco and Sacramento into a book. When *Barrio Boy* was finished, Samora released it in his series "United States–Mexico Border Studies Project" with the University of Notre Dame Press. Samora described it as fitting the profile of "Chicanos who have lived through and survived the acculturative process," and "who appreciate the numerous obstacles to, and the struggle for, self-identity in a strange culture, while resisting complete 'Americanization.'"

Samora's statement is thought-provoking. Among other things, it begs for a comparison of acculturation with Americanization. Are they one and the same? Or does the boy undergo acculturation but reject Americanization, as Samora suggests? If anywhere, the answer, I believe, is in the language in which Galarza's memoir is delivered: neither Spanish nor Spanglish (writing it in the latter would have been heresy for an educator of Galarza's type), but a straightforward, unadulterated English, which he learned in his teens but in which, at the time of writing, he felt at home. Insightfully, at the end of the memoir he included a glossary. Its role is crucial because, throughout the thumbnail sketches turned into a full-fledged autobiography, Galarza insists on using italicized Spanish words, which he seldom explains—for instance, *asqueroso* ("a most filthy person, a person so untidy or of such unhygienic habits as to make one's skin creep") and *pizarrín* ("a small slate used by schoolchildren instead of paper and pencil; could be wiped clean with a wet rag, a sponge, or with the tongue"). These explanations go beyond a standard dictionary: they are deliciously idiosyncratic. All this is to say that the language in which *Barrio Boy* comes to us, and the glossary it includes, allow us a glimpse of who Galarza's target audience was: the Americanized reader.

Not an American per se, but an *Americanized* person, like Galarza himself, with an abundance of self-esteem, one capable of understanding what immigration as a story is all about.

This was the journey he remembered.

The actual journey may have been quite different. . . .

The memory was all that mattered.

———

HENRY ADAMS

Barrio Boy began as anecdotes I told my family about Jal-cocotán, the mountain village in western Mexico where I was born. Among this limited public (my wife, Mae, and daughters, Karla and Eli Lu) my thumbnail sketches became best sellers. Hearing myself tell them over and over I began to agree with my captive audience that they were not only interesting, but possibly good.

Quite by accident I told one of these vignettes at a meeting of scholars and other boring people. It was recorded on tape, printed in a magazine, and circulated among schools and libraries here and there. I received letters asking for reprints and occasionally a tempting suggestion that I write more of the same, perhaps enough to make a book.

Adding up the three listeners in my family and the three correspondents made a public of six. I didn't need more persuasion than this to link the anecdotes into a story.

But a book is more than a family affair. To make it a public affair I needed more weighty excuses. I thought of two—one historical, the other psychological.

What brought me and my family to the United States from Mexico also brought hundreds of thousands of others like us. In many ways the experiences of a multitude of boys like myself, migrating from countless villages like Jalcocotán and starting life anew in *barrios* like the one in Sacramento, must have been similar. So much for the historical.

Now for the psychological. Of those boys, the ones who are still living are grey-haired, slightly cantankerous, and in all probability creaking at the joints, like myself. But the worst thing that has happened to them is that some psychologists, psychiatrists, social anthropologists and other manner of "shrinks" have spread the rumor that these Mexican immigrants and their offspring have lost their "self-image." By this, of course, they mean that a Mexican doesn't know what he is; and if by chance he is something, it isn't any good.

I, for one Mexican, never had any doubts on this score. I can't remember a time I didn't know who I was; and I have heard much testimony from my friends and other more detached persons to the effect that I thought too highly of what I thought I was.

It seemed to me unlikely that out of six or seven million Mexicans in the United States I was the only one who felt this way. In any event, those I knew and remember and tell about had an abundance of self-image and never doubted that it was a good one.

That is all there is to the plot of *Barrio Boy*: our home "In the Mountain Village"; the "Peregrinations" of a family uprooted by a revolution; their escape as refugees, "North from Mexico"; their new "Life in the Lower Part of Town" in a city in California; and their joys and tribulations "On the Edge of the Barrio."

This, then, is a true story of the acculturation of Little Ernie.

Part One

IN A MOUNTAIN VILLAGE

UNLIKE PEOPLE WHO are born in hospitals, in an ambulance, or in a taxicab, I showed up in an adobe cottage with a thatched roof that stood at one end of the only street of Jalcocotán, which everybody called Jalco for short. Like many other small villages in the wild, majestic mountains of the Sierra Madre de Nayarit, my pueblo was a hideaway. Even though you lived there, arriving in Jalco was always a surprise.

From Tepic, the nearest city to the north, you came down a steep mule track, careful not to step on the smooth round rocks that could send you spinning, or the sharp, flat ones that cut your feet. If you were traveling first class on a mule, or tourist class on a burro, you gave the beast a free rein to pick his way among the rolling stones and small boulders. The trick was to lean back slightly and ride loose so you could fall free if you had to. The trail fell away in front under a high gloomy vault of foliage that hid the sky. The trees made a stockade on both sides that gave the trail the look and feel of a winding tunnel. Loosened rocks rattled downhill, the echoes growing fainter with every bounce, until they got lost in the forest.

Unlike most tunnels, there was no patch of sunlight ahead to spot the end of the trail. It just twisted to the right, and there was Jalco, viewed from the north end of the street.

Coming in from the south end it was uphill for man or mule. The trail, called a *brecha*, climbed the mountain steadily from the pueblo next below, Tecuitata. In this direction, the forest was less dense. The palisade of pines and cedars was broken now and then where hurricanes had smashed it, leaving jagged gaps through which you could see the blue peaks of the Sierra Madre. The mule path stayed close to a stream that pell-melled its way from Jalco to the sea the year around. At the edge of the village, where the stream spread into a pond of still, hazel water, the trail broke to the left and heaved itself over the crest of the grade. You were looking at Jalcocotán from the south.

Whether you came to the pueblo from Tepic or from Tecuitata, you could surmise at once several things about the village. The Indian ancestors who had founded Jalco intended that it should be a place that would be difficult to get to. They had chosen a narrow rocky terrace parallel to a protecting gully that the arroyo had gouged out of the mountainside. Two humps of the ridge, or *cerros*, covered the flanks of the terrace. The forest fenced in the hollow, which lay under the open sky like the palm of a long, thin hand cupped to shelter the village and its people. The choice of the founding fathers had been wise. The Sierra was sometimes swept by storms that could wrench huge trees from the earth, roots and all. The sensible thing for a village to do was to squat in some natural storm cellar like the scoop in which Jalco lay, and let the hurricane pass overhead.

Shelter from the summer sun was also important. From May to October it burned, climbing the sky until it scorched, straight down, the adobe cottages and the corrals of the village. Until mid-morning the overhanging fringe of the forest filtered the hot sunlight. The arroyo, springing among the boulders in its course, pulled a cooling draft the length of the pueblo. Where the huge walnuts spread over the arroyo, children waded and men squatted until high noon had passed.

Besides providing shelter from wind and sun, the location of Jalcocotán was meant to give protection against outsiders. The old men of the pueblo told it the way it had been. And it was true, because they had heard it from the old men before them, and they in turn from the old men who had founded Jalco in the days of the Spaniards, perhaps even before that. The first settlers were refugees from the fertile river bottoms and the coast lands, taken from them by force. They had moved into the rugged mountains of the Sierra Madre, founding their villages where attack was difficult. A few hundred yards above and below Jalco, the trail squeezed through natural strong points, bottlenecks where rocks were plentiful and from which boulders could be rolled on approaching enemies.

If the invaders broke through, they would find a deserted village. A hundred footpaths, the *veredas*, unknown except to the *jalcocotecanos*, snaked away from the corrals, winding deeper into the forest and higher up the mountain. The families would wait there, watching from hidden lookouts, until the invaders left. These events had happened years—maybe centuries—before I came to live in Jalcocotán.

I also learned very early that the forest, *el monte*, was a dangerous place. Hunters told of narrow escapes from boars and mountain lions that prowled on the other side of the arroyo. The *gato montes*, the mountain cat, was a mean marauder. On the trail between Jalco and

Tecuitata a five-foot rattlesnake had been killed. These were warnings for small boys, to be heeded until you became a man and learned to get along with the forest.

Jalcocotán and the forest had always been a part of each other. "El monte," the old men said, "no es de nadie y es de todos"—the forest doesn't belong to anyone and it belongs to everyone. Like those of my pueblo, the men of Tecuitata and the other villages on the mountain talked vaguely of boundary lines between their portions of the *monte*. But when anyone asked how far the village timber extended, the *jalcocotecano* would answer with a sweeping wave of the hand. The gesture could mean that it all belonged to us, even the farthest ridges of the Sierra Madre, even to Jalisco. It really didn't matter. The only part of the forest that was useful to us was the farthest point you could walk to and get home by sundown.

El monte was a place of wonders as well as of dangers. The pines, the huge umbrellas of the elms, and the shaggy cedars were the tallest things in the world. The pine kindling was marvelously aromatic and sticky. The woodsmen of the pueblo talked of the white tree, the black tree, the red tree, the rock tree—*palo blanco, palo negro, palo colorado* and *palo de piedra*. Under the shady canopies of the giants there were the fruit bearers—*chirimoyas, guayabas, mangos, mameyes,* and *tunas*. There were also the coffee bushes, volunteers that straggled here and there in an abandoned coffee patch.

The deep woods also gave the pueblo the songs and colors of the flocks of parakeets, macaws, and *loros* that chattered and squeaked on the fringe of the forest; in flight over our house they sounded like little rusty hinges. Springing suddenly from the tree tops into the sunlight over the village street, a flock of *loros* looked like dabs of bright green enamel streaking in formation across the blue sky.

But of all the creatures that came flying out of the *monte*—bats, doves, hawks—the most familiar were the turkey vultures, the *zopilotes*. There were always two or three of them perched on the highest limb of a tree on the edge of the pueblo. They glided in gracefully on five feet of wing spread, flapping awkwardly as they came to rest. They were about the size of a turkey, of a black-ish brown color and baldheaded, their wrinkled necks spotted with red in front. Hunched on their perch, they never opened their curved beaks to make a sound. They watched the street below them with beady eyes. Some-time during the day, the *zopilotes* swooped down to scav-enge in the narrow ditch that ran the length of the street, where the housewives dropped the entrails of chickens among the garbage. They gobbled what waste the dogs and pigs did not get at first. These tidbits were enough to keep the *zopilotes* interested in our town and to accustom them to the presence of people. Grim and ugly though they were, the vultures were regarded as volunteer gar-bage collectors who charged nothing for their services and who, like good children, were seen but not heard.

The one and only street in Jalcocotán was hardly more than an open stretch of the mule trail that disappeared into the forest north and south of the pueblo. Crosswise, it was about wide enough to park six automobiles hub to hub. Lengthwise, you could walk from one end to the other in eight minutes, without hurrying, the way people walked in the village. The dirt surface had been packed hard by hundreds of years of traffic—people barefooted or wearing the tough leather sandals called huaraches; mule trains passing through on the way to the sea or to Tepic; burros carrying firewood and other products of the forest; *zopilotes* hopping heavily here and there; pigs, dogs, and chickens foraging along the ditch.

There was a row of cottages on each side of the street, adobe boxes made of the same packed earth on which the houses stood. At one end of the street wall of every cottage there was a doorway, another in the wall standing to the back yard corral. There were no windows. The roofs were made of palm thatch, with a steep pitch, the ridge pole parallel to the street. Back of the houses were the *corrales*, fenced with stones piled about shoulder high to a man. Between the *corrales* there were narrow alleys that led uphill to the edge of the forest on the upper side of the village, and to the arroyo on the lower side. The eaves of the grass roofs hung well over the adobe walls to protect them from the battering rains. In the summer time the overhang provided shade at midday, when it seemed as if all the suffocating heat of the heavens was pouring through a funnel with the small end pointed directly at Jalco.

Since there were no sidewalks, from the front door to the street was only a step. Our pueblo was too high up the mountain, the connecting trails were too steep and narrow to allow ox carts and wagons to reach it. Like the forest, our only street belonged to everybody—a place to sort out your friends and take your bearings if you were going anywhere.

Midway down the street, on the arroyo side, there was a small chapel, also of adobe, the only building in the town that had a front yard, a patch of sun-baked clay squeezed between two cottages. Back of the patio stood the squat adobe box of the chapel, with a red tile roof and a small dome in one corner topped with a wooden cross. Once upon a time the walls of the chapel had been plastered and whitewashed, but the rains and the sun had cracked and blistered them. The adobe was exposed in jagged patches with flecks of grey straw showing like wood grain on the ancient mud. The base of the walls, pelted by the rain, was chewed as if beavers had worked on it.

Directly across the street from the chapel, the row of cottages was interrupted by the plaza. In any pueblo of some importance this would have been the *zocalo,* or the *plaza mayor,* or more grandiloquently, the *plaza de armas.* In Jalco it was a square without a name, about forty steps wide along the street and as many deep. Once, so it was said by the oldest people in the village, there had been a fountain in the center of the plaza, and a collection had been taken to buy a bust of Benito Juarez for a centerpiece of the park. When I knew the drab little plaza, there was no fountain and no bust. The surface of the square was, like the street, a sheet of hardpan. Holes had been chopped in it and some trees planted. An acacia shaded one corner of the upper side of the lot. Three smaller trees lined one side of the square; in the spring they flamed with brilliant crimson blossoms like cups of fire, which is why they were called *copas de fuego.*

In a village like Jalcocotán there was little use for either the chapel or the plaza. We had no resident priest; *jalcocotecanos* with serious matters to lay before their patron saints or the Virgin of Guadalupe walked to Tepic, forty kilometers to the north, with its magnificent basilica. If it was a matter in which the whole village was concerned, a pilgrimage was organized to the shrine of Nuestra Señora de Talpa, where couples were married and babies baptized. Even less ever happened in the plaza than in the chapel. There was no police, no fire department, no post office, no public library. No one was ever elected mayor or sheriff or councilman. There was no jail or judge or any other sort of *Autoridades,* which explained why there was no city hall in Jalco. The shrunken, sun-beaten plaza was there nevertheless, solitary except when children played in it or passing mule drivers rested under the shade of its trees. It was a useless spot in our everyday life, but just by being there, the public square, like the chapel, gave our one and only street a touch of dignity, the mark of a proper pueblo.

Like the plaza, the street had no name. On a nameless street the houses, naturally, had no numbers. The villager was indoors and in bed after dark so there was no need for lights, of which our street had none.

Having a single gutter in the middle of the street instead of one on each side was a piece of simple and practical engineering. The shallow ditch made a slightly crooked dividing line through the center of the town. On either side of it each family took care of its frontage on the street, sprinkling it to settle the dust in the dry season, or sweeping the litter into the ditch. When it rained the trench collected the runoff, making a small torrent that scoured the gutter clean. During a downpour people stood in the doorways to watch the stuff that passed bobbing on the chocolate water—corncobs, banana peelings, twigs, an old huarache, or a dead rat drowned in the flash flood.

Whatever happened in Jalcocotán had to happen on our street because there was no other place for it to happen. Two men, drunk with tequila, fought with machetes on the upper edge of the village until they were separated and led away by the neighbors. A hundred faces peered around doorways watching the fight. When someone died people joined the funeral procession as it passed by their doors. If a stranger arrived on horseback, the clopping of horseshoes on the rocks of the trail announced his arrival before he could turn into the street. Arriving in Jalco was like stepping on a stage. The spectators were already in the doorways, watching.

The narrow lanes between the corrals on the lower side of the street led to the arroyo which ran the length of the village. The turbulent waters, even in the dry season, twisted and churned among the boulders, slapping them and breaking into spray, or dividing around them in serpentines of blue-green foam. Below the village the arroyo was checked by a natural dam of rocks and silt, over which it dropped into a quiet pond before rushing on to the sea.

On both sides the arroyo, here and there, had slammed boulders into the bank or against the trunks of trees. Downstream from these rocks the water formed small ponds over a floor of white sand and speckled pebbles. In these nooks the women of the village washed clothes, kneeling waist high in the water.

On the edge of the pond, at the far side, there was an enormous walnut tree, standing like an open umbrella whose ribs extended halfway across the still water of the pool. The scars on the trunk of the mighty bole showed where the arroyo had bashed it during storms of former years. But the nogal had always won these battles. The arroyo, when the storms had passed, gave up and backed away, leaving around the trunk a small beach where the pond lapped gently on the gravel.

The arroyo was as much a part of the pueblo as the street. Like the street, it had no name; it just tumbled into town from the timber stands up the mountain that fed it the year round, and tumbled out from the pond to pick up and carry to the ocean the seepage of the forest below. It could rage dangerously in the summer freshets, called *avenidas*, pounding at the lower side of the village with boulders and ramming it with tree trunks a man could hardly circle with his two arms. Most of the year, it brought driftwood downstream and delivered it to the *jalcocotecanos* who chopped it into kindling. It supplied the pond with fish, but most important of all, it piped the sweet seepage of the forest to our town, always cold, transparent, and greenish blue. We called it *agua zarca*, good for drinking and washing.

Like the *monte* and the street, the arroyo was common property. Those who lived along the upper side of the street used the lanes between the cottages on the lower side on their way to wash, to fill their red clay *cantaros*, or to water their stock. Going to the arroyo from the street was called *bajar al agua*. Going up the lanes to the forest was called *subir al monte*. Taking the trail to Tepic was *cuesta arriba*. Taking it down to Miramar was *cuesta abajo*. These were the four points of the compass for Jalcocotán. If you followed them you could always find your way back home.

It was in the evening, when dusk was falling and supper was being prepared, that Jalco shaded itself little by little into the forest, the arroyo, the sky, and the mountain to which it belonged. Westward toward the sea, a rose and purple mist nearly always lingered after sunset.

The eastern slopes of the range became patches of black-blue. From the slant of the shadows and the signs in the sky, everyone knew when this would happen— almost to the minute. The men and the boys of working age came down or up the trail at about the right time to reach the street a few steps ahead of or a few steps behind the dusk. They walked, each man and his sons, to their cottages. On both sides of the street the doors were open. In the kitchens, the coals glowed in the adobe *pretiles* where the cooking was done, illuminated by the tin oil lamps, three inches round and two deep, the *candiles* that swung from the ceiling.

Through the doors, opened to receive the returning toilers and to freshen the air inside the cottages, came the sounds and sights of the street at sundown. There was the soft clapping of the women patting the ration of tortillas for the evening meal. The smoky light from the wicks of the *candiles* flickering through the doorways cast wobbling shadows on the threshold as people moved about. The air outside was a blend of the familiar smells of supper time—tortillas baking, beans boiling, chile roasting, coffee steaming, and kerosene stenching. The hens were clucking in their roosts in the corrals by the time the street was dark.

After supper, if the weather was warm, the men squatted on the ground, hunched against the wall of the house and smoked. The women and the girls ate supper and put away the kitchen things, the *candiles* turned down to save kerosene. They listened to the tales of the day if the men were in a talking mood. When they pulled on their cigarettes, they made ruby dots in the dark, as if they were putting periods into the low-toned conversation. The talk just faded away, the men went indoors, the doors were shut and barred, and there was nothing on the street but the dark and the rumble of the arroyo.

Our adobe cottage was on the side of the street away from the arroyo. It was the last house if you were going to Miramar. About fifty yards behind the corral, the forest closed in.

It was like every other house in Jalco, probably larger. The adobe walls were thick, a foot or more, with patches of whitewash where the thatched overhang protected the adobe from the rain. There were no windows. The entrance doorway was at one end of the front wall, and directly opposite the door that led to the corral. The doors were made of planks axed smooth from tree trunks and joined with two cross pieces and a diagonal brace between them hammered together with large nails bent into the wood on the inside. Next to each door and always handy for instant use, there was the cross bar, the *tranca*. On both sides of the door frame there was a notched stub, mortared into the adobe bricks and about six inches long. The door was secured from the inside by dropping the *tranca* into the two notches.

All the living space for the family was in the one large room, about twelve feet wide and three times as long. Against the wall between the two doorways was the *pretil*, a bank of adobe bricks three feet high, three across, and two feet deep. In the center of the *pretil* was the main fire pit. Two smaller hollows, one on either side of the large one, made it a three-burner stove. On a row of pegs above the *pretil* hung the clay pans and other cooking utensils, bottom side out, the soot baked into the red clay. A low bench next to the *pretil*, also made of adobe, served as a table and shelf for the cups, pots, and plates.

The rest of the ground floor was divided by a curtain hung from one of the hand-hewed log beams, making two bedrooms. Above them, secured to the beams, was the *tapanco*, a platform the size of a double bed made of thin saplings tied together with pieces of rawhide. The top of a notched pole, braced against the foot of the back wall of the cottage, rested against the side of the *tapanco*, serving as a ladder. Along the wall opposite the *pretil*, in the darkest and coolest part of the house, were the big *cántaros*, the red clay jars; the *canastos*, tall baskets made of woven reeds; the rolled straw *petates* to cover the dirt floor where people walked or sat; and the hoes and other work tools.

There was no ceiling other than the underside of the thatch, which was tied to the pole rafters. On top of these, several layers of thatch were laid, making a waterproof cover thicker than the span of a man's hand. The rafters were notched and tied to the ridgepole and mortared on the lower end to the top of the walls. Between the top of the walls and the overhang there was an open space a few inches wide. Through this strip the smoke from the *pretil* went out and the fresh air came in.

It was the roof that gave space and lift to the single room that served as kitchen, bedroom, parlor, pantry, closet, storeroom, and tool shed. The slender rafters pointed upward in sharp triangles tied at the peak with bows of darkbrown rawhide that had dried as tight as steel straps. Strings of thatch hung from the ceiling like the fringe of a buggy top, making it appear that the heavy matting of grass did not rest on the rafters but tip-toed on hundreds of threads. It was always half dark up there. My cousins, Jesús and Catarino, and I slept in the *tapanco*. More than a bedroom, to us it was a half-lighted hideaway out of sight of parents, uncles, aunts, and other meddlesome people.

The corral was the other important part of a Jalco home. Ours was enclosed on three sides by stone walls and shut off from the street by the house. The only entrance to the corral was through the back door of the cottage. The ground sloped up toward the edge of the monte. A ditch along the back wall stopped the runoff water and sluiced it toward the lane between our house and our neighbor's. Close to the house, there was a corn-crib built like a miniature adobe cottage with the walls sloping inward at the bottom. It was raised on stilts and covered with a grass roof.

The only landscaping of the corral was a willow tree that stood half as high as the house roof. It always looked yellowish and limp, as if it had too much sun and not enough water. For beauty it was not much, but as a hen roost it was the best there was in Jalco. During the day, especially at high noon when the willow stood deserted in the baking sunlight, the round shadow of its crown was mottled with chicken droppings continually changing in pattern.

The color and the charm of the corral were along the back wall of the house, adorned by a row of geraniums, herbs, and carnations potted in jars of many sizes and five-gallon kerosene cans. Some of the pots were on the ground, others were raised on one, two, or three adobe bricks. The thatch eaves protected the sprays of bright green and red and pink from rain and sun. When the herbs were pinched off for cooking there was a faint aroma of oregano, thyme, and mint. The herbs and carnations were on the higher bricks, to keep them out of reach of the hens.

The utensils and the furniture were matched to the cottage, as if everything had been made at the same time by the same people out of the same materials of the earth. The three-legged *metate* on which the corn for the tortillas was ground, a small, oblong sloping platform of black rock speckled with grey dots, stood on one side of the *pretil*. The *comal*, a round griddle about two feet across, hung from a peg looking like a black shield with a red rim. The beds were hewn frames of poles standing on short legs. The sides and ends of the frames were girdled to hold the loops of rawhide stretched between them, making the small squares of the bed spring. The bows where the rawhide was tied were like those that held the rafters to the thatch and the ridge pole. The straw mats were partly the color of the floor, partly the color of the thatch where it was less sooty. Who had built and designed and made all this nobody knew. We had just moved in; if we ever moved out it would all be left as it was, soaped and scrubbed to look and smell clean.

I never thought to count them, but there could have been forty such homes in Jalcocotán when I lived there. Some cottages were deeper and longer than others, some corral walls were patched with poles and adobe bricks, some roofs rested on straight-up gables and others on slanting ones. But every cottage seemed built and placed to look like every other one. There were no building codes in the pueblo about where to set the walls, or how high they must be or as to the pitch of the roof. The houses made an almost solid front on either side of the street except for the breaks of the lanes, the plaza, and the chapel.

We moved to Jalco—my mother, my uncle Gustavo, my uncle José and I—several weeks before I was born. They walked, with a few clothes and some food, from Miramar, about twenty miles away down the mountain. Under the circumstances, the journey was no problem for me.

My father, Don Ernesto, senior, was not in the small caravan. He had stayed in Miramar, where he kept books and supervised the peons of an hacienda. My mother and he had been married in San Blas, but only *por lo civil*, not *por la iglesia* because my father was a Lutheran and my mother a Catholic, and he would not have a priest. As it turned out, and as often happened in such a place as Miramar and such times as I am telling about, my father got around to thinking that a civil wedding was not much more for keeps than one in church. The divorce was a simple matter. He wrote my mother a letter and she wrote one in return. Aunt Esther and Uncle Gustavo went to Miramar to talk the matter over. It was arranged that the ring which my father had given my mother was to be kept by her. She was also to keep the sewing machine he had given her for a wedding present. And as part of the property settlement, I was to remain with my mother.

I was told years later by Uncle Gustavo and Aunt Esther that the most important part of the agreement was what to do about me, whenever I should come around. The ring and the sewing machine were negotiated to make the change in our lives somewhat easier. The ring, a simple gold band, could be pawned when we needed money. My mother was an expert seamstress; she could sew and mend for wages at home. It was arranged that the sewing machine, with the trade name *Ajax* in cast iron letters on the treadle, and painted in gold leaf on the plate, was to be delivered to Jalco on muleback.

As I grew older and could put together the bits and pieces that adults allow children to have about family histories, it was clear to me that even though I was something less than an infant, I had played an important part in the negotiations. My mother could have made her way alone, but with me on her hands the gold ring and the sewing machine would help. My needs, moreover, turned out to be modest. For several months they were provided by my mother and a small pile of diapers made from *manta*, the cotton stuff of which the *calzones* and the shirts of the *jalcocotecanos* were made. When the gold ring was pawned, as it often was, the loan money was used to buy food for the entire family. The wages my mother made sewing and mending were put into the *alcancía*, the fat clay pig painted in bright colors which served as the family bank. It was in this way, as I see it, that I earned my way from the start.

The move to Jalcocotán was the only way out of Miramar for the four of us. My grandfather, Don Felix, and his wife, Doña Isabel, had died. Their few possessions had been sold to pay off debts, out of which Don Felix did not seem able to keep. We had relatives in San Blas, but none with room enough for three people and possibly four.

Aunt Esther had married Don Catarino López, one of a numerous family of Jalco. Don Catarino, his father, and brothers worked the corn patches and the *milpas* on the mountain, tilled and harvested bananas deep in the forest and earned a living in other ways from the countryside. Don Catarino had brought his bride, Esther, to the pueblo where they were living with their two boys— Jesús, a year older than myself and Catarino junior, a year younger. The four of them hardly filled the one big room of the cottage. The extra beds behind the curtain and the *tapanco* could accommodate us all, cramped or cozy, depending on how you looked at it.

Don Catarino became the head of our household. He was a dour man of middle height, with a skin sunburned to a chocolate brown. He talked slowly, drawling in a soft, pleasant rumble, but when he was angry he could clench his voice as quickly as his fist. Like a true *campesino* and *jalcocotecano*, he always seemed to count to a hundred before speaking and when he did speak it was a decision, not a discussion. What he decided he backed up with some ancient proverb that everybody knew and everybody believed. With his voice, his way of looking at you and his proverbs Don Catarino left no doubts in my mind that he was the *jefe de familia*.

Doña Esther, my Aunt Tel, as I called her, was a small person. Something over five-feet-five, she was fair-skinned and hazel-eyed. She seldom laughed, for when we came to Jalco she had already had enough grief to last a person a lifetime, the least of which was the responsibility for two younger brothers and a sister after the death of Grandfather Felix. He, too, had been a rigid *jefe de familia*. She had lived all her life under authority but it had not bent her will; standing up to it she was more than a person—she was a presence. When she was alone in the cottage with us she told jokes about animals and foolish, stuck-up persons. She smiled mostly with her eyes.

We belonged to an even larger family than the eight of us who lived in the cottage. Don Catarino's father and brothers were also settled in Jalco. We, the Galarzas, became a part of this network. Even though they were all poor, I could say from the start of my life that on the López side I had connections. It seemed that every village on our mountain had a López or two in residence, with whom you could be sure of a place to sleep and something to eat away from home. I heard of López's in Miramar and in Tepic, which meant that our connections extended at least forty kilometers north and south. Taken together this was my *parentela* on my aunt's side. On my mother's, it stretched to San Blas which I never saw as a child.

As members of Don Catarino's household my mother, Doña Henriqueta, my Uncle Gustavo, and my Uncle José became *jalcocotecanos* by adoption. Doña Henriqueta was not even as tall as Doña Esther, but plumper. She had a light olive complexion and a mass of dark brown hair so wavy it burst when she undid her braids. She never did household chores without singing, accompanying herself by imitating a guitar that plinked and plonked between the verses of her song. Her features were good-looking, almost soft, not much like her temper. Doña Henriqueta knew about people in deep trouble for she was one of them. But unlike most of them, she believed in rebelling against it, in resisting those who caused it. As the oldest of the four migrants from Miramar, Doña Henriqueta stood between us and Don Catarino when he was in one of his cantankerous moods. She drew a line between respect, which we were expected to show, and fear, which we were not.

My Uncle Gustavo, next youngest of the four Galarzas, was chunky and cheerful, with red-tinged hair as kinky as my mother's. As a young man he carried the heaviest responsibilities for the family—traveled farther for a job, moved the household goods from one place to another, walked for miles to earn a few centavos. He was sunny and humorous, but he would blow his temper over small things. Doña Henriqueta handled his outbursts with a firm hand and a gentle scolding.

In Jalco people spoke in two languages—Spanish and with gestures. These signs were made with the face or hands or a combination of both. If you bent one arm and tapped the elbow with the other hand, it meant "He is stingy." When you sawed one arm across the other you were saying that someone you knew played the fiddle terribly. To say that a man was a tippler you made a set of cow's horns with the little finger and the thumb of one hand, bending the three middle fingers to the palm and pointing the thumb at your mouth. And if you wanted to indicate, without saying so for the sake of politeness, that a mutual acquaintance was daffy, you tapped three times on your forehead with your middle finger.

Gustavo taught me these important signs and refined them into a secret code that only he and I used. To boast of something clever I had done, I opened my mouth and tapped a bicuspid with my forefinger. Gustavo explained to me that this meant: "With such a wisdom tooth as I have, I can't help it if I am smarter than you." If we were being watched, the warning was to place a forefinger under one eye and pull down lightly. If it was time to get out of there, you walked two fingers of one hand on the palm of the other, fast. When we had an understanding about something both of us, in perfect time, closed one eye tightly and made a horrible grimace with the mouth.

The youngest of the four, and my closest contact with the grown-up world of Jalcocotán, was José. When I was born he was twelve, already a man by all the standards of our town. He was wiry, tough, talkative, and sharply tuned to the sounds of people and of nature. He was an artist at whittling and at putting together odds and ends in useful and curious ways. It was José who interpreted for me, in a highbrow, know-it-all manner, the sayings and doings of the pueblo, such as why so-and-so beat his wife so often, why the *zopilotes* liked guts, or why Don Catarino kept a bottle of tequila under the bed. By orders of Doña Henriqueta, when José was not working he was directly in charge of my security. This put me altogether at the foot of the family totem pole, and I was lucky that the one next above me was José.

Somewhere between my third and fifth birthdays I began to have a memory. The forest trail, the street, the *zopilotes*, the arroyo, my mother's potted garden, the summer showers, José whistling an imitation of a song bird—these were some of the earliest pictures and sounds which for some reason I could recall whenever I wanted to.

The little tin portraits—daguerreotypes—that my mother kept in a small cedar chest wrapped in tissue paper were among these first recollections. There were two—Grandmother Isabel and Grandfather Felix on their wedding day. It astounded me that my grandparents could have been so diminutive as to fit into a metal tab, two inches by three. The doll in a plaid dress that covered her from throat to toes was fourteen years old. Her bridegroom posed like a dandy, stiff in tight pants and a bolero jacket, leaning on a bamboo cane.

The cedar chest from which these treasures were taken out on special days was itself a relic of the happy days of Doña Isabel and Don Felix. It held other heirlooms—handkerchiefs Doña Isabel had embroidered, some tooled leather bits of my Grandfather's, a dress pattern and a bundle of New Year's cards with doves and roses in brilliant colors and sprinkled with grains of golden sand. Whenever the chest was opened I sniffed the inside of the box, taking deep breaths of the unvarnished wood. Between these occasions the cedar box stood in a far corner of the room, behind the curtain, on top of the *petaca*, the family trunk. Both were locked, and my mother carried the keys on a string around her neck. The *alcancía*, the clay pig with our savings, was kept in the bottom of the trunk, under the clothes, the lacework, and the fabrics for my mother's sewing.

Breakfast was before daybreak and regularly announced by our rooster, Coronel. He was always a half hour ahead of the dawn, crowing lustily in our back yard. It was the signal to get up. Up in the *tapanco* we stirred on our mattress of cornhusks and mats, sitting up hunched in our sarapes, listening. In the corrals of the village the other roosters picked up the reveille, trumpeting as if this was the first dawn of time and a marvelous sight to see. Up and down the mountain the cocks of the ranchos and the other pueblos took up the fanfare, their calls fading with the distance.

One by one we came down the notched pole, still snug in our sarapes.

"Buenos días, muchachos."

"Buenos días, Don Catarino."

"Buenos días, Tía."

"Buenos días, Tío."

"Buenos días, mamá."

We huddled around the fire in the *pretil* as close as we could without getting in the way of the business of preparing breakfast. Over our heads the oil lamp sputtered, giving off more smoke than light. My mother stirred the coals she had bedded down the night before under a thick bank of ashes. On top of them she dropped small splinters of pine heavy with resin, the pungent *ocote*. With a small mat she fanned the splinters into a flame, feeding it with larger pieces of *ocote* to set the fresh charcoal on fire. From the center pit coals were scooped and transferred to the side burners. On the three fires now going the pots were arranged, their black bottoms sitting on the ruby coals. The tortillas were already warming on the *comal*, the beans coming to a boil in one pot, the coffee in another.

Don Catarino was usually moving about in the corral, getting ready for the day's work. My uncles would be with him or back of the corral on the edge of the forest, where the bushes and the darkness gave privacy.

We ate breakfast in silence. The men, sitting on the edge of the beds, were served first—a plate with beans and red pepper rolled in tortillas, a large bowl of coffee, still boiling, to warm their hands and burn their stomachs on account of the early morning chill. The tacos for their lunch were already rolled in cornhusks and a napkin, tucked into the haversacks of woven hemp. My aunt took down the crossbar from the front door and the men stepped out into the dark, wrapped in sarapes. Their huaraches sandpapered the hard surface of the street, the white stuff of their clothes disappearing like dim blobs into the night. They would be in the fields by daybreak.

My aunt closed the door and served breakfast to the three boys, huddled around the *pretil*. It was a bowl of coffee, a tortilla with beans and pepper, and a few sucks on a chunk of brown sugar, the *panocha* that was kept in a clay pot on a shelf out of our reach. The women always ate last.

"Now, up the *tapanco* and raise your bed." I could never understand why Aunt Esther always said "raise your bed." *Al tapanco y alzar la cama* was what she called this part of the morning routine. We climbed up the notched pole again, to spread the cornhusks evenly, lining up the woven mats on top, like a bed cover. We did this crawling on all fours, butting one another like goats. By the time we came down it was time to round up Coronel and his hens in the corral for their daily ration of maize. When the chickens were fed we called Nerón, our dog, to the kitchen door for a tortilla dipped in bean juice. In one swallow Nerón finished his breakfast and he chased us to the edge of the woods back of the corral. While Nerón stood by, as if he understood what was going on, we lined up along the wall for a minute or two. Whoever won the race back to the kitchen when my mother called would get the first licks on the *panocha*.

Doing chores and chasing one another we warmed ourselves during the morning chill, playing as much as possible between the routine jobs we were assigned. Most of these jobs were as agreeable as the games we made up. When it was full daylight, both doors of the cottage were opened. Jesús and I walked Nerón up and down the street so he could explore the fresh garbage in the gutter. He was then left on his own, except when he got into a fight and barked for help. Coronel and his hens were ushered through the kitchen into the street to scratch in the litter. Some time during the morning we had to sprinkle the street directly in front of our house.

The protection of Coronel and his hens and the supervision of Nerón were two of the important tasks assigned to us. There was one other—to look after Relámpago, the burro that didn't belong to anyone in particular.

Ours were by no means the only hens and roosters and dogs in Jalco. They all used the street living in peace most of the time, but sometimes not. When fighting broke out over scraps in the gutter, we knew it by the cackling and the growling and grunting up the street.

From among these noisy arguments we could make out Nerón's bark or the unmistakably López cackle of our hens. It was our duty to look over the situation and fix it, or to run back home and ask for help if necessary.

It was our way of protecting Nerón, our watchdog and playmate; Coronel, our chanticleer, and his wives; and Relámpago, to whom we belonged more than he to us.

Nerón came to live with us when I was about a year old. He was a gray mongrel puppy, assigned to grow up with and keep an eye on me. He developed into a husky mix of breeds, with the alert look of a shepherd, the body of a runty St. Bernard, and the friskiness of a terrier. If I bawled when I was put down in the hammock, Nerón would push it with his paw—a trick José taught him. By the time I first remember Nerón, I understood that I had been assigned to grow up with and keep an eye on him.

Coronel was not only the principal rooster of Jalcocotán; Jesús, Catarino, and I strongly believed that he was the champion rooster of all the pueblos on the mountain. Don Catarino had brought him home from one of his trips. He grew into a proud red cock standing nearly as high as my waist. Strutting in the sun, Coronel flashed the ochre rainbow of his feathers—orange red, brick red, ruby red, geranium red, and blood red. Coronel always held himself like a ramrod, but he stood straightest when he was on top of the corral wall. From up there he counted his chickens, gave the forest a searching look, and blasted out a general challenge to all the world. With his flaming red crest and powerful yellow spurs, Coronel was the picture of a very *jefe de familia*.

Relámpago, the other member of our family, was a distant sort of relative. He was a small, brownish-grey donkey. His left ear always drooped and he didn't swish his tail like other burros. Nothing in Jalco moved as slowly and deliberately as Relámpago, for which reason he was called "Lightning." He didn't belong to anyone and no one knew where he had come from. But his way of gazing at people, of stopping in front of doors to stare, and his willingness to give the small children rides, made him at least a cousin to every family in the village. José hoisted me on Relámpago's back now and then, walking us from one end of the street to the other. No reins, no saddle, no stirrups, almost no hands, except that José would be alongside to steady me on top of the burro. Whenever Relámpago cared to do so, he was welcome to walk through our cottage and into the corral to spend the night.

Don Chano, who lived at the other end of the street from us, was one of the elders of Jalco. He had been to Guadalajara when he was a young man. "Don Chano," said my mother to Aunt Esther once when Jesús and Catarino and I were up in the *tapanco*, supposedly asleep, but eavesdropping, as usual, "tells that nothing ever happens in Jalcocotán."

The remark made no sense. If we had been as old as Don Chano we would probably have argued about it. For the three of us, important things happened in the cottage, on the street, in the corral, along the arroyo, and on the edge of the forest. Not only that. Most of the things that happened, happened every day. Coronel started them, bugling to all the other roosters on the mountain. Nerón ran races with us in the corral when the sun was hardly up. We got our licks at the *panocha* without missing a day. Moreover, in Jalco the happenings stopped when night fell, so you would not miss any of them while you were asleep.

Whether we were playing in a neighbor's corral, or on the street, or down by the pond, we knew the afternoon was about over by the voices. "Juan." "Neto." "Chuy." "Melesio." They were calling our names, the voices of mothers and aunts poking their heads out of doorways or over the walls of the corrals. The voices were not shouts. They were tunes. And we knew when we heard them—being only five or six years old—that we had to dance to them, at once. "Si, señora." "Ya vengo." "Voy." When we answered we were already on the trot. We obeyed by trotting. We showed respect by answering. Failure to do either could mean that you would have your ear pinched at the doorway or be asked that ominous question that nobody knew how to answer and had better not try to: "Qué pasó?"—how come?

The voices always called about the time the shadows began stretching from the forest side of the pueblo over the cottages. After reporting in, Jesús and Catarino and I looked after Coronel and the hens. Usually they were on their way home, dawdling as they scratched. If Nerón wasn't around he had to be caught and turned home by the scruff of his furry neck. We herded all of them—usually Nerón first, the hens next and Coronel last—through the doors and into the corral. From then until supper we hopped to chores and errands—some charcoal for the *pretil*, bringing in the straw *petates* that had hung freshening in the sun on the walls of the corral, stopping a ruckus between Nerón and Coronel, or propping the rickety ladder the hens climbed to roost in the willow tree.

While supper was being prepared, a quietness settled on the family waiting for the men to return from work. On one corner of the *pretil* there were the freshly baked tortillas, wrapped in a double jacket of napkins and stacked in the cream-colored basket with the musical name, the *chiquihuite*.

Don Catarino was always the first to walk in out of the dusk, if he and Gustavo and José had been working the same field. Gustavo was second and José last. They unfastened the machetes and hung them in their sheaths on pegs by the back door. They dropped the sarapes, folded, on the beds. Without a word they stepped into the darkening corral to wash from clay bowls. We stood by, a boy to each man, holding the chips of soap and the mended towels.

In the same order as at breakfast, the men were served first. The food was laid out on a side table not much wider than a shelf. As the men ate they tore the fresh, warm corncakes into halves and quarters and eighths, making tiny spoons with which they scooped the food, eating the spoon along with it.

When they finished, the men rose from the table. Don Catarino rumbled "Buen provecho," which was a Jalcocotán way of wishing the diners a comfortable digestion of the meal.

Jesús, Catarino, and I took the places of the men. The beans came steaming out of the tall pot, red-brown, *frijoles de la olla*, sprinkled with browned rice and washed down with coffee, but no pepper. With the last tortilla spoon we sopped up the bean juice and nit-picked the last grain of rice on our plates. When my Aunt Esther said "Buen provecho," the meal was over. While the women ate, we loitered, any place where the men were not.

In the corral, by the bright orange light of a long stick of flaming *ocate*, they sharpened the machetes, or secured a hoe handle that had come loose. We could watch, careful not to get under foot, for we knew the men were irritable at the end of a bone-tiring day in the *milpa*. Don Catarino looked menacing with the shadows the dancing *ocate* flame made on his dark face. Gustavo hummed as he whetted his machete. José tested the edge of his blade, feeling it gently with his thumb crosswise, licking it before testing—one of the tricks of a good *machetero*.

Except for the candil turned low indoors, it was pitch dark when the men sat down or squatted along the front wall facing the street. Only Don Catarino smoked.

Gustavo and José were not allowed to—at least not in the presence of my Aunt Esther and Doña Henriqueta. As the men relaxed they talked in low voices and short sentences. We sat on mats just inside the doorway, the women on the edge of the bed or standing behind us in the gloomy room. When Don Catarino was in an easy mood he told about things that had happened when he was a boy, such as the flood that carried away his father's mule. His voice, low and pebbly, came to us in the darkness mingled with the chirping of the crickets and the croaking of the frogs in the pond.

At a signal from Doña Esther we turned in, climbing the notched pole to the *tapanco*. Wrapped in our sarapes we settled quickly into the cornhusk mattress and the mats and stopped squirming the better to hear the low-keyed talk that continued below us. It was easier to hear up there. The words climbed up the wall and in through the space between the thatch and the top of the adobe wall.

What we heard were bits of village gossip, the names of people we didn't know, talk of things that had happened somewhere else a long time past, or things that might happen in a day or a year or two. Even though we understood little we knew we were listening secretly. The grown-ups were in no hurry to talk. They, too, seemed to be listening to the sounds of the night—the rumble of the arroyo, and the stirrings of the forest.

Eavesdropping on talk that crept from one word to another down there in the darkness, my attention wandered to other matters. I listened to the chirping all around the cottage and thought it came from the stars. They and the crickets always came together after dark, the cricket calls blinking in the silence just as surely as the stars seemed to chirp in the darkness far above us. When I raised this question with José or my mother they said "Que ocurrencia," pointing out that I had caught crickets but never stars.

But lying quietly in the *tapanco*, undisturbed by the scoffing of adults, it seemed to me quite possible that I was right. If I was still awake when the front door creaked shut and the cross bar thumped into place, I knew that was the end of the day.

The morning of one memorable day Jesús, Catarino and I climbed down from the *tapanco* as usual. Bundled in our blankets, we scrunched ourselves against the wall as close as we could to the warmth of the fire without getting in the way.

By the light of the *candil* overhead I saw the dim outlines of familiar things. The small basket for the long red peppers reflected on its glossy yellow weave the flicker of the *candil*, like the tongue of a cat licking its paw. Next to the back door, on a wooden peg, hung the *bule*, a large gourd mottled gray and brown. The *bule* was a dry, leakproof container about eight inches across, with a wide belly and a short neck cut at the tip and plugged with a cork. Drinking water kept cool and sweet in the *bule*. Aunt Esther tipped it from time to time over her cupped hand to sprinkle the cornmeal.

Doña Esther was already at the *comal*, making the fresh supply of tortillas for the day. She plucked small lumps, one by one, from the heap of corn dough she kept in a deep clay pot. She gave the lump a few squeezes to make a thick, round biscuit which she patted and pulled and clapped into a thin disk. The corncake grew larger and larger until it hung in loose ruffles around her hands. She spread her fingers wide to hold the thin, pale folds of dangling dough which looked as if they might drop off in pieces any moment. As she clapped she gave her wrists a half turn, making the tortilla tilt between each tat-tat of her palms. On each twist the tortilla seemed to slip loose but she would clamp it gently for another tat-tat. When the tortilla was thin and round and utterly floppy, she laid it on the comal. My aunt worked on the next tortilla as she turned those already on the griddle, nipping them by the edge with her fingernails and flipping them over fast. When they browned in spots, she nipped them again and dropped them into the *chiquihuite*, covering them with a napkin to keep them hot.

Breakfast over, the men left, and pink shafts began to show through the gray sky over the corral. Nerón was standing at the back door, observing the food on the *pretil* and waiting for his tortilla dipped in bean juice. That day it was my turn to run with it to the back wall of the corral, tantalizing Nerón until he managed to grab it from me.

Coronel and the hens were already scratching in the patio. They were used to the daily commotion of Nerón's tortilla, but they always made one of their own, cackling and flapping their wings as they scattered.

Coronel himself was always cool and dignified. He circled around the hens, high-stepping carefully between them and me and Nerón, his body stretched tall. Wobbling his comb from side to side like a red pennant he turned his head to watch us now with one yellow, beady eye, now with the other. It was a mean look.

More than the *jefe de familia* among his hens, Coronel was part of the security system of the family. With Nerón he patrolled the corral when he was not on the street, as puffy and important as an officer of the watch. In Jalco any boy or man who was not afraid of anything was known as *muy gallo*. Coronel was the most rooster of them all.

After Jesús and Catarino and I had done our morning chores that day, I went to the corral to escort Coronel and his household through the cottage and into the street. He was circling one of the hens, making passes at her, his neck feathers ruffled. She ducked and swiveled away from him, but Coronel drew nearer and nearer. Suddenly Coronel was on top of her, his yellow beak clamped on the hen's crest, his talons and spurs on her back.

I ran to the back door, excited and angry. My aunt was tidying up the kitchen. "Tía, tía," I yelled. "Coronel is squashing the hen. Shall I hit him?" My aunt stepped to the door and looked at the scene. She didn't seem worried. She turned to me and said matter-of-factly: "Leave Coronel alone. He knows what he is doing. The hen will be all right."

The hen, after her horrifying experience, had straightened up and gone about her pecking and scratching as usual. Coronel renewed his strutting. He did, indeed, seem to know what he was doing, but what was it? It was one of those things that adults were always leaving half explained. I would have to think about it in the *tapanco*.

My mother called out, "Take the hens out." I rounded up Coronel and his flock and shooed them through the cottage into the street. Nerón followed us.

Up and down the street the chickens of the pueblo had begun their daily search along the gutter. The pigs and dogs had spotted themselves where the garbage looked most promising. Halfway up the street, a *zopilote* was already pecking at something.

I sat down at the corner of the house in the sunlight. It was our favorite spot for watching what went on. Now and then a housewife stepped out of her front door to swing a jug of dishwater, spilling it in a sparkling arc over the street.

Nerón lay beside me, on the shady side of the corner. That morning I was his favorite playmate, since it was I who had given him the juicy tortilla. With his furry head between his paws he blinked and looked at me sidelong, screwing his eyes around, too lazy to raise his head. He knew my name, for whenever my mother called "Ernesto-o-o-o," lifting and holding the "o-o-o," Nerón came running from wherever he was, pretending, I suppose, that he had been watching over me all the while.

On mornings like that one Nerón and I sometimes walked down to the arroyo to watch the spumy water dash by. We would take the lane by Doña Mariquita's house, to whom we reported after a respectful *saludo*, and who watched us from her back door as we watched the torrent. But that day I had decided to just sit and see what happened on the street.

Coronel and his hens were making their way up the street between scratches. The hens kept their beaks down, pecking; and he paced this way and that, flaunting his comb, his feathers glistening in the sunlight.

When they were a few steps from the *zopilote*, the hens became alert. They stood still, some on both legs, some on one, looking intently at something that lay between the talons of the buzzard, which held his attention completely. He lowered his bald white head and tore at the garbage with his hooked beak. Among the pigs and dogs and chickens there seemed to be an understanding not to bother the *zopilotes* that came down to scavenge. To all the residents of Jalcocotán, including the domestic animals, the vulture's looks, not to mention his smell, were enough to discourage sociability.

Nerón and I were watching when one of the hens left the flock and went in for a peck at the *zopilote*'s breakfast. She moved head low, neck forward, more greedy than afraid.

The buzzard struck. With a squawk the hen flipped over and scratched the air madly, as if she were pedaling a bicycle.

Coronel sailed in. His wings spread, his beak half open and his legs churning over the hard earth, he struck the *zopilote* full front, doubled forward so that his beak and his spurs were at the *zopilote*'s breast feathers. The buzzard flapped one great wing over Coronel and bowled him over. The rooster twisted to his feet and began making short passes in cock-fighting style, leaping into the air and snapping his outstretched legs, trying to reach his antagonist with his spurs.

Up and down the street the alarm spread. "Coronel is fighting the *zopilote*."

"He is killing Coronel."

"Get him, Coronel. *Éntrale, éntrale.*"

A ring of small children, women, pigs, and dogs had formed around the fighters. Nerón and I had run to the battleground, Nerón snapping at the big bird while I tried to catch Coronel.

As suddenly as it had started, the fight was over. The *zopilote*, snatching at the heap of chicken guts that had tempted the hen, wheeled and spread his great wings, lifting himself over the crowd. He headed for a nearby tree, where he perched and finished his spoils.

Coronel, standing erect among the litter, gave his wings a powerful stretch, flapped them and crowed like a winning champ. His foe, five times larger, had fled, and all the pueblo could see that he was indeed *muy gallo*.

Seeing that Coronel was out of danger, Nerón and I dashed back to the cottage to tell the epic story. We reported how our rooster had dashed a hundred times against the vulture, how he had driven his spurs into the huge bird inflicting fatal wounds. Nerón, my dumb witness, wagged his tail and barked.

My mother had stepped to the door when she heard the tumult. She had seen it all and heard me through my tale solemnly. Coronel himself was strutting home prodding his flock and followed by the children who had seen the fight.

That night, after Jesús and Catarino and I were in bed in the *tapanco*, we heard Doña Esther give the men an account of the battle. Coming through to me in the dark, the story seemed tame, nothing more exciting than throwing the dishwater into the street.

"The boys think Coronel was magnificent," my mother commented.

Gustavo chuckled. Don Catarino drew on his cigarette and said: "Coronel is smart. *Zopilotes* are very chicken. They will fight among themselves, but if it's alive they won't even fight a fly."

The next day I asked my mother what it meant that somebody was chicken if he was not a chicken.

"It means he is not very brave," she explained.

"Is Coronel chicken?"

She guessed what was troubling me. "In no way. He is not chicken. He is the most rooster in Jalco. And I think he is the most rooster from here to Tepic."

I looked out into the corral. Coronel was standing on one foot, erect and watchful, under the willow. I knew something that he didn't—that people were talking about him as the only *gallo* that had ever beaten up a *zopilote*—something to be proud of even if a *zopilote* was, in some fashion, chicken.

Like many other mountain pueblos, Jalcocotán had no school. Once the village had sent a committee to Tepic to petition the government for a teacher. The committee assured the government that the neighbors would be willing to build the school themselves and to provide the teacher with a place to live. Once in a great while, when the *Jefe Político*, who represented the government, visited Jalco he would be asked very discreetly and courteously about the petition. The answer was always the same: "It is under consideration." Many years had passed—how many no one really knew—and Jalco still had neither teacher nor school when we went to live there.

Reading, writing, and arithmetic were held in great esteem by the jalcocotecanos. A few adults in the town had finished the third or fourth grade somewhere else. They taught their own children the *a*, *b*, *c*'s and simple arithmetic with the abacus. For writing they had the *pizarra* and the *pizarrín*—a small square of slate with a decorated wooden frame and a slate pencil.

Books were rare. My mother had one, which she kept in the cedar box. It had a faded polychrome drawing on the cover with the title *La Cocinera Poblana*, a cookbook which had belonged to Grandmother Isabel. We did not need it for cooking the simple, never-changing meals of the family. It was the first book from which Doña Henriqueta ever read to me. The idea of making printed words sound like the things you already knew about first came through to me from her reading of the recipes. I thought it remarkable that you could find oregano in a book as well as in the herb pot back of our house. I learned to pick out words like *sal* and *frijoles*, *chile piquín* and *panocha*—things we ate. From hearing my mother repeat the title so often when she read to us, and from staring at the cover drawing, I guessed that the beautiful girl in the colorful costume was the *Cocinera Poblana*. The words above her picture were obviously her name. I memorized them and touched them. I could read.

For me and my cousins until we were six, book learning was limited to a glimpse now and then of my mother's cookbook. Our school was the corral, the main street of Jalco, the arroyo, and the kitchen.

We learned to roast coffee on the *comal*. In the back of the house we kept a large basket of green coffee beans covered with a straw mat. Every few days my aunt scooped a bowl of the beans and spread them on the hot griddle. We took turns stirring them with a long wooden spoon. When the beans were toasted to a shade of rich brown, which my aunt called *el punto*, she took over. Too much brown and the coffee would taste burnt. Too little and it would taste raw. While this was going on the incense of coffee filled the house.

The toasted beans were then stored in an earthern pot covered with a cloth and a lid. Every afternoon a portion of this supply was measured out and chucked into the coffee grinder with the bronze cast-iron dome, the crooked handle, and the tiny wooden drawer. We took turns at the daily grind to give us enough fresh coffee for the next three meals.

The green coffee and the other staples of corn, beans, and rice were kept in rattan baskets along the back wall where it was always coolest and darkest. From a rafter there usually hung a stem of bananas, the king-sized ones called *platano grande*. Braids of red peppers hung there also, and white onions. Three boards resting on pegs made a shelf where we kept the bundles of corn-husks and the dried herbs. Stashed somewhere in the larder there was always a jar of raisins and some vanilla pods which appeared in the kitchen only on special occasions. From this storehouse came the foods and aromas of Doña Esther's kitchen.

Watching her, I learned to cook rice. She poured a cup of water into the rice bowl and churned it with a spoon to rinse it. In a clay frying pan the cooking oil was already sputtering, and in it the washed rice was spread and stirred constantly until it turned a light brown. The rice was then covered with boiling water, salted, peppered, seasoned with minced onions and set on a side burner of the *pretil* to simmer. The grains of rice came out of the pan crisp and whole, the mark of proper Mexican rice.

Our cooking lessons included roasting *pinole*, brewing *atole*, steaming tamales, and barbecuing the big bananas.

Pinole was for birthdays, the only production in which my cousins and I had more to do than my aunt or my mother. On the *comal* we roasted a cupful of dried corn, which we passed through the coffee grinder; on the *metate* we ground vanilla pods, lemon leaves, and raisins which had been dried in the sun until they were brittle. My aunt added a few scrapings of chocolate. We tightened the coffee grinder and put the mix through again. It came out *pinole*, a fine brownish powder that we ate a pinch at a time and that required much chewing and a great deal of saliva.

As a combination, *atole* with *panocha* was almost in the same class with *pinole*. The *atole* was a thick gruel of plain cornmeal. By itself it was ordinary stuff. But with *panocha* it was delicious. On Sunday evenings or on birthdays, instead of coffee we were served, in the same big earthen cups, steaming *atole*. Between careful nips of it Jesús, Catarino, and I passed around a chunk of the brown sugar cone for a suck and a lick. How you handled your *atole* marked the difference between a man and a boy. A man would gulp the thick, scalding liquid and crunch his own *panocha*. A boy sipped between licks at the sugar cone; a child would be given lukewarm *atole* dipped out of the cup on his mother's finger. For this we had a saying, "I gave him *atole* with my finger," which meant someone was a babe in the woods.

If we were in luck the *atole* and *panocha* were served with tamales. The day special visitors came we had a *tamalada*. It was an all-day affair; getting the cornhusks down from the back shelf; washing them until they bent without cracking; grinding the corn to make the *masa*; boiling the chicken; smearing the husks with moist cornmeal; tucking a bit of chicken into each chunk of *masa*, with a raisin or two; doubling the ends of the corn wrappers back and tying them in the middle of the *tamal* with a strip of husk.

The magic of the *tamalada* was not in all this preparation but in the *olla*—a huge earthen pot made of red baked clay like the rest of our kitchen ware, rough outside, glazed inside, and burnt black on the bottom. Into the belly of the olla went three or four small flat rocks. These were covered with water; on top of them a layer of shredded green banana leaves; on top of the leaves layer after layer, each crosswise to the next, of raw tamales. Some folded cloth napkins were battened down on top of the loaded *olla*. Set on the main burner of our stove, it became a pressure cooker, spitting steam around the edges of the napkins.

The visitors were served first, along with the men of the household. They took their *atole* boiling and crunched the *panocha* instead of licking it. When everyone had been served, the corn wrappers were dumped in the corral under the willow. Coronel, the hens, and Nerón soon scattered them, sniffing and pecking for bits of cooked *masa* that had not been scraped from the husks.

Even less frequent than the *tamaladas* were the banana barbecues which we called *tatemas*. Somewhere up on the mountain my Uncle Gus cut down a stem of the *plátanos grandes*. It was hung from the beam in the back of the house. Its long green fingers turned in, tight and solid, with straight brown ridges showing like veins from tip to tip. A cluster of these fingers was called, naturally, a hand.

In the corral the men dug a large round hole. The bottom was covered with rocks, and on top of them we burned *ocate* and charcoal.

When the stones were at top heat a thick pad of banana leaves was laid on them, followed by a layer of bananas, another layer of leaves, and so on until the hole was packed. Level with the ground a mattress of leaves and dirt was laid, weighed down by short, heavy poles.

The hard part came next—to wait overnight until one of the men began the unpacking. From between the layers of steaming leaves the huge *platanos* came forth, dripping in their own syrup. My aunt laid them inside the *olla*, from which she would take them one by one and serve them sliced, with *atole*. As they came out of the pit some of the bananas were wrapped in leaves, and we were sent to take them to the neighbors. This was better than taking cups of rice or beans because we could suck our fingers returning home.

Like the cooking, whatever went on in the cottage was serious business—making things or repairing them for the use of the family. We boys could watch, and often we were allowed to help, or to run errands. When the straps of rawhide broke on the bedsteads, Gustavo repaired them with new thongs. The straw mats that were laid on top of the rawhide springs were mended every so often. The oil lamp was lowered now and then to trim the wick and refill the tiny tank with kerosene from the green bottle on the shelf.

When my mother sewed or mended on the Ajax in the dim light of the back room, it was my task to lay mats all around the sewing machine to keep the garments from touching the dirt floor. That remarkable piece of machinery we were forbidden to touch, but we could watch the treadle see-saw dizzily, the belt whip around the balance wheel, the thread jerk and snake from the spool, and the needle stab the cloth with incredible speed.

Even Relámpago, the indolent burro, was my teacher. The rides on him up to the other end of the street and back were the beginning, I thought, of a heroic career as a cowboy. What I learned best from him was patience. With his droopy ear leading the way, Relámpago behaved more like a snail, continuously looking back at a small boy slouched on his rump. Back there you had nothing to take hold of, no mane, no ears. You either learned to balance or you fell off. Relámpago moved so seldom that I had time enough to shift on his grey, furry butt between jogs.

In Jalco it was easy to think about what you would be when you grew up. On the street, in the *corrales*, and in the family workshops people who had decided what they would be and had become what they had wanted to be, showed you how, if you watched.

On the other side of our street, next to the chapel, lived Don Crescencio, who made bedsteads out of ash poles and rawhide. Don Chencho, as everyone called him, brought the rough poles out of the forest and trimmed them and sized them with his machete. Under the eaves of his cottage he always had strips of rawhide exposed to the sun, and he took them down when it rained. Don Chencho notched and girdled and bored the poles, joining them to short legs, weaving the rawhide back and forth, up and down and across to make a pattern of small squares which was the spring of the bed. When they dried, the thongs became as taut as steel rods. Anyone could fix a broken rawhide spring, but only Don Chencho could make one properly.

Don Aparicio made *huacales* and wove *reatas*. The *huacales* were crates made of branches tied with rawhide or hemp rope. Inside the *huacal* you could crowd eight or ten hens to take them to market, or two large *ollas*, or a couple of dozen small ones. The *reatas* were ropes of woven cowhide made from thin strips and used for cinching loads on donkeys and mules. The strips gave off the stink of the tallow that Don Aparicio was constantly rubbing into them.

Up and down the street, there was somebody who could weave the shoulder bags in which the men carried their lunch to the fields; or cut, trim, and fit a pair of huaraches. We saw the butcher kill a steer, rip open its belly, yank out the guts, hang the carcass on a crossbar, peel off the hide with a knife, and cut up the raw red meat into strips for drying in the sun.

The girls of Jalco learned from the women of the pueblo how to sew and embroider. But my cousins and I, like the rest of the boys, paid no attention to such matters. An exception to this was my mother's letter writing. When she wrote one for a neighbor, she explained to us that in the large cities there were *escribanos* in the public squares who wrote letters for people who didn't know how. Since the *escribanos* were men, I thought that letter writing might also be a worthy profession for me.

It was the outsiders, the people who passed through town, who gave us some notion of other occupations besides those we saw in the village.

That is what Relámpago and I observed when the manager of the hacienda de Los Cocos rode through town. With me straddling his rump, my burro was standing stock still in the middle of the street staring into space. I was bending forward, grasping his shaggy coat as well as I could and giving his flanks gentle kicks with my heels. Out of the trail and into the sunny street rode the *Señor Administrador*, as he was respectfully addressed. He was on a horse twice as tall as Relámpago, a black beauty that glistened with sweat and bubbled white foam around the bit. The steed nodded from side to side as he stepped, shaking his mane and flashing a silver medallion in the middle of the strap across his forehead.

The *Administrador* sat on a horned saddle, a rifle in a sheath of tooled leather hanging from the cantle. The coil of the reata was looped over the horn. He rode as if he were standing tiptoe in the stirrups, his spurs jingling. His face was almost as dark from sunburn as his brown hat with a cone-shaped crown. The chin strap tied under the jaw ended in two strings dangling below the knot. Watching him pass, I conceived a vague notion that Relámpago and I could grow up to be *administradores*.

The *varillero* was another possible ideal. He came one day to the door of our cottage—a tall man wearing *huaraches* with thick soles and the loose cotton shirt and pants of the peasants. Doña Esther invited him in. He unstrapped a flat wooden box from his back and laid it on the bed. The box contained a pair of large trays filled with glittering gifts—combs studded with sequins, bracelets, buttons, party fans for ladies, rosaries, medallions with the picture of El Santo Niño de Atocha, needles, spools of colored thread, coils of bright ribbons, earrings, thimble-sized bottles of perfume, and mouth organs.

Our neighbors already knew the notions man was in our cottage. They came to our door, said "Con su permiso," and walked in, making a circle around the *varillero*. Cut off from the sparkling display of the trays on the bed, Jesús and Catarino and I climbed into the *tapanco* and had a birds' eye view of the houseparty: the *varillero* picking up and passing the trinkets around, the smiles of delight on the faces of the women, the girls giggling. The *varillero* made a bow with a red ribbon on his thumb and wiggled it. He blew a scale on the harmonica, which we bought for José, who had been wanting one a long time.

After the party at our house, he stopped at other cottages and by mid-afternoon took the trail in the direction of Tecuitata, where he would exchange, as he did with us, the gossip of the pueblos where he stopped.

But what I wanted most was to grow up and drive a donkey train, like the one that camped one evening on the edge of the pond near our house.

We heard them, the *atajo*, coming down the trail. The stumbling beasts set the rocks clattering, alerting the whole village. The cries of the *arrieros* came nearer—"Arre, f-z-z-t," sharp, spiraling whistles, and now and then the crack of a whip. They filed down the street between doorways crowded with women and children. Each donkey carried a brace of sacks or crates roped together, one on each side. The sweat blankets over the backs of the burros were tattered sarapes, padded with strips of canvas and rags. At every step the little beasts looked as if they would break under their huge wobbling loads.

The *arrieros* trotted alongside, zig-zagging, backtracking, running ahead to keep the donkeys in line and moving. Their tattered cotton *calzones* and shirts were flecked with mud, their faces covered with a makeup of sweat and dust. Some of them walked barefooted to save wear and tear on their huaraches, which they carried slung over one shoulder.

To my way of thinking, the *arriero* was the most one could grow up to be. He commanded not one burro, like Relámpago, but many. He could trot, sidestep, spring, and jump like a dancer. He could explode his long whip like a firecracker smack on the rump of a misbehaving burro. When he whistled he pulled his lips tight, showing his snow-white teeth, and the signal came out like

— 43 —

a whip, "Whee-oo-wheet." It was the *arrieros* who carried up and down the mountain more corn, more beans, more charcoal, more bananas, more coffee, and more coconuts than all of Jalcocotán could ever use. With nothing more than a rope or a rawhide reata, he could cinch a load on a donkey so tight it seemed glued in one piece to the animal. Besides, the *arriero* shouted words we were not allowed to repeat—words, in fact, we were not supposed to know.

The *arrieros* pitched camp by the pond, unloaded the animals, tethered them, and made a fire for their supper. A young drover came to our door to buy a penny's worth of salt. My mother gave it to him and added some fresh tortillas. After dark, Don Catarino, Gustavo, and José went down to talk with the *arrieros*. They brought news from other villages, rumors and wayside tales from far-off places like Compostela and Guadalajara. From the cottage we could hear José playing the harmonica for them.

They were gone in the morning before Coronel crowed. Behind the corral that afternoon Jesús and Catarino and I played donkey train. Up and down back of the wall, hidden from the house, we rode herd, snapping pretended whips and swearing at our imaginary donkeys: "Arre burro pendejo, f-z-z-t-." Doña Esther looked over the wall. "What are you saying? Inside the house, all of you. Quick." She met us at the front door after we circled the corral on the double. As we filed in she gave us each a sharp pull on the ear. Up in the *tapanco* for punishment, the three of us were silent, wondering how you could grow up to be an *arriero* unless you could talk like one.

Growing up in the pueblo, we would become like the *jalcocotecanos*. But two of our fellow citizens, who belonged to the past, knew how it once was. They were Don Cleofas and Doña Eduvijes.

Don Cleofas (nobody knew his last name) was certainly the oldest person in the pueblo. He didn't know how old he truly was, except that he had been born "before the time of Don Porfirio, much before." He had sons and grandsons and great-grandchildren who lived in other villages in the Sierra Madre. We used to see him sunning himself by the wall of his cottage when the days were cool. In the hot days of the summer he reposed in the farthest, darkest corner of the house, resting on a bed or a hammock. The hair on his head was almost white, smoothed down all around like a close-fitting knitted cap. His nose was sharp and smooth, in contrast with the wrinkles of his face, like those of a dry prune. He was beardless. His moustache, the color of his hair, drooped on either side of his mouth. Like many such old people born before the epoch of Don Porfirio, he was not missing any teeth, and why his thick eyebrows never turned white was one of the things that puzzled us about Don Cleofas. Under them his coal black eyes never looked at anything but the clouds, the stars, the forest, and the distance. Everyone called him "Tata."

The story of Jalcocotán was stored in Tata Cleofas's head. He never told it to boys or girls, but we got it secondhand from the talk that my uncles and Don Catarino had with the old, wise man, who was very much respected by everyone.

In this roundabout way with the explanations and comments of our own elders, we learned that there had been a time called Before the Conquest, when the Indian tribes had their own kings and emperors. Then the Spaniards had come, killing the Indians with guns and running them down with hunting dogs. The conquerors took the land along the rivers where there was water and

rich soil, flat and easy to farm. On these lands the Spaniards set up their haciendas, where the Indians were
forced to labor for nothing or were paid only a few centavos for a hard day's work. Don Cleofas had been a peon
on one of those haciendas. He had run away and hidden in the mountains until he was forgotten. Jalcocotán
was a *pueblo libre*, a free village, where people worked for
themselves and not for an *hacendado*.

According to Don Cleofas and our parents, the Indians had fought valiantly against the white invaders.
When they were overcome, those who were not killed or
captured fled into the Sierra Madre to places like Jalcocotán. "The Huicholes and the Coras," said Don Cleofas,
"are from the ancient times." The proof of this were the
Coras and Huicholes themselves. They passed through
Jalco from time to time along our street, silent and shy,
dressed in embroidered cotton clothes and wearing flat-
brimmed hats decorated with feathers.

There had been famous *caciques*, Don Cleofas said,
in those olden times—famous ones like Nayar, who had
taught the *Nayaritas* to make tools, to farm on the steep
mountain sides, and to fight. Old men who had fought
with Nayar had told these things to their children,
and they to their children, and so on until it was Don
Cleofas's turn to tell them to us.

He could remember—so he said—the time of the
war against the French. But the French never got as far
as Nayarit; he knew only that General Porfirio Díaz had
helped defeat them and then became the president of
the Republic. And Don Porfirio, as even Jesús and Catarino and I knew, was still president.

Doña Eduvijes was not, like Don Cleofas, an historian. She told stories like that of La Llorona, the Weeping Woman, who walked at night through the forest
chilling your blood with her wail. When she was heard

in the village it meant someone was about to die. The Devil himself appeared, as Doña Eduvijes told it, carrying a bag into which he stuffed children who had not been baptized and he took them off. It was she who told us stories of buried treasure and of el Capitán Espanto, the most dreaded ghost of all the Sierra Madre.

Doña Eduvijes always told these stories sitting on a bench of adobe bricks under the tree in the plaza nearest her house. When we saw Doña Eduvijes walking up the street to her seat under the tree, we knew she was in a mood for storytelling. She wore a cotton blouse tucked under the waistband of her numerous skirts, which showed in various colors at the hem. They bulged from her hips to the ground, barely touching it, so that we never saw her actually walk. She rather floated along, the skirts hiding her bare feet completely. As she walked, her heels broke the circle of the hems behind her with each step, and these slight kicks were how we could tell she had feet. Except for the one-two-left-right motion of those taps, she could have been moving on a dolly pulled without a sound by someone you couldn't see.

The younger children of the village gathered around Doña Eduvijes, sitting on the ground at her feet. From where I viewed her she looked commanding. She parted her grey hair in the middle and like all the women in the pueblo, let it fall in two tight braids down her back. She tied the tips with strings, not with ribbons like the *varillero* sold. Her face was moon-round and full, not wrinkled like Don Cleofas's. On her left cheek she had a hairy black wart, which was the spot I looked at most.

Before beginning a story, Doña Eduvijes reached down between the folds of her skirts and pulled out a small bag of tobacco and a pad of rice papers. With her left hand she rounded the paper lengthwise and with the right she tipped the tobacco over it, tapping the bag with her forefinger to make the brown crumbs drop into the paper canal. She rolled the paper into a little curved tube, licked one edge to make it stick, and pinched the ends to keep the tobacco from spilling. She struck a match, drew on the cigarette, and looked at us through the curls of blue smoke.

"This happened after the time of the French," she would begin.

"There was a captain of all the pueblos in the Sierra Madre. He rode a magnificent white horse and a saddle covered with silver medallions. I myself never saw him, but that is what I have been told. They called him el Capitán Espanto." And she related how the captain discovered the treasure of the three Indian kings, how he lost it and died, returning to haunt the Sierra Madre on a white horse.

When Doña Eduvijes drew the last puff from her cigarette and brushed the ashes from her lap, we knew the tale was over. We broke away from the circle, one by one. Like the others I walked home through the growing darkness, looking up the lanes to the forest or down to the arroyo, thinking I saw a captain on a white horse, my skin slightly crinkled and my heart thumping.

Doña Eduvijes sat on the bench and smoked until the last child had started home. She got up and padded on her invisible feet across the street to her cottage.

If you were past six and going on seven, life in Jalco could be made disagreeable by neighbors who seemed to think that they could scold you and tell you how to behave. You never knew when a *compadre* or *comadre* of your aunt, or your uncle, or your father, or your mother was watching. For that matter, even people who were not *compadres* to your family thought they had some sort of rights over you. If you did or said something slightly irregular at the farthest end of the street from your cottage, where your legitimate bosses lived, somebody would be watching and ready to call out: "Mira, que muchachito tan mal-criado." And if the offense was considered serious, the voice would say, "You will see, I am going to tell your mother." In a village so full of snitchers and busybodies you could get an extra ear-pull for any trivial breach of good manners—the *buena educación* which the adults prized so highly.

As a result you paid attention to what was expected of a *muchachito muy bien educado*. You never broke into an adult conversation. This was called putting your spoon in, or the way I remember the rule: "Los muchacitos bien educados no meten su cuchara." No one ever entered a house, or left the room without saying "Con su permiso." It was "with your permission this" and "your permission that" practically all day long, unless you were playing with your friends. Whoever called you, for whatever rea-son, if you answered "what do you want?" you were in trouble. You had to answer by asking for a command: "Mande Usted?" People talked to one another on the street in low tones; only drunks and *muchachitos mal educados* raised their voices, or the *arrieros* when they shouted to their donkeys.

Every mother in the village could ask you to do an errand. If I was in the middle of a game, or just sitting in the street watching the *zopilotes*, some neighbor would call me: "Ernesto, come here and take this to Doña Edu-vijes." What right she had to order me around no one ever explained, but I was taught to move right up, an-swer "Sí, señora," and do the errand.

In fact, running errands was the special business of any boy or girl between the ages of four and six. When you delivered something you always began by saying: "My mother sends greetings and says may God give you a good day, and here is an egg." When you reported the accomplishment of your mission, you repeated the other half of the ceremony by heart: "She says that she sends greetings, how is the family, and many thanks for the egg." Any neighborhood courtesy—an exchange of a banana for a red pepper, or the return of a borrowed utensil—was sure to pass through our messenger system.

Some errands were special. Going for milk was one. There was one cow in the village. She was stabled in a corral on the arroyo side of the town, where she could be walked across the stream and tethered in the pasture beyond. No family drank milk every day, only when there was pudding or chocolate to make on feast days. It seemed to work out smoothly, with just enough milk whenever it was wanted, because nobody wanted much. I went to the one-cow dairy with a small pitcher about quart size. The cow was milked straight into it, nobody minding the flies or manure among the cornhusks that littered the corral. On the walk home the important thing was to avoid the pigs and dogs and hens with strict attention to getting the milk home unspilled.

We did not have an orchestra in Jalco, though even the Huicholes had them in their villages. But there was always music. Somebody on the street owned an ancient guitar that Doña Henriqueta said was from before the time of the Aztecs, which was several hundred years. The *jalcocotecano* who owned the guitar tried hard year after year to learn to play it. In a feeble voice he sang to the "kaplink-kaplunk" of his instrument, and everybody on the street listened, mostly out of sympathy.

In a class by himself as musician was my Uncle José. The mouth organ we bought for him from the *varillero* became, under his direction, as close as anything we ever had to a town orchestra. José never had any lessons. He heard the *arrieros* whistling on the trail, the ballads the mariachis played in San Blas and Tepic, the country poems set to music which the women sang, and the cries and calls of the birds. He imitated pig grunts, Relámpago braying, Coronel sounding his morning call, and the "kaplink-kaplunk" of his fellow artist down the street. Out of the double row of small square holes of his harmonica, José sucked and huffed the repertoire of *corridos* and lullabies and marches he carried in his head. He gave concerts for me and my cousins back of the corral or down by the arroyo, as we watched the harmonica flash back and forth cupped in his long thin fingers. José always began by working his mouth as if he was rinsing it, clearing his throat, and spitting with an explosion of his cheeks. He tapped the harmonica, which he kept wrapped in a piece of cloth, holding it upside down, then giving each side of the instrument a swipe on his pants. When he played, his Adam's apple bobbed up and down, keeping time to the music.

These recitals were special events. The music we heard every day were the songs my Aunt Esther, my mother, and the other women of the village sang. Singing went along with the washing of clothes in the arroyo and the kitchen chores. If there was a baby in the house, there were songs for rocking, the dinner music for breast feeding. In one of these songs, a cicada who lived in a chink of a wall piped a sad tune that always ended up with "chee-ree-bee, chee-ree-bee." There was one about a learned crow who made pens out of his quills and earned a comfortable living writing letters for people who had never gone to school. Another was about a peacock who snubbed everybody because he roosted at night in a Cup of Fire tree all by himself, a splendid perch for a magnificent bird. A hurricane blew the tree down and the peacock had to sleep on the ground "just like any other animal," said the song—a lesson for egotists.

Doña Henriqueta sang about an ugly dwarf who hid in the top branches of a *guamuchil* whenever six lovely elves danced around the tree to their musical rhymes. Their favorite was the one that went:

> "Mondays and Tuesdays and Wednesdays make three;
> Thursday and Fridays and Saturdays, six;
> We are as happy as happy can be."

Everything depended upon keeping the rhythm perfect, but the old imp high up in the tree would groan at the end of the verse:

> "And Sunday's seven."

This, my mother explained, was like poking your spoon into a conversation and had to be punished. The elves finally caught the mischievous dwarf one night when he was climbing the tree, and they beat him with a stick until he promised to cooperate. They made him learn a new punch line, which he sang out from the top of the *guamuchil*, so that the song now sounded like this:

> The elves: "Mondays and Tuesdays and Wednesdays make three;
> Thursdays and Fridays and Saturdays, six:
> We are as happy as happy can be;
> The dwarf: "I'm in a terrible, terrible fix."

When some of the *compadres* got drunk, usually on Sundays, there was singing in some corral or in the plaza. Women and children took no part in these affairs, which sometimes ended in fights with machetes. We couldn't help hearing the men's songs, which became louder with the drinking. They sang the *corrido* of Catalino, the bandit who stood off hundreds of *rurales*, the mounted police who chased him up and down the Sierra Madre year in and year out. In his last battle, Catalino was cornered in a canyon. From behind a boulder he picked off dozens of *rurales* with his Winchester, taking a nip of *aguardiente* between shots, and shouting to his persecutors : "Acérquense, degraciados, aquí está su padre." The *rurales*, like anybody else, did not like to be called wretched punks especially by an outlaw who boasted he was their father. In Mexico for such an insult you paid with your life. They closed in until Catalino lay dead. They chopped off his head and showed it in all the pueblos of the Sierra Madre, which made Catalino hero enough to have a ballad composed about him. It was generally agreed that he was from Jalcocotán where the bravest men were to be found, especially on Sunday nights when they were drunk.

Without *aguardiente* the *compadres* could hardly have annihilated hundreds of *rurales* in one evening, even with the help of Catalino. Inside of the tall green bottles in which it was sold, the "burning water" was as innocent as a Coke. Inside of a man it turned his guts into rattlesnakes, ready to strike with the deadly fang of a machete. It rose like tear gas to their heads making the *compadres* cry and sing weepy love songs like "La Rancherita": "I loved a little country girl / she was so shy / she couldn't even talk to me / I would take her hand / and she would sadly cry / Now go away / My mother will be scolding me."

Rowdiness of this sort stopped when the priest came to visit Jalco, which happened once or twice a year. Instead of drinking songs, we heard the chants and the litanies that he sang with the chapel choir.

José, besides serving as an altar boy, sang in the choir, and for a time his future as a chorister looked promising. But he composed comical Spanish versions of *Dominus vobiscum* and other Latin bits of the ritual. The priest heard about this and expelled him because his translations were disrespectful. One of them was to the effect that "if you are an awful sinner, just invite the priest to dinner." José was scolded (but not very severely) for entertaining us with his sing-song imitations of religious rites.

The expulsion of José made it much less likely that we would be sent to mass or that the priest would receive from us the gifts that the *jalcocotecanos* usually presented him on his visits—a roasted chicken, a pot of tamales, a comb of honey, and other savory foods that kept him overweight. He never visited a cottage without sending advance notice, so that when he knocked on the door there would be a milk pudding or a whole barbecued banana dripping with syrup ready to serve. José's humiliation put a stop to these visits to our family. After that we heard more and more family criticisms of the religious man. He charged too much for funerals. He collected fees for baptizing children as well as for blessing pigs and goats and other domestic animals. He sold scapularies which, my mother said darkly, a seamstress in San Blas made from his underwear. My cousins and I vowed that if José was not reinstated in the chapel none of us would ever become a priest.

For nearly everyone else in town the infrequent visits of the priest, his sermons and incantations, and his sprinkling of holy water in places where a ghost had appeared were serious matters. People spoke of *El Diablo* and of *La Muerte* as if they were persons you might run into any moment. The Devil could descend on you from a tree in the shape of a monstrous lizard or block you on the trail dressed in flames and aiming a spear at you. Death was a gangling skeleton who perched her rattling bones (Death was always a She) on the roof ridge of your cottage, or signal you with a bony finger to follow her into the forest. Against the powerful black magic of *El Diablo* and *La Muerte*, the *jalcocotecanos* needed the equally powerful protection of their scapularies, the sign of the cross, and Our Lady of Talpa and the Holy Child of Atocha, the most revered saints among our neighbors.

Pictures in polychrome colors of the holy ones of Talpa and Atocha were carried at the head of funeral processions that went by the front of our house. When a playmate died down the street, I saw the small coffin wrapped in a white sheet carried by a man on his shoulder. People stood in their doorways and made the sign of the cross and prayed silently as the procession passed. I didn't know the prayers exactly, which sounded to me between a whisper and a mumble, so I bowed my head and whispered and mumbled. The next day we made a bouquet of geraniums and carnations from the pots in our corral. We took it to the mother when we went to offer our *pésame*, the mourning visit to the family of my dead friend. My mother spoke, and I repeated the traditional words: "I come to keep you company in your grief. May he rest in peace." My mother was dressed in black and there was a narrow black ribbon around my arm. When she walked me home I complained that she was holding my hand too tightly. I looked at her face. She was weeping. The dead boy had been about my own age.

Up to the time a boy was between five and six years old, Jalcocotán was for the most part an easy place in which to live. The neighbors and *compadres* and *comadres* who scolded you for your bad manners or sent you on errands did not interfere much if you were respectful and stayed out of the way. With my two cousins and other boys of my own age I always had something to watch or to do.

The near side of the pond was shallow and fringed with reeds and tall clumps of grass that blossomed with plumes of cream-colored fluff. Around them the pond was always muddy and cool. In your bare feet you sank up to the ankles and by wriggling your toes you could raise oozy, iridescent bubbles. Trampling and squishing the mud, we made plopping hollow sounds and pretended we had gas on our stomachs. Pulling your foot out of the soft gumbo while your friends listened closely made a noise remarkably like the mules in the corrals when they dropped manure.

Although we never collected polliwogs or frogs or lizards we chased them along the mud flat until they hopped into deep water or slithered away in the grass. Water snakes were everywhere, which we imagined were poisonous *víboras* or copperheads, like those the *jalcocotecanos* found in the forest. We spiced our play with a legend about an alligator that had crawled all the way up from Miramar and lay in wait for us somewhere in a deep pool of the arroyo—a monster no less real because he lived only in our imagination.

When the older boys of the village came to the pond on Sunday afternoons we watched them swim and dive. From a high branch of the big *nogal* they dropped a swing made of bush vines we called *liana*, braided like the women of the pueblo did their hair. The boy who was to dive next waited up in the *nogal*. Another handed him the end of the *liana*. The diver kicked off and let go as high as he could swing, his naked brown body twisting through the air like a split string bean. On our side of the swimming hole the smaller boys stripped and paddled while the divers yelled instructions on strokes and kicks.

Once in a great while the older boys would also allow us to join them in the bullfights they organized in one corner of the pasture. The bulls, the matadores, and the picadores were the ten to twelve-year-olds, and the master of the fight was the oldest of the gang. We were permitted to take part only as fans or *aficionados*, to provide the yelling, the catcalls and the cheers. The master of the *corrida* directed us to sit on the ground on the upper slope of the bullring, which was entirely imaginary.

From behind a tree a trumpeter stepped to the edge of the ring. Blowing on a make-believe bugle he sounded a call and the bull rushed in—a boy with a plain sarape over his shoulders, holding with both hands in front of his chest the bleached skull of a steer complete with horns. Between the horns a large, thick cactus leaf from which the thorns had been removed, was tied. It was at the cactus pad that the matadores and picadores aimed their wooden swords and bamboo spears.

If the fight went according to the rules, the master declared the bull dead after a few rushes, by counting the stabs into the cactus, and the dead bull was replaced by a live one. Sometimes a sword or a spear missed the cactus pad and poked the bull in the stomach or some more sensitive spot. If the bull suspected that the miss was on purpose and dropped his skull to charge the to-rero with his fists, there was a free-for-all. We *aficionados* fell on one another with grunts and kicks, wrestling on the ground to increase the bedlam. If the commotion got out of the hands of the master of the *corrida*, there was always an adult watching from the village across the arroyo, who would walk over to the ring to scatter the rioters and send them home.

The girls of the village, needless to say, did not take part in the swimming parties or in the action of the bullfights. Neither did we, the boys who were under seven years of age.

This by no means put us in the same class. Up to his third year, a boy could still be led by the hand or undressed by an older sister. He was a *chilpayate*, a toddler who could play on the street naked without anybody noticing it. Little by little the *chilpayates* became men of sorts. They noticed that only girls had their earlobes pierced, wearing bits of string until their parents could afford genuine rings. They had to sit for hours to have their hair braided. At five years of age girls began to learn to carry water up from the arroyo in *ollas*, holding them on top of their heads with both hands, something that no man in Jalco would think of doing. They played silly games like La Ronda, hopping around and around, we thought, like *zopilotes*. Boys did girls' chores only if, and everybody knew that it was only if, there were no girls in the family—like shaking and sunning the bed mats or sprinkling the street in front of your cottage.

Between five and six, the fact that girls belonged to a lower class became even more obvious. Boys went into the forest to gather firewood. If their father's *milpa* or banana patch was not too far away they would be sent off before noon with a hot lunch in the haversack. They picked coffee beans on the lower branches of the bushes. They were taught to halter the burros and water them at the arroyo. They cut and bundled weeds in the *milpa* to feed the hens and the stock.

When a Jalco boy was passing six years of age and had become used to such jobs, he spent more and more of his day with the men and less time with the women. He was given more important tasks, which had a great deal to do with his becoming a man: "para que se vaya haciendo hombre." At six, a boy stood about as tall as a machete, but he would not be able to use one for several years. By the time he was fourteen he would be a man, complete with a machete of his own, working the *milpa* or the coffee patch or the banana stand by the side of his father, and able to do it by himself, if necessary.

Somewhere between seven and fourteen the village noticed other signs of his coming manhood. The surest of these was his watching the girls when they went to the arroyo to scrub clothes and bathe. We under-sixers could do this anyway without anyone paying attention or chasing us off. Sitting high on a boulder just above the pond I could see them, with a white skirt pulled up and pinned over one shoulder, slapping the clothes on the rocks, dipping them in the water and wringing them. When the washing was over they slipped off the skirt and slid into a pool, dunking themselves, chattering and laughing above the noise of the current. That was how I found out, without my folks making any particular fuss, that there were at least two important differences between boys and girls besides the braids and the perforated ears.

That was not, however, real girl watching. Around twelve years, boys stood away, behind a tree or a bush. If someone noticed, they pretended that they were going into the forest or to the *milpa* to work.

After you picked out a girl you began watching her in the village, coming closer step by step until everybody knew it. In this way the girl was staked out and every other young man in the pueblo was on notice. Any other watcher would have to fight for it sooner or later. All this took time; if you began watching when you were around twelve by the time you were sixteen you could propose, asking your parents to ask hers for permission to get married.

All this happened only if the parents of the girl liked you. If they didn't, her father would let you know. Jalco was a small, tight town and you could easily be caught shadowing the girl or even speaking to her. She would most likely get a beating, and you might be chased away by her father or brothers.

But you were not ready to take the risks of going steady in Jalco until you had proved yourself a man at work. At six years of age or thereabouts you stopped being a playmate and became an apprentice. Jacinto and his father were a good example of this.

Chinto, as we called him, became an apprentice *campesino* when he was only a little older than I. I saw them pass in front of our cottage in the early dawn, Chinto following his *jefe* to their corn patch down the mountain. The man walked ahead, his cotton pants cinched tightly to his waist, one side of the fly crossed over the other and tucked into the waistband. The legs of the *calzones* were wound snug to the ankles, like puttees. At this time of the day the grass along the path to the *milpa* would be heavy with dew; the puttees soaked up less moisture than the bell-bottoms of the pants legs when they were loose. The soles and leather thongs of the huaraches the father wore were the soiled brown color of his ankles and toes. The hat was the usual ice cream cone of straw set on a wide brim curving down over the eyes and upward above the neck. He carried a machete in a sheath with the rawhide loop over one shoulder, and over the other the lunch bag.

Jacinto walked behind, dressed exactly like his father, except that he did not carry a machete. Several paces behind, he trotted to keep up with the steady gait of the man, learning the first lesson of his life as a *campesino*: that he would spend the rest of his life walking, walking, walking. "Ay va Jacinto con su papá," someone said in the gloom of our kitchen. It was the end of another boy and the beginning of another man.

They came back at nightfall in the same way, the man leading the boy. Both had rolled their pants legs above the knees, their white cotton shirts open in front, their hats tilted back. The man carried his huaraches over his shoulder. When the trail had roughened and calloused the feet of the boy, he would do the same.

The daily rounds that Jacinto and his father made were either to the cornpatch, the *platanar* where they cultivated banana trees or to the few rows of peppers and *jitomate* they tended. We knew the day that Jacinto went to pick coffee berries with his father, because they both carried wicker baskets, the man a large one, Jacinto a small one. When they left the village for several days to herd cattle for a *patrón*, father and son carried rawhide slings, the father a long sling, the boy a short one. Rounding up heifers and calves, the father taught the boy to whirl the sling and let one end go, timing it so the pebble would strike the target. Jacinto showed us how, when he was practicing in the pasture.

Jacinto and the other seven-year-olds who were growing into manhood lost no time in making it clear to the rest of us that we were nothing but stay-at-homes. As we felt more important than girls, so Jacinto and his fellow apprentices felt more important than us. It took courage to walk toward the *milpa* through the forest where you could step on a rattler any moment, if you didn't see it coiled in the path or hear its tall buzzing. It took stamina to weed the corn hills and the banana trees under the broiling sun. Only a boy with manstuff in him could walk down the mountain and up the next ridge to spend the night tending heaps of burning wood to make charcoal that the burros carried to Tepic and San Blas. At night from Jalco we could see the orange bonfires high up on the mountain to the east. We saw Jacinto come back with his father from such work—jaunty *carboneros* with rolled-up pants legs, hats tilted back, face and legs and arms smeared with charcoal, dust, and sweat.

It was in the cultivated patches in the forest that boys grew into men. With machetes they cleared the steep slopes and the hollows, setting fire to the brush and the stumps. In the ashes they planted corn, beans, peppers, *jitomate*, and bananas. Under the shade of a tall tree they grew coffee bushes. The forest provided the rest of Jalcocotán's living—timber, charcoal, wild fruit, herbs, boars, deer, and hides from alligators and cougars.

Out of the forest a man took out only what he and his family could use. Not all the *campesinos* in Jalcocotán, or in all the pueblos on the mountain together took out so much that the *monte* and the arroyo could not replenish themselves. In the conversation of the townspeople there were ancient sayings—*dichos*—that showed how long the people and the forest had lived together : "Agua que no has de beber, déjala correr"—at the arroyo drink your fill, let the rest run down the hill. "El que a buen arbol se arrima buena sombra le da"—the shade beneath a goodly tree is good for you and good for me.

Other than the stone walls of their corrals, the *jalcocotecanos* did not build fences to separate one man's property from another's. When the soil wore out in a *milpa* and another one was cleared, there were no old fences to take down or new ones to put up.

The world of work into which Jacinto and the other seven-year-olds were apprenticed was within sight and sound of the pueblo. It was work under blazing suns, in rainstorms, in pitch-black nights. It was work that you were always walking to or walking from, work without wages and work without end. It was work that gave you a bone-tired feeling at the end of the day, so you learned to swing a machete, to tighten a cinch, and to walk without lost motion. Between seven and twelve you learned all this, each lesson driven home when your *jefe* said with a scowl: "Así no, hombre; así." And he showed you how.

But he knew that there was another world of work beyond Jalco. Over in Miramar, Los Cocos, Puga and such places there were haciendas where peasants from the pueblos could work for money. Some *jalcocotecanos* did this kind of hiring out. They cut sugarcane, herded cattle, butchered steers, tended the crops, gathered coconuts for the soap works, and cleared land *a puro machetazo*—with your bare hands and a machete.

Boys who went with their fathers to the haciendas soon learned the differences between making a living on the mountain and working for the *patrones*. One was that on the mountain you took home corn, bananas, peppers, coffee, and anything else you had raised, but never money. From the hacienda, when your contract ended, you never took anything to eat or wear except what you paid for at the *tienda de raya*, the company store. A peon could make as much as ten pesos a month at hard labor working from dawn to dusk, seven days a week, four weeks every month. It came to about two or three centavos per hour, plus your meals and a place to spread your straw sleeping mat.

The most important difference, however, was the *capataz*, the riding boss who watched the laborers all day long, just as the *guardia* watched them throughout the night. The business of the *capataz* was to keep the *peonanda*, as the crews of field hands were called, hustling at the assigned tasks. He carried a machete slung from his saddle, a whip, and often a pistol: the equipment of a top sergeant of the hacienda. The captain was the *Administrador*, who in turn took his orders from the *patrón* who probably lived in Tepic or Guadalajara or perhaps even in La Capital, as everyone called Mexico City.

The men who had worked on haciendas knew of these matters. We heard snatches of firsthand reports from them but mostly we learned from Don Catarino, José, Don Cleofas, and the muleteers who passed through Jalco. Whoever had been there came back cursing it. The riding boss was the Devil on horseback; in the company store every centavo you earned was taken back by a clerk who kept numbers in a book that proved you always owed him something. If a peon left the hacienda before his contract was over and his debts were paid, he became a fugitive. He either returned to his pueblo, his *compadres* and his *milpa* in some far-off place in the mountains, or he scratched for a living, lost in the forest. Old men in the village talked of the time they had worked on a hacienda as if they had served a sentence in prison or on a chain gang. They remembered capataces who had whipped them or cursed them fifty years before, and they still murmured a phrase: "Algún día me la pagan." There were a hundred blood debts of this kind in Jalcocatán, Doña Esther said, thousands of them in all the villages of the Sierra Madre, and millions in all the pueblos of Mexico.

"Algún día me la pagan."

"Tía, what does that mean?" I asked her more than once. She always sent me to my mother with the question. Her answer was: "It means that somebody owes him something."

"But what does somebody owe him?"

The anger and the foreboding in "algún día me la pagan" was in my mother's voice: "Something that hurts." She did not explain, just as she would not tell me why Catalino the bandit hated the *rurales* and shot so many of them.

Guessing at what people meant, I came to *feel* certain words rather than to *know* them. They were words which came from the lips of the *jalcocotecanos* with an accent of suspicion, of fear, and of hatred. These words were *los rurales*, the *jefe político*, the *señor gobernador*, *las autoridades, el gobierno.* When a stranger rode into Jalco, people stopped talking. Every detail about him and his horse was observed for a clue as to whether he was one of the *autoridades.*

It was the same with all outsiders. They always came asking questions, which the *jalcocotecanos* answered politely but roundabout. For me the world began to divide itself into two kinds of people—the men on horseback and the men who walked.

Whether the flood happened before Nerón was killed, or the *rurales* descended on Jalco before the flood, I don't remember. These troubles, along with the appearance of Halley's comet were crowded into the last year we lived there. The most memorable of them was the death of Nerón.

As a good watchdog he stayed in the corral all night. When he sensed prowlers from the forest padding down the lane on their way to the arroyo, or sniffing near the willow where Coronel and his hens roosted, Nerón growled. Nobody paid any attention to him unless he barked repeatedly, running to and from the back door. If a mountain lion or a timber wolf was in the vicinity, Nerón joined the dogs in the other corrals in a commotion of barks, yips, and whines. The men could tell from the way the dogs barked whether it was a predator stalking the hens or only a deer going down to the arroyo for a drink.

After his morning tortilla, Nerón usually found a place in the corral where the first rays of the sun would warm him. He pulled in his hind legs and arranged his front ones so he could rest his head on his forepaws, always pointing his nose toward his tail. His grey coat was the color of the hard earth of the corral, which he swept with his bushy tail when he wagged it as he lay resting. With his short fur, his alert pointed ears, and a way he had of standing at attention on three paws Nerón was easily the prize dog of Jalcocotán.

When he tired of watching us do the morning chores, and being ordered here and there to get out of the way of the housework, Nerón loped down the street to visit his friends. Between his own social life and playing with us, Nerón passed most of the day. About mid-afternoon he was in the habit of trotting off into the woods. Now and then we heard him baying excitedly.

It was Don Catarino's opinion that on one of these expeditions Nerón was bitten, perhaps by a skunk, and that was how he got rabies. Doña Esther saw him walk slowly up the lane one afternoon, wobbling on his legs. She called us and we saw him stumble near the corner of the corral and hunch himself against the wall. He snarled as my aunt approached him. "Nerón," she called out. Instead of trotting up as he usually did, tail wagging in obedience to the command, the dog growled and slavered. We were kept in the house, behind closed doors, and my mother walked up and down the street warning the village.

José was sent for. When he arrived Nerón was still humped by the wall of the corral. We heard my aunt tell him about Nerón's behavior.

We watched him until Don Catarino and Gustavo arrived. José armed himself with a big stick and they went out to the lane. We were ordered to stay in the house, but from the back door we could see the heads of the three men above the wall of the corral wall, moving slowly up the lane. They stopped. José called, "Nerón," and the dog snarled. Gustavo came back. "Rabies," he said. He pulled his machete from the sheath and started back to the lane. "Not with the knife," my aunt said.

My cousins and I listened to all this, perplexed by Nerón's behavior. Now we watched in terror from the far end of the lane. Don Catarino and Gustavo stood back while José advanced slowly. He was holding the stick above his head, ready to strike. "Nerón," he called. The stick fell swiftly on the dog's head. He was too weak to attack or avoid the blow that crushed his skull.

The men came back and José went to the back of the house. From beneath the bench on which the grain baskets stood he pulled a sack. We watched him walk back up the lane and step cautiously near Nerón, moving his hind legs with the stick. The dog did not stir. José slipped the open end of the sack over Nerón's head and jerked it little by little over his body. He picked up the sack, twisted the open end, hoisted it over his shoulder and walked into the forest.

That night, before we were sent up to the *tapanco*, Doña Esther explained it to us.

"Rabies," she said. "Nobody can cure rabies. Animals get rabies from other animals and people can get rabies from animals. They die. An animal with rabies does not know what he is doing. He is mad." She paused and added: "Poor Nerón."

Up in the *tapanco*, we tried to figure it all out. My beloved José had killed my beloved Nerón with a stick. Where had he taken Nerón? Would the *zopilotes* devour him? Could Relámpago get rabies? Could Coronel? We whispered these questions to one another until my mother spoke quietly from below, "Go to sleep."

The night of the flood we were not sent to bed in the loft. Instead of undressing we wrapped ourselves in our sarapes and sat quietly where we were told—in the corner of the kitchen by the *pretil*, out of the way, but ready to leave.

Outside, the hurricane was howling and crackling through the forest. We could hear the whoosh of the windstorm coming closer until it swept over the cottage, whistling through the cracks of the doors and along the open space between the roof and the walls. The flame of the *candil*, hanging from a beam, bent this way and that with the gusts of wind. Through the cracks beneath the eaves we could see the purple flashes of lightning, and we sat watchful and alert, like the grown-ups, waiting for the thunder to crash over our heads.

The downpour had started early in the afternoon. The men knew that this was going to be no ordinary summer shower. It had been thundering far up the north end of the mountain all morning. Throughout the day the wind picked up steadily from the west. There were no hawks gliding far up in the sky and the *zopilotes* were gone from their perches. Instead of rolling, the clouds piled higher and higher and turned to a charcoal grey color. Coronel and his hens did not go out into the street, but squatted close to the back wall of the house inside the corral, as if they wanted to be closer to the family.

The men started arriving at the village before mid-day. Every one of them was a weather man and they all knew this was a time to be in the pueblo and not in the *milpas*. They passed our house in the drenching rain, some with soaked sarapes over their shoulders, some wrapped in capes of banana leaves tied in a peak over their heads.

By late afternoon the street was already under water. On the down side the doors of the cottages were closed and barred and the chinks of the threshholds stuffed with rags. Being on the upside of the street, our front sill was above the tide. We left the door open through the afternoon and watched the slanting rain streak hard into the flood. Each plopping raindrop punched a round dent into the sheet of water that covered the street, raising a silver purl like a crown that disappeared instantly. The street, as far as we could see, was a carpet of ruffled crowns, rippling and sliding in the direction of the arroyo.

By early evening we could hear the roar of the creek above the pounding of the rain on the roof and the drumming of the thunder. The hurricane had passed, bouncing off the hills all around us, unable to dig its terrible claws into the hollow where Jalco was safely tucked. Now the danger was in the arroyo.

The pleasant stream where women washed clothes, girls bathed, and naked boys belly-flopped was now a giant brown dragon growing wider, higher, and wilder by the hour. In this condition the waters of the freshet were called *aguas broncas*, for they were like a stampede of broncos pounding the pueblo. Down the lane between the two cottages opposite our house we could hear the roar of the torrent and the banging of timber which the arroyo had wrenched from its banks upstream.

Every man, woman, and child was up that night. The dogs and hens were brought indoors; neighbors who lived on the arroyo side of the street took theirs to the houses on the upper side. The cow, the burros, and the mules were tied in the corrals across the street away from the torrent.

It seemed we had been waiting hours for something to happen when there was a knock on the door. Don Catarino unbarred it, and opened it a chink.

"Don Evaristo's corral is down. The water is up to the back wall," a voice yelled out of the darkness above the racket.

"We're coming," shouted Don Catarino.

Wrapped in sarapes, the men of our family and Don Evaristo's hurried back and forth between our cottage and theirs. It was the last house on the low end of the street, as ours was on the high side. In bare feet, with their pants legs rolled tight above their knees, the men moved beds, pots, pans, chickens, the dog, tools, machetes, and baskets filled with food. Should the water reach our own house we could move things to the upper end of the corral, and if necessary over the wall and up on the rising slope of the forest. Among the jumbled heap of furniture and animals we kept watch. Doña Henriqueta served coffee and *atole* through the night. One of the men dashed across the street now and then to check on the arroyo.

I awakened sitting against the wall at the end of my mother's bed, wrapped in my sarape. Both doors of the house were open. Outside the sun was shining. The men were moving everything back to Don Evaristo's. Jesús, Catarino, and I were put to work carrying small objects across the muddy street, and it was my job to clean up the droppings that our hens and the neighbors' had deposited where they had spent the night. As a child, whenever I came near a mess my mother always said: "Caca." I chased Coronel and his hens into the corral, yelling "caca" at them.

That day the men did not go to the *milpas* which would have been flooded or damaged by the hurricane. There would be time enough to learn the worst. Moreover, there was more urgent work to be done in the village: cleaning up and fixing after the rampage of the arroyo.

Don Evaristos's corral had been swept away, the lower wall bashed in. The cresting waters had chewed away the foundation of the back wall of his cottage, crumpling it. The beams of the roof on that side were slanting steeply and resting on a pile of mud at a crazy angle, looking more tired than battered. The men were already notching poles and fitting them to the under side of the fallen beams to hoist the roof back into place. The women, including my mother, were getting the kitchen back into shape, and neighbors were already bringing pots with hot food.

It was many days before the waters of the arroyo settled and cleared and became friendly and pleasant again. The tops of the biggest boulders began to show above the muddy tide, and the trunk of a huge tree, wedged between two boulders, was left high and dry behind the chapel. The pond shaped up slowly out of the muck and the *nogal* stood once more dry and serene. The women rebuilt the arbors of boughs to protect them from the hot sun where they did their laundry. The girls glided slowly up the ramps of the lanes with *ollas* full of water on their heads, the pot sitting on a coil of their shawls. They went back to bathing in the pools, and I went back to sitting on my favorite boulder to watch them.

Don Cleofas told stories about the *aguas broncas* of many years ago that had wiped out whole pueblos, by which he probably meant that what we had seen was nothing worth speaking of. Everybody seemed to agree with him, except the boys of my own age. We were certain that the first *aguas broncas* we had experienced were the most formidable, the most treacherous, the most devastating, altogether the most of any *aguas broncas* there had ever been. Having lived through that terrible night was enough to make heroes of us.

Telling tales about our heroism would have been enough to keep us boasting and arguing for a long time in a quiet town like Jalco, where notable events happened once or twice in a lifetime. But the village did not settle into its usual ways of taking for granted that the next hundred years would be just like the last hundred.

In the beginning it was mostly rumors. A family received a letter from a son who had left Jalco and had gone to work somewhere in the north. My mother read the letter to the family and she said it was from Sonora where they had public letter writers in the plazas and her son, who himself did not know how to read or write, had the letter written for him. In it he said he was going to the United States because in Sonora there had been a strike in the mines where he worked, and men had been killed.

Arrieros who passed through the village said that the government was rounding up young men in the towns and drafting them into the army. The *varillero* told us that Don Francisco Madero had been in Mazatlán campaigning for president of the Republic against Don Porfirio. Everybody in Jalco knew about Don Porfirio, although nobody had ever seen him, and only the old men could remember a time when General Porfirio Díaz had not been president. Nobody knew Don Francisco Madero.

News always reached us in bits and pieces—when the *arrieros* passed through the town, when the *varillero* appeared with his gee-gaws or when *jalcocotecanos* returned from their long hikes to Tepic or San Blas to buy and sell. The news spread without newspapers or telephones. In the village no one ever kept news to himself; while you were telling it you were paid attention to, especially if you added comments of your own.

It was over this grapevine that our family heard of the first stirrings of trouble through the countryside. It was said that the *maderistas* had formed a party against the *porfiristas*. The farmhands of the haciendas were running away and gathering in bands in the mountains. One of these bands had held up a stagecoach bound for Mazatlán. A regiment of soldiers had arrived in Tepic to defend it from attack by the peasant guerillas. The *administrador* of Las Varas had packed his goods and he and his family had disappeared. Young men were leaving the *milpas* to join the guerillas, which they called "bolas." A *bola* could start in any pueblo and take off for the hills, to join other *bolas* and form a command under a *jefe revolucionario*.

In Jalco a new fear was growing in the village. It came home to all of us the day José brought word that the *rurales* were riding toward our town. He had met a peasant on the trail who told him they had been seen moving out of Ixtapa the day before.

We heard José telling the family the news. Then, without waiting for their supper, the three men left the cottage. The rest of us stood at the front door, watching as they stopped to chat with other men in the street or in the doorways. Some of Don Catarino's *compadres* and their *compadre's compadres* came to our house and stepped into the corral, murmuring to the women as they passed "Con su permiso." They carried machetes. There was quiet talk for a while, like all the conversation in Jalco—someone saying something, a silence to think it over, a question.

It was pitch dark when our visitors left. The women served supper. My mother packed tortillas, a pot of beans, some salt, and a few strings of jerked meat into José's shoulder bag. The same rations were prepared for Gustavo. They picked up their sarapes and machetes, and stepped out the front door without a word. José turned into the lane towards the woods, Gustavo heading up the street toward the trail for Tepic. Except for Don Catarino, who squatted under the eaves to smoke, the rest of us stood in the doorway looking into the darkness where Gustavo and José had disappeared.

The *rurales* rode into Jalco before Coronel crowed the next morning. We heard the clopping of the horses' hooves as they crossed the arroyo below the pond, and the jingling of spurs and the rattle of sabers as the troops passed by. The ponies whinnied and somebody cursed in front of our house. Jalco was occupied before the men would be starting out for the *milpas*.

It was barely light outside when Don Catarino unbarred the front door to answer a knock. Doña Esther and my mother and we three boys stood well back in the shadows of the room. By the light of the lamp we saw a *rural* standing in the doorway, in the uniform of Don Porfirio's mounted police—peaked sombrero, tight pants, bolero jacket, riding shoes.

"Good morning," he said, his thumbs hooked on his ammunition belt. "By order of my Sergeant, no one is to leave the pueblo." He paused. "The Sergeant requests, if you will be so good, to prepare breakfast for the troop." The *rural* turned on his heel, his spurs jingling as he walked away.

On the spot, Jesús, Catarino, and I were given our own orders. We were to stay in the house unless called. Coronel and the hens were to be kept in the corral. We were to answer no questions whatsoever.

While Doña Esther busied herself with breakfast for the *rurales*, my mother opened the cedar box and brought out the clay pig bank and a leather wallet. "Help me," she commanded. We stepped into the back yard. She handed me the pig bank and the wallet. Straining, she lifted a geranium planted in a five-gallon tin. Beneath it was a hollow in the ground. "Quick, in the hole." I put the wallet down and the pig on top. She lifted the can so as not to drag it over the ground and leave marks and set it over the hole carefully. My mother bent over me. "Not a word. To any one. Do you understand?" The sharpness in her whisper not only bound me to a secret; it also made me understand that I was taking part in dangerous events.

The troop of some twenty *rurales* went about the business of taking over a pueblo. We saw them walking their ponies down the lanes to the arroyo to water them. The mounts were tethered in the plaza and given grain provided by the *jalcocotecanos* on orders from the Sergeant. The women served the soldiers, who squatted or sat in the shade of the trees. The Sergeant and two *rurales* rode up and down the street, noticing everything. They turned up our lane and rode back to the street, looking over the walls into our corral.

We were at the back door, watching intently. The Sergeant rode by our door. He was on a black pony not nearly as big as the horse of the *administrador* of Los Cocos, and uniformed like all the *rurales*—gray jacket like a bullfighter's, tight pants with two rows of buttons down each leg, and a felt hat with a tall pointed crown and wide brim. A rifle in a sheath hung from the saddle. The bullets inserted in his belt showed with their round brass bottoms up and their tiny gray teeth down. Besides his rifle and pistol, the commander of the troop carried a saber dangling from his belt.

Half of the *rurales* remained in the plaza while the others searched the houses one by one. They asked us, "Arms?" "No, sir, we have none." "How many people live here?" "Five, not counting the children." "Where are the others?" "They are working." It was no use for us to lie about how many of us lived there. The police could easily tell from the beds, the *tapanco*, the pots and pans and other telltale details. But we could lie about Gustavo and José. At that moment nobody could have found them.

The search of our house ended with a short speech by the *rural*. "We have orders to protect the pueblos. The government desires the cooperation of the citizens to maintain peace and tranquillity."

"Si, señor."

"You will be so kind as to prepare a lunch for one man and bring it to the plaza."

"Si, señor."

Toward noon the *rurales* rode out of Jalco, taking the trail down the mountain. After the last invader had disappeared the talk went the rounds of the village, mixed with jokes, a kind of quiet celebration over the defeat of the *rurales*. They had not found what they most wanted—arms and young men. Nor had the *rurales* found *aguardiente* in the cottages on which they could get drunk and shoot up the town.

The men prepared to go to the *milpas*, but some did not go to work that day. Along the *veredas* that short-cut the trail to the villages and the homesteads up and down the mountain they hurried ahead of the *rurales*, to pass the word that they were coming.

"Malditos," my mother said that night at supper.

I knew the word. When we played war on the pasture, we drew straws to choose sides of good *jalcocotecanos* and bad *rurales*. When it was my turn to be a *campesino* chasing *rurales* and killing them, I yelled "malditos" adding the worst insult of all: "aquí está su padre," like Catalino.

José came back to the village a day or two after the *rurales* left. He had circled the mountain, talking with the peasants. He said that the *bolas* were forming, and that people were asking whether there would be one in Jalcocotán. Gustavo had not returned. It had been decided that he would go to Tepic and let us know what was happening there.

The villagers were still talking about the occupation by the mounted police when Halley's comet appeared. Only old Don Cleofas claimed that he had seen anything like it before, when he was a boy.

Every man, woman, and child gathered in the plaza to stare at the heavenly kite with the bushy tail. Shooting stars we saw every night, streaking across the most un-expected places of the sky. They came in a wink and were gone in another. A comet was something else. Don Cleofas said it was bigger than the earth and that the tail was so long nobody could guess how many millions of kilometers it was from tip to tip. Jesús and Catarino and I were called down from the *tapanco* the first night the comet appeared. I caught the awe of the older people who were listening to Don Cleofas tell that a comet fore-told something important, and serious. He said that this one meant *La Revolución*.

Gustavo returned from Tepic a few days later. He, too, had seen the comet. He said that soldiers had ar-rived in Tepic, that guards were traveling with the stage-coaches, and that the *rurales* were taking young men to the regimental barracks to be drafted into Don Porfirio's army. The rumors about Don Francisco Madero were true; in the marketplace he had heard that the *maderistas* had already fought the *porfiristas* in the north. A peasant from Escuinapa said that he had himself seen the *rurales* set fire to a village.

Evenings after supper the conversation was about these matters, and important decisions were made. It was agreed that Gustavo was to leave for Tepic. José, my mother, and I would follow him. The four of us would find work and a place to live for the whole family in the city.

Doña Henriqueta made a bundle of Gustavo's belongings and he said good-bye to his friends in town. We three were still asleep in the *tapanco* when he left one morning before dawn.

Part Two

PEREGRINATIONS

EVEN THOUGH IT was only a long day's walk to Tepic we did not hear from Gustavo for several weeks. Some *arrieros* said the trail was closed halfway to the city by a landslide. We saw fewer peasants pass through the village prodding their donkeys on their way to the towns along the coast.

The *varillero* arrived in Jalco one morning with his wares and a message for my family. The *varillero* had talked with Gustavo in Tepic a few days before and wanted to inform us that he had found work and a place for the four of us.

Unusual things began to happen in the household. My mother and Doña Esther sat and talked a great deal more. It seemed they were making up their minds about many things. If we came close enough to hear what they were saying we were ordered off to play.

Don Catarino came back one day driving a horse and a mule which he walked through the house and tied in the corral. Coaxing him with a ration of corn I had my last ride on Relámpago. My mother worked long hours at the Ajax, mending and sewing, not singing, as she used to, above the whir and clicking of the machine.

I let every boy in Jalco know that we were moving to Tepic. Carrying over my shoulder a multi-colored sarape of brilliant red, green and orange stripes that my mother had given me, I strutted up and down the street. I repeated words I picked up from household talk about what Tepic was like—the cathedral, the *plaza de armas*, the *palacio* of the governor.

But when I found out that Relámpago, Coronel, and the hens were not going with us, I did not feel important over our coming departure. I knew that Jesús and Catarino were staying behind, but it had not occurred to me that we would not be sleeping together in the *tapanco*.

The day we left Jalco everyone was up long before Coronel crowed. Doña Esther was already cooking at the *pretil*, the flame of the oil lamp, as usual, flickering in the gloom beneath the thatch roof. My mother was busy folding clothes and packing the few things we were taking. Both doors were already unbarred and open. In the street, directly in the light of the *candil*, Don Catarino and José were harnessing the mule and loading it with our belongings. The stars were shining in the pitch dark sky.

The horse on which my mother and I were to ride stood in the doorway where the light from the kerosene flame fell on it, looking eerie and huge. Don Catarino heaved a saddle to the back of the beast, securing it under the bulging belly with straps, loops, and rings. Except for Don Catarino's crisp, quiet orders, and brief questions and answers between Doña Henriqueta and Doña Esther, no one had spoken. Everything had already been said and decided.

Don Catarino was standing by the doorway, looking up at the stars, the way *jalcocotecanos* told time at night.

"It's getting late" he said. My mother embraced my Aunt Esther. "Adios, Tel." "Adios, Queta." They said good-bye using their family nicknames. Doña Henriqueta pushed me gently toward her sister. She bent over me for our last *abrazo*, a gentle throwing of the arms over the shoulders and a flutter of pats on the back. "Say good-bye, boys." "Adios, Jesús. Adios Catarino. Adios Ernesto."

My mother stood in the doorway, the two sisters looking at each other for a moment. Her hair was wound in two tight braids pinned to the back of her head, the strings of her straw hat tied under the chin. Over a cotton blouse with long sleeves she wore a shawl. She was wearing the riding skirts I had seen her make on the Ajax, divided in the middle like baggy pants. The black high-buttoned shoes she wore were her Sunday best, the ones I had often polished and put back on the shelf in the back of the cottage.

José stepped out of the darkness. He stood close to the horse and laced both hands like a stirrup. My mother put one foot into them and he lifted her to the side-saddle position proper for a lady, then lifted me in front of her, straddling the horn of the saddle. Don Catarino came up. "You hold on to the horn. Don't touch the reins," he said to me.

We waited for Don Catarino to check the cinch on our mount by the light of the lamp. Aunt Esther, Jesús, and Catarino stood framed in the doorway backlighted dimly by the *candil*.

"Arre," said Don Catarino to the lead mule. José standing behind our horse repeated, "Arre." They stepped off and we headed up the street between the double row of adobe walls for the trail going north. In the dark of the early morning we kept together more by sound than by sight. Coronel had not yet crowed. Jalco was still asleep.

When we came to the end of the street and picked up the trail, the horses slowed down. Their iron shoes clopped and clinked against the rocks in their path. Climbing against the grade they strained forward and slackened the pace to feel their way, swaying right and left by the feel of the earth beneath them and humping as they pitched gently. I hung tight to the horn of the saddle between the reins.

We moved slowly up the trail. I got used to the bobbing of the horse, the chirruping of the saddle leather under me, and the sour smell of the sweating beast. The calls of the men—Don Catarino ahead, José behind—reassured me like the touch of my mother's arms. "Arre," "f-z-zt." "mula-a-a-a." I fell asleep, hunched over the horn of the saddle, propped and safe from toppling to either side and backstopped by my mother.

I awakened in bright daylight where the trail leveled into a meadow surrounded by pines, on the far side of which there was a brook. We crossed the meadow and tied the horses in the shade of a tree. José helped us dismount. Don Catarino was already checking the cinches, the halters, and the bits, tugging here and pulling there on the belts and straps. Doña Henriqueta crossed the brook and disappeared in the woods. José said to me: "Come," and I followed him in the opposite direction into the trees. Waiting for him, I stood in the deep shadow of the forest. The air smelled of damp earth, damp bark, and damp leaves. Between the trees I looked back at our camp and the sky above it, turning the pale blue of a hot day.

Back at the brook we washed in the ripples between the rocks, now that the horses had been watered and were crunching their ration of corn, their noses deep in the feed bags. José made a fire pit with rocks while my mother warmed our lunch of tacos, tortillas, and a pepper for each of the men. As we ate, the grass around us had begun to steam in the early sun. My mother pointed to the sky and we looked up. "A *zopilote*," she said. High above us it glided in circles above the pasture, as I had often seen them do over Jalco. The clearing was as silent as Jalco when we had left it a few hours ago. Don Catarino rolled a cigarette and smoked. My mother turned to look for a bird that screeched in the woods.

Don Catarino was speaking, brief and to the point, a little gruff. "We will get to the pass by early afternoon so we can cross it before dark. We will camp on the other side and start early and get to Tepic before noon." The plan took care of the important things—a long rest for the horses, crossing the most dangerous part of the trail in the cool of the afternoon with plenty of sunlight, time enough to find a rancho where we could ask for permission to camp, and arrival in Tepic in broad daylight, when the military patrols could see us plainly and would not challenge or fire on us.

My mother and I mounted and our journey continued. Ahead I could see Don Catarino leading the load mule by a rope. Now and then he gave it a tug to keep the mule to a steady pace. On one side of the animal a large box containing our clothes, the cedar chest, and cooking utensils was strapped to a wooden frame secured to the back of the mule. On the other, wrapped in straw mats and a saddle blanket, hung the Ajax, balancing the load. On top, between the cross arms of the frame, bundles were piled and held in place by ropes.

Besides the two of us, our horse carried an assortment of bags and a bedroll back of the saddle. Between its ears I watched the back end of the mule, glistening with long black streaks of sweat. The load see-sawed sidewise as the mule maneuvered its way patiently over the rough trail. Don Catarino, now leading the mule, now following it, tugged at the halter, and slapped it on the rump by turns.

From my perch behind the saddle horn I could see an arroyo rushing to the sea. On the other side the canyon rose straight up, the ridge topped by a green comb of forest against the sky. All along the trail footpaths branched away into the bush, packed hard by the tramp of men in huaraches. These were the *veredas*, narrow and crooked, that criss-crossed the forest like a spider web. A few feet off the main trail only the natives who lived on that particular mountain could find their way.

I saw wooden crosses, their arms tipped or broken, stuck into mounds of rocks along the trail. They marked the place where a traveler had stumbled to death into the canyon below, or had been killed and robbed.

In the stretches where we rode through thick woods, it was dank and gloomy like the *monte* behind our corral in Jalco. Don Catarino guided the mule as the path twisted between the trees. We rode under a dark ceiling of foliage that smelled warm and wet. The horse and the mule seemed to step faster through these places, and I certainly wanted them to hurry. We broke out of these fearsome places suddenly, coming out into the bright sunlight of clearings where robbers were not so likely to be waiting in ambush.

In the meadows it was hot, and the flies swarmed around us. The green-bellied ones stung the animals, keeping their ears twitching and their tails swinging. Our horse wrinkled his withers in nervous spasms trying to shake off his tormentors. I fought the green demons with a switch.

As we ambled through a clearing where the forest fell away from the trail, we had glimpses of the Sierra Madre. The ridges piled up one after another, blue-gray and smoky, until they became lost in the haze of the distant skyline. Tepic, I began to think, was beyond the farthest of those ridges, and we would never get there. "Where is Jalco?" I asked my mother over my shoulder, hoping she would order Don Catarino to turn back. She merely said, "Way back there," and I felt wretched. The Sierra Madre, stretching from us without end in every direction, had swallowed both Tepic and Jalco and we would never find either again. With every bump of the saddle horn between my burning, itching legs I got madder and hated everything and everybody—my mother, the horse, Don Catarino, the flies, and the desolate mountains.

At mid-afternoon we came to the devil's backbone. That was what Don Catarino called the most dangerous passage of our trip. The trail came to the edge of a grassland and jutted beyond into space. It was a rocky path atop the crest of a dam which had been piled up by the convulsions of the earth and the hurricanes between the two walls of the canyon we had to cross. The dam looked to me hundreds of feet high.

Don Catarino stopped us at the rim of the gigantic hole. He said that he and the mule would lead well ahead. My mother was to give the horse a free rein and under no circumstances spur him. If he stopped we were to wait. José was not to start across until we were on the other side.

The crossing was only about the length of the street in Jalco but it seemed miles to the other end. Step by step the mule followed Don Catarino. Our horse started after them, picking his way between the cliffs on either side of the narrow crest, so close we could look down on the tops of the trees far down in the bottom of the canyon. He kicked loose pebbles and rocks that rolled and clacked their way to the bottom, striking other rocks as they fell. The horse stopped several times, then moved ahead cautiously, Doña Henriqueta holding the reins loosely around his neck. I held on, gripping the saddle horn for dear life.

Halfway across, the mountain came out to meet the razorback, making an almost perpendicular wall up on our right. Now we could only fall to one side, but stones could fall on us from the other, and even a small one could frighten the horse or stun you.

We reached the end of the cliff. Don Catarino had tied the mule to a tree and was ready to take the reins of the horse to lead him well away from the edge of the canyon. He helped us dismount and we waited, hot and shaky, for José to cross over. He was already coming, as straight down the middle as he could, avoiding the loose rocks and keeping his eyes on the ground ahead. We watched him in silence, as we had crossed, remembering what Don Catarino had told us—that in such places a shout could set a rock slide in motion as easily as the kick of a mule.

Together we sat down in the cool shade to rest ourselves and the animals from the strain. Don Catarino plotted the last leg of the trip. We would go a short distance to a rancho where he knew the people. We would spend the night there and reload early so as to arrive in Tepic before the noonday heat.

Our caravan arrived at the homestead long before sunset. It was like all the other mountain ranchos I had seen around Jalcocotán. On a terrace back several yards from the trail there was a hut built of thin poles tied together and driven into the ground. You could poke your fingers through the cracks between the poles. The roof was of palm thatch with a wide overhang of scraggly grass on all four sides. Front and back of the hut there were stake doors hinged to posts by means of leather straps. Behind the hut there was a clearing with a patch of vegetables. Along the side some geraniums were in bloom in earthen pots.

We held back while Don Catarino stepped up the terrace. A dog barked and there was a stir among the chickens back of the hut. A woman in white blouse and white skirts came to the front door. She and Don Catarino exchanged greetings.

"Good afternoon, señora."

"Good afternoon."

"Is your husband home?"

"He is in the *milpa*. He will be here in a very little while."

Don Catarino walked back and said, "We will wait." The "very little while" could be one minute, it could be one hour, it could be two.

While he smoked and José stretched himself on the ground well away from the hut, my mother took me to a brook below the hut. She sprinkled my head with cool water, scrubbed my face, and refilled our water gourd.

It was nearly dark when the man of the house returned from the *milpa*. José had slept, Don Catarino had rested in a shady nook of the trail, my mother had watched, and I had played in the brook.

Don Catarino exchanged greetings with the man, keeping his distance and speaking quietly, as mountain people always did. He asked permission for us to spend the night and to unload the mule in the corral. As we listened, he asked for the favor of a few fresh tortillas for supper, for which we would be glad to pay.

The ranchero and his wife knew why we had stopped, and just what we would say. We knew that they would give us permission, that they would not take any money for the tortillas, and that we must leave some gift before we left. I had watched these formalities before, the signs of courtesy and hospitality of the mountain people. We said "thank you" all around and retired with the mule and the horse to our camp behind the corral.

Don Catarino and José unloaded the mule and unsaddled the horse, fed them and watered them at the brook. The Ajax was unpacked, and with the straw mats and blankets in which it was wrapped my mother made our beds on the ground. Some pots were placed over an open fire to warm our supper. The lady of the rancho appeared with a stack of tortillas wrapped in a napkin. My mother asked her if she would do us the favor of accepting two cones of *panocha* and some salt.

It was nearly dark when my mother returned with the cups and plates she had been washing at the brook. The mats were spread around the coals of the firepit and we covered ourselves with sarapes and blankets. I was told to go to sleep at once, but I had catnapped all along the trail and I wanted to listen to the voices of children in the hut. Sneaking looks from under my covers, I could see the kitchen fire in the center of the dwelling flickering between the palings of the wall. I had seen the rooster and hens in the yard, and a skinny dog, the color of Nerón. I liked the rancho and decided we should stay there instead of going on to Tepic.

When my mother awakened me, the mule was already loaded and the horse saddled. There was coffee on the coals, with tortillas and warm bean tacos. Inside the hut the fire was still flickering through the chinks. The rooster crowed and the man came to the back door to see us off. My mother and I mounted and we were on the trail again.

It was downhill the rest of the trip, easy for the horses, the trail getting wider until it became a genuine road of hard-packed brown earth. We could see other travelers ahead of us, on burros or horses, but mostly walking. The people and the animals carried loads, sacks, crates, earthenware, and *huacales* filled with chickens. A burro train passed us going the other way. The donkeys carried piles of empty sacks in which charcoal had been delivered to the city. The *arrieros*, powdered with coal dust, kept them at a trot with shouts and whistles and snapping whips. A boy about my age skipped along the line of burros, helping the two men.

The road became busier with foot travelers and pack animals. They trotted or bounced along the crest of the hill ahead of us. We rounded a knoll at the top of the grade, and as our horse kept an easy pace, I looked down into a bright and endless valley that fell away gently in fields laid out in squares. The other side of the valley was cut off by high mountains with jagged peaks, unlike the smooth-timbered hills back of Jalco. In the midst of the green and brown fields of sugarcane, corn, and pastureland I saw a checkerboard of white and red, tiny blocks of whitewashed houses with tile roofs. My mother reined the horse and pointed. In the middle of the checkerboard I spotted two grey towers not much longer than my little finger.

"Tepic. The cathedral," my mother said.

As we descended, the country road straightened out into a lane enclosed by low walls and one-story houses, their roofs slanting this way and that. The tops of the walls were set with pieces of broken glass and splintered bottles that glistened in the morning sun. Women with blue shawls draped around their heads and shoulders walked close to the adobe walls carrying wicker baskets filled with fruit, meat, and vegetables. They were coming from the market with the day's food supply for the family—the *mandado*. Donkeys loaded with straw, firewood, and *huacales*, charcoal, green bananas, and lumber passed by. Rancheros returning to the mountains cantered on nags that looked too small for the riders. I had never seen that many people in my life.

Our horse's shoes began to clack as we came to a street paved with stones. Along the middle of the street they were flat, at the sides they were cobblestones, rounded and neatly laid. The walls of the houses echoed the clatter of the traffic, so that people indoors could tell whether horses or mules or burros were passing, whether they were coming or going, and how many there were. Everything that passed over such a pavement made a characteristic sound, even the bare feet of people.

Don Catarino turned us into a cross street. He slackened the pace, looking at the houses as we went by. We stopped alongside a long low wall with scaly whitewash and a coping of red tile. Midway along the wall there was a high, weather-beaten plank door wide enough for a wagon to pass. This was the *zaguán*. In the planks of the right hand side of the *zaguán* a smaller door was framed, the *postigo*, for people to go through, one at a time.

The *postigo* was open, and Don Catarino stepped in. He came back with a fat lady in calico skirts, blue shawl, and long braids. She was the caretaker and landlady of the *casa de vecindad* where we were to stay.

Our landlady went inside and opened the *zaguán*. We rode in, following Don Catarino and the mule, between two rows of adobe rooms, each with a door to the corridor which was open to the sky. In the back there was a large patio enclosed by high walls and planted erratically with trees and bushes.

Don Catarino and José busied themselves unloading the mule after helping us dismount. Instead of stepping around to stretch my legs as I had wanted to do, I promptly sat on the ground. I was stiff and raw from the waist down and I didn't want to say precisely where it hurt most, especially in the presence of the landlady.

Guessing what was wrong, as she always did, my mother spread one of the straw mats and José carried me to it. I knew better than to whimper from the bruising I had received all the way from Jalco, jouncing on the saddle horn. It was not so much a matter of principle as of *vergüenza*. I remained on the mat convalescing while everybody else worked. The landlady laid out four bowls of hot soup, tortillas, coffee, and mangos on a rickety table in the patio. Feeling very inadequate I waited for José to carry me to the table but my mother merely said, "Come to eat." I up-ended myself as well as I could and managed a side-winding hobble to the table. I was excused from doing errands and I lay on the mat all afternoon, napping and fighting the flies.

Don Catarino left for Jalco early next morning. At the door of the *zaguán* my mother said, "May it go well with you." He rode off on the horse, leading the mule. We watched him down the street until he turned a corner.

While José went to look for Gustavo, we inspected our new home.

Gustavo had rented two of the rooms in the *vecindad*, one for himself and José and one for my mother and me. The rooms were more like cells, four adobe walls with a single door to the corridor. An oil lamp was suspended from a peg in the wall. The beams of the ceiling slanted toward the back, supporting the planks on which the roof tiles were laid. The dirt floor was cool and hard. In the corner by the door stood a thick pole and there was a shallow hole in the floor for the brace when the door was shut at night.

The furnishings were as plain as the room. In one corner there were two low sawhorses with planks on top. The straw mats and a blanket laid over the planks made my bed. In the opposite corner there was a wooden frame with a rawhide criss-cross spring like our beds in

Jalco. The Ajax was placed next to the doorway and on top of it everything else we had brought—clothes, blankets, pots, and the cedar chest.

The adjoining apartment that Gustavo and José were to share was even less luxuriously furnished. Each had some straw mats in a corner for a bed. A bench along the front wall served as a dresser, closet, and table. There were pegs to hang clothes, and the oil lamp overhead. The other rooms were occupied by families living temporarily in the *vecindad*, like us.

The landlady's helper, a boy two or three years older than myself, ran errands, chased the hens away from the corridor, watered down the street in front of the *zaguán*, and mopped the red brick pavement of the corridor with a long rag tied to the end of a broomstick. The step-and-swing rhythm of this operation seemed to me the cleverest I had ever seen.

The women cooked on a row of *pretiles* built against the wall of the patio around the corner from the row of apartments. The laundry was done in stone tubs in the patio, where the housewives scrubbed and slapped and lathered the clothes as they chatted or scolded the children. Nearly every day the shrubs in the patio were draped with garments set out to dry. The toilets, two-hole privies separating the men from the women by a curtain, were in one corner of the patio.

To take a bath we used a wooden tub placed in the center of our room on top of straw mats. Water was heated over a fire in the patio and hauled to our room in pails. I was the only one of the family who did not take his bath in privacy. Doña Henriqueta's excuse for this indignity was that I did not scrub myself clean enough with the straw washrag. This was a piece of soap wrapped in hemp, the purpose being to make the soap last. I unwrapped the soap and used it without the straw, which scratched me.

An old lady who lived alone in one of the back rooms was the first absolutely toothless person I had ever seen. When she gossiped with my mother I stood close to watch her lips curl over her gums and flap as she blew them out of the way to get the words out. My mother treated her with much respect, as did everyone else in the *vecindad*.

At night, the landlady propped two poles against the wings of the *zaguán* and barred the *postigo*. Each family slept behind the barred door of its own room. Through the night the watchmen on the street blew their whistles as they walked their rounds, stopping at every corner. The military patrols clattered by on their ponies, ready to challenge anything that moved on the dark streets with the fearful "Quién vive."

We settled a week before my Uncle Gustavo showed up. He had a job in a sugar mill north of the city. On Sundays he walked to Tepic to see us and walked back the same afternoon. The conversation on these weekly visits was about the family back in Jalco, how long it would take to reunite us, our trip over the mountains, the revolutionary *bolas* that robbed the stagecoaches to Mazatlán, the difficulty of finding work, the low wages. There were more questions than answers—how much the two men could earn, how much could be saved.

Another important problem was where to keep the small change that we saved from day to day. In the *vecindad* there were no loose bricks behind the *pretil* or secret holes under geranium pots. Someone remembered a cousin who had moved to Tepic from San Blas many years before and it was decided to locate her and consult her on the matter.

José, like many other young men from mountain villages who were drifting to the cities one step ahead of the *rurales*, scrounged for odd jobs. He left every morning with his lunch and ten centavos that my mother allowed him. On lucky days, when he came home with wages jingling in his pocket, he did a bit of stage business that we all enjoyed. He announced his good fortune by standing in the doorway, tapping the coins in his pants pocket with his knuckles and saying: "I'm standing in water, and it comes up to here." In Spanish it went like this: "Hasta aquí me llega el agua." Together we counted his earnings. When they reached one peso it was fantastic. When he had spent the ten centavos he had taken in the morning, my mother shrugged off his disappointment by quoting some helpful proverb, like: "It's better to be young than to be rich." She served supper and José told us what he had done, if he had worked—carrying bricks on a construction job, cleaning carcasses at the slaughterhouse, repairing a street with cobblestones, or helping a tanner spread hides in the sun.

Being in a strange city, with no one to look out for me, my mother took me with her wherever she went. Together we located people in another *vecindad* who knew our relative from San Blas. We found the distant cousin, a middle-aged lady who did washing and ironing for rich people. She told us we could leave our savings with her and that they would be kept in a place that only she knew. Our money was to be wrapped and tied in handkerchiefs and we could have it any time we needed it.

Finding our cousin helped in another way. She could send us to ladies who had sewing and mending to do. Listening to the two women talk, I understood that this meant we could get our Ajax into production. Our cousin banker gave us names and addresses, and with these connections Doña Henriqueta found work she could do at home.

Picking up and delivering garments and visiting our cousin, we explored Tepic. First we located the central park, called the *plaza de armas*. The main square of the city was a terrace surrounded on all four sides by wide cobbled streets. The sidewalk around the terrace was an ample promenade, with green iron benches set along the edge. Like a garland around the promenade a border of Cup of Fire trees bloomed in crimson. In the center of the square there were rose beds and grass plots setting off the *kiosko* where the military band played on Sundays and the authorities made speeches.

People came to the plaza to sit or to walk around and be seen. Gentlemen in suits and round black hats sat on the benches and had their shoes shined. Women with braids and bare feet sat on the edge of the terrace nursing babies wrapped in blue shawls. Men in the straw hats, huaraches, and the loose dress of the mountaineers talked, standing or sitting on benches apart from the gentlemen in tailored suits. Vendors went up and down the walk and criss-crossed the square carrying trays of sliced coconut meat, sticks of brown taffy, popcorn dipped in molasses, and gum. The man with the push-cart and the bottles with the colored water passed along, calling out refreshments of pineapple, coconut, barley, orange, and lemon. On one end of his cart he carried a metal tray lined with gunnysacks. When a customer asked for a *raspada* he uncovered the block of ice under the sacks and with a tool like a small carpenter's plane in the palm of his hand he grated the ice, scooping it into a paper cone and sprinkling it with colored juices from his bottles.

On our visits to the plaza I was given a penny to spend—a large, heavy coin of dirty copper that was much less important than it looked. With that one centavo I had to make hard choices among sugared bananas, gum, and peeled mangos on a stick. Because the brown sugar sticks, the *largas*, provided more licks per centavo I usually spent my allowance on them. Sitting on a bench with my mother, listening to her comments and dangling my legs, I sucked on a delicious *larga* until there was nothing left of it but the treacle on my fingers. Life was never like that in Jalcocotán.

On two sides of the square were the most important stores of the city, standing back from the street so that the arches and columns made the sidewalks into shady corridors. These were the *portales*, with shops, booths, stands, counters, and displays where a multitude of things were sold. We liked to push our way through the crowds of the *portales*, looking at the stunning sarapes of green and gold and orange designs; the new huaraches laid out in rows on the sidewalk; the yardage store, with its piles of bolts laid neatly on top of one another up to the ceiling; the paperback novels in the book shop in illustrated covers of bandits robbing and stabbing travelers. Under a canvas shade an elderly man sat writing a letter for people who didn't know how. We always watched him, for that was what my mother had done in Jalco. While the customer dictated, the scribe designed the words slowly and neatly, decorating them with curves and loops to make the letter look pretty. My mother pointed out to me that the person sending the letter always put a cross at the end instead of his name. That was his signature.

On the days we shopped for food we walked around the plaza in front of the Palacio de Gobierno to the market place. The *mercado* was an enormous building of corrugated iron that covered the entire block. The roof slanted up more than two stories high, supported by iron beams and trusses laced with cobwebs. Walking around inside the *mercado* the people seemed like pigmies wandering in a huge cave. At the ends of the building the sunlight came through the high doors in shafts that pierced the twilight of the interior.

To me, the *mercado* was a remarkable place. The aisles were crowded with people, sacks, crates, dress racks, and piles of sarapes. The tradesmen greeted us endearingly, calling us *marchantitos*. Live hens and roosters were tied in pairs by the legs and held up for our inspection. At the egg counter we could buy one or two or a dozen.

The trick about shopping in the *mercado* was to buy in the right order. First, we bought red beans which were poured into the bottom of our market basket. On top of them we laid the solid vegetables like potatoes and carrots. Next came the meat, then the soft ripe fruit, and last of all the eggs. By this time the basket was filled with the *mandado*—our groceries for the next day or two.

To maneuver ourselves out of the maze of the *mercado*, we had to sidestep sweepers pushing heaps of garbage along the aisles and *mozos* bent double carrying heavy loads on their backs. We walked home, Doña Henriqueta explaining the remarkable sights we had seen in the market, such as the fortune-telling canary and the man who breathed flames from his mouth.

Between trips to the market we were supplied by the baker, the milkman, and other tradesmen who came to the door of the *vecindad*. The dairyman came on a disheartened old mule loaded with two cans of milk, one on each side. By the door of the *postigo* his customers held up jars, *ollas*, and pots which he filled with a long-handled dipper. The baker came on foot, with a large tin pan on his head and a folding stool hooked over his arm. Like all the other vendors he made his sales at the *postigo*. Squatting carefully, he unhooked the stool, set it firmly on the ground, and lowered the pan with both hands. The customer took his choice from a heap of hard rolls, called *birotes*, the kind that were pointed at both ends with a curly flounce between. To select a *birote* you turned it over to make sure the bottom wasn't burned. If the flounce and the tips were crisp and golden brown it was good. On Sundays we dunked them in hot chocolate as a special treat.

We knew who was at the *zaguán* selling something by the commercials of the hawkers and the peddlers. The bread man cried "Calientito-o-o-s," singing about "the little warm ones" piled on his tray. Our milkman bawled out, "de la vaca," everybody knowing what it was of the cow he was selling. The pushcart vendor with the colored waters went by calling out in a high tenor, "fresca y de seis colores" meaning that he offered cool drinks in six flavors. But the prima donna of the street singers was the candy man who brought the children of the *vecindad* to the *zaguán* with his trills and obligattos about *largas* and *caramelos*. The one street crier we paid no attention to was the advertisement man who stood on street corners announcing that such-and-such a store was offering bargains in this or that. Like a pitchman at a circus, he commanded people to "hurry-hurry-hurry" or they would miss the wonderful bargains.

In the daytime the market and the streets were busy with people, horses, burros, and carts on the move. In contrast, the Alameda, which became our favorite park, was a quiet woods on top of a low hill close to the city. The grove of thick, high-crowned, elegant trees could have been a patch of the forest around Jalco carved out and moved to Tepic. It was a long, hot walk from the *vecindad* to the Alameda. We went there to sit on a bench, listening to the calls of the birds and to the silence between.

On the far side of the valley from where we lived was our other favorite spot, the river. We never went beyond the bridge where soldiers with rifles at the guardhouse always lounged. They stopped mule trains and wagons and horsemen coming into town, searching the loads and asking questions.

On our visits to the market, the plaza, the Alameda, and the river I discovered that Tepic had a thousand times more people than Jalco, including genuine *charros* who rode around the plaza on Sunday mornings. Anyone could see that they were showing off. Their tight pants legs were decorated with double rows of brightly polished silver discs. Their jackets were covered with curliewurlies of platinum and gold thread, like the brims and crowns of their hats. The saddles, reins, and straps of the harness were decorated with brass and silver medallions and buttons and with lassos of filigree. The *charros* glittered as they passed, their rowels jingling, spurring their mounts into fancy dance steps, wiggling their rumps, and snapping their heads up and down to make their manes flutter. Pedestrians on the street had to scamper out of the way of the *charros*. I asked my mother, watching the show, if they were *rurales*. She shushed me the way she always did to let me understand that she would tell me later, when we were alone.

Close about the plaza and the cathedral were the townhouses that intrigued me greatly. These were the homes of the rich, *los ricos*. The high front walls were neatly painted brown, grey, pink, or light cream. The street windows were even with the sidewalk with long iron bars that reached almost to the roof. Lace curtains, drapes, and wooden screens behind the bars kept people from looking in. Every townhouse had a *zaguán* and a driveway cutting across the sidewalk, ramped and grooved so the carriages could roll in and out. On hot days the *zaguánes* were left wide open, showing a part of the patios with their fountains, rose gardens, and trees. The walls and the floors of the corridors were decorated with colored tile in solid colors and complicated designs. Between the open *zaguán* and the patio there was the *cancel*, a grill of wrought iron that was always kept closed and locked.

By quick looks through the *zaguánes*, since my mother would not let me stop and stare, I began to have some idea of how *los ricos* lived. They rode in carriages directly into their houses. Servants opened and closed the grill and led the horses to the stable in a back patio. The *mandado* was always brought from the market by kitchen maids and cooks. The ladies and gentlemen had barbers and hairdressers come to their homes. Seamstresses and menders made deliveries to a servant at the *cancel*, not being allowed beyond that point. The bright patios, sometimes filled with the singing of canaries and warblers and the screeching of parakeets, settled in my mind another difference between people—those who lived in these *casas solariegas* and those who lived in *vecindades*. People who had townhouses and horses and carriages called themselves the *gente decente* of Tepic.

The patios of the rich, glimpsed from the street, charmed me, but it was the sights of the market, the plaza, and the streets that amazed me. Among the stalls that crowded the market I saw a boy about my own age eating fire and begging for centavos. In one of the *portales* a man sold medicine in brown bottles, pointing with a stick to a large poster in color on the wall that showed the insides of human beings. On the way to the river we saw carts loaded with sugarcane pulled by pairs of oxen, their heads bent low under the wooden yokes and boys stabbing their bloody humps with a pointed pole. In front of a saloon I watched for the first time a mariachi playing the marimba, harp, fiddle, trumpet, and guitars marvelously keeping the same tune and the same tempo. I saw a group of Huichole Indians sleeping on the ground back of the cathedral, with their shoulder bags for pillows and their ponchos partly covering their ragged clothes. On the way to the bridge we looked in at the tanners dipping hides into vats that smelled putrid, and cobblers cutting out and sewing huaraches. My mother explained all these sights and my repertoire of games increased. Back in our huge patio I played *charro*, ox-cart driver, cobbler, and fire eater.

Ever since I could remember I had heard about schools and that some day I would be sent to one. In Jalco the closest thing to a school were the catechism classes that the priest taught on his infrequent visits, and these I did not attend; first, because I could not, being too young, and second, because I would not, after José's expulsion from the chapel. There was no education going on in the pueblo, other than being alert to whatever was going on.

In Tepic there were private *colegios* but they were for children from the houses with patios and servants. On our walks around the city I saw these *niños decentes* dressed in starched clothes, long stockings, and patent leather shoes. They carried haversacks of writing pads and books on their backs. They were not to be seen except going to or from the *colegios*, the younger ones accompanied by maids in uniform. While they were in school the boys of the *vecindades* were shining shoes in the plaza, carrying trays of candy on their heads, helping the tradesmen, sorting pieces of stinking leather at the tanner's, and jamming a goad into oxen to make them move faster. I began to understand a difference between boys—those who went to school and those who worked.

I would have preferred to go into any of the professions of my friends in the *vecindad*, but Doña Henriqueta had other plans. She set up a *colegio* for me in our apartment, equipped with a new slate, slate pencil, and abacus. The slate was set in a wooden frame decorated with red and green stripes. In one corner there was a small hole in the frame for the string to which the slate pencil was tied. Thin as a soda straw, the slate pencil was wrapped in red, white and green paper, the colors spiraled as on a barber's pole. The abacus also had a wooden frame, with a handle like a hornbook. The beads of different colors were strung crosswise on copper wires with space to move them back and forth.

With this equipment my school days began in the *vecindad*. Classes were not scheduled; they happened as my mother sewed or mended, and were interrupted for our daily errands about the town. Her household chores gave me frequent breaks to play in the patio or to stand at the *zaguán*, watching the traffic and waiting for my favorite hawkers, the man with the caramel *largas* and the pushcart with the colored juices. When I was called for class, I sat on a straw mat in the doorway near Doña Henriqueta.

My first lessons were demonstrations on the slate and the abacus. On the slate my mother drew horizontal lines between which she wrote the letters of the alphabet. With a damp rag that was part of my equipment she wiped the *pizarra* clean and drew designs such as she embroidered on handkerchiefs and scarves. From the remarkable tip of the slate pencil in her hand there came outlines of oxen, a donkey's head like Relámpago's, carnations, trees, and bananas. She drew numbers and gave their names to each of the beads on the abacus. Up and down and across she made the beads bounce and add up to fantastic sums that sounded like rhymes—"cientos y miles y millones."

In class some technical details were settled her way. When the rag eraser began to dry, I preferred to spit on the slate rather than bother to get up and soak the rag again. Little by little our free-style introduction to learning changed to regular lessons in writing, reading, adding, subtracting, and multiplying.

As she sewed, my mother dictated the review of the previous lesson. In numbers she called out: "Dos y dos." I moved the first two beads on the lowest wire of the abacus to the left and then two more, repeating the name of the last bead—*cuatro*. So two and two made four. On the next wire up, the beads were moved in threes so that the last bead from the left was *seis*, and three and three were six. Giving the beads different names each day soon led to drawing the numbers on the slate, and I began to have some idea why ten centavos was more than five centavos.

We combined writing and reading and spelling as my mother called out the combinations she had already written for me at the top of the slate. I learned vowels and consonants in surprising arrangements, writing the syllables as I heard them and then combining them to make complete words. In English it would have sounded something like: "b-a-m—bam; b-o-o—boo; bam-boo," or "h-a-m—ham; b-u-r—bur; g-e-r—ger; ham-bur-ger." We always started with the easy ones I had already learned, and which I wrote down and read from the slate. The new ones I had to listen to first, putting them together as well as I could from the sounds. At the end of the lesson I had to listen to formidable words that sounded more like trapezes in full swing, like *ca-pi-ro-ta-da* or *Po-po-ca-té-petl*. Doña Henriqueta repeated them every so often until I was able to put them together. The sound and the rhythm of the words intrigued me more than what they meant.

Between lessons I discovered that the abacus also made a good rattle. On the slate I learned to draw a small cannon on the left-hand side with a Mexican artillery-man. On the right-hand side I drew tiny Frenchmen, the invaders Don Porfirio had beaten in Puebla. By placing the tip of the slate pencil at the mouth of my cannon, closing my eyes and drawing the pencil across the slate I could fight a war by myself. When the lines of fire crossed every one of the enemy, I turned the slate over and began another battle.

I measured my progress in our one-man *colegio* by the speed with which I made the beads on the abacus spin without mistakes, and by the paper I peeled from the slate pencil to keep the point sharp. With a shake I could demolish a multiplication table on the abacus and begin another. At a swipe of my wet rag, words disappeared, gently or with a vengeance, depending on how much trouble they had given me. I was eager to learn words like Relámpago and Coronel and Nerón which my mother called out in syllables; and they usually stayed on my slate longer.

It was about this time that my progress as an intellectual took a nearly fatal blow. I had fallen into the habit of asking our landlady questions, as I did my mother and my uncles. One day she did not answer a question but said scowling, "Que muchachito tan preguntón." When I sat down with my slate in the doorway I told my mother what the landlady had said, and asked: "Am I?" She explained, "*Preguntón* means nosy and minding other people's business. *Preguntar* means just to ask about things you don't understand. It is not good to be nosy. It is good to ask. Just be careful who you ask and what you ask. You can always ask me or your uncles."

"Do you and my uncles know everything?"

"No, but we know many things you don't and that is enough for now."

There was a certain way to deal with the problem of questions and answers, which I discovered. If there were people around to hear me I was to be quiet, look and listen, and ask later. Adults were queer. They were offended if they heard me ask why they had a wooden leg or why they were bald or why they had such black warts. Keeping to this rule I looked and listened and waited, like the day the four of us went to the ceremony at the plaza.

It was late in the afternoon when we wedged our way into the crowd that packed the *portales* around the square. Soldiers with rifles and fixed bayonets were lined up along the arches keeping the crowd off the street. José maneuvered me to the edge of the sidewalk where I could see. Carriages were pulling up across the street. Ladies in long dresses decked with ribbons and hats covered with artificial plumes and flowers were handed down from the carriages and up the platform by gentlemen in stiff round hats and black coats that came to their knees. The *Autoridades* were gathering in front of the Palacio de Gobierno before a mounted troop of spick-and-span *rurales*. On the opposite side of the plaza, by the cathedral, a corps of buglers and drummers with red chevrons on their sleeves kept up a deafening racket. Surrounding the important people in the center of the square was the military band of the Tepic regiment. A huge flag hung on the mast of the Palacio. Black wires were strung like ropes between poles and trees. To them were attached glass bubbles that bobbed and swayed in the wind.

The drums rolled and the bugles blared. An officer in a uniform with more gold and silver decorations than I had ever seen on the *charros* stood up and yelled:

"Viva México." The people, packed like sardines under the *portales*, yelled back: "Viva" and I cheered with them. The soldier shouted: "Viva El Presidente Díaz." Everybody answered "Viva" and so did I. A bald gentleman dressed in frock coat and spats, his neck cinched by a stiff white collar, read a speech, after which a parade of soldiers circled the plaza.

While the band played, the elegant ladies and gentlemen left the *kiosko*, got into their carriages, and were driven out of the square. The soldiers kept pushing the people back under the arches with the butts of their rifles. When all the important people had left and only the band was left on the stand the soldiers marched off and the people, including ourselves, were allowed to walk around and around the plaza, listening to the music.

It was dusk when my greatest surprise of the fiesta came. The glass bubbles strung on the wires suddenly glowed. They made a light like *candiles* but they did not flicker or smoke. That evening at supper I was told that electricity went through the black wires and that it came from a machine somewhere in the city, making the light in what my mother called *bombillas*.

José answered the questions I had been waiting to ask. The *rurales* and the soldiers with rifles and bayonets were there to protect *los ricos* from *los pobres*, who were ourselves and all the others jammed under the *portales*. What it had to do with the spectacular ceremony of that afternoon I could not tell, but José was talking about the *bolas* that were gathering in the mountains. "One of these days," José predicted, "they won't be yelling Viva Don Porfirio." What would the *bolas* do to *los ricos*? "Make them work like everybody else," José said emphatically.

The family's plan to move by stages to Tepic and settle there was not working out very well. Ever since Halley's comet the question in our family was not whether a revolution was coming but when and where. To keep the two women and three boys out of the violence that everyone was expecting was the first concern of the men; their second was to find steady work. In Tepic the family had no land to produce its own food. We did not own a house and had to pay rent.

The city was peaceful while we lived there but in the *vecindad* there was the talk and the feeling of trouble. My mother lived in dread that José would be picked up and taken away as a draftee to fight for Don Porfirio. No one could enter or leave Tepic without being stopped by the patrols. Morning and night we could hear the bugles of the regiment a few blocks away. We saw the platoons drilling on the parade ground in front of the state penitentiary where the regiment was quartered. The building, two stories high and a block long, with gun turrets at the corners, looked like a fortress. Under the clock tower in the center of the prison was a *zaguán* four times larger than ours. Men in huaraches and ragged clothes passed in and out of it, guarded by soldiers. We heard the patrols ride by our *vecindad*, their mounts clopping along the dark streets, their sabers clinking.

José brought home the news of what was happening around the city. There were signs on fences, painted at night, "Viva Madero." He brought home a printed paper which he had torn from a wall. My mother read it aloud, something from the *Autoridades* addressed to the citizens of the city of Tepic praising President Díaz. José had seen soldiers cross the bridge on their way to the penitentiary with a contingent of draftees. At the plaza he heard that the people of Ixtlan del Río—even the women and children—had revolted and were fighting the federal soldiers. José was not the only one who talked with excitement about these events. There were arguments in the *vecindad* between those of us who were red-blooded *maderistas* and people who weren't, or were afraid to admit it.

Another kind of news that José brought was about the scarcity of work in the town. More peasants were coming down from the mountain villages to find a safe place for their families and to work, like us. Gustavo came back one weekend from his job at the sugar mill to tell us he had been laid off. The police had come, the manager and his family had left, and some of the peons had been taken away.

These reports were exchanged when we were in our room, eating supper. Unlike the way things had been in Jalco, now I sat at the table and ate with the men, hearing all the important family conversation. Though I did not understand a great deal of what was said, I knew that along with the excitement there was fear. Now my mother got into the habit of standing by the *zaguán* until Gustavo and José returned home. I sat near her, looking up and down the street—waiting for them to appear or to hear José, who always whistled a tune coming home.

Living cramped in the two rooms, eating with the adults, hearing all the family conversation and going with my mother everywhere I had a fairly good sense of how we were managing. When we delivered work to my mother's customers I saw them pay her in pesetas or tostones and centavos. The quarters, half pesos and copper coins went into a handkerchief, which she knotted and dropped out of sight into her bosom. Gustavo and José brought their earnings to her, from which she gave them back an allowance for the next day, keeping the rest for our expenses. Several times we visited the elderly cousin to deposit our savings, but there were not many of these visits. If there was sewing or mending, our income increased and my lessons on the abacus and the slate became longer. The *varillero* we knew from Jalco stopped once in a while to bring us messages from the family, and to take back to them, tied in a handkerchief, a few pesetas and centavos. I felt like the assistant treasurer of the family when I helped my mother sort the coins on the top of the table in making out the budget.

After much discussion the decision was reached that things were getting worse in Tepic. Gustavo announced one night that he had talked with a labor recruiter for the Southern Pacific Railroad. The *enganchador* had told him that the railroad company was laying track between Santiago and Tepic, at which he could find steady work and good wages. More than that, the company would give him an advance in cash which could be paid back later. After a while he could get a pass for the family.

It was the *enganchador* who changed the family plans. He persuaded not only Gustavo but also José to sign up. The arrangement was that Gustavo and José would give us the advance from the Southern Pacific on which we could live temporarily. The work, the *enganchador* said, would be steady. My uncles would soon have passes on the train, so that both ourselves and Aunt Esther's family could travel north. In Mazatlán we had a cousin, Doña Florencia, who was married to a merchant and who would help us find work and a house.

Though my opinions about what should be done made no difference, I immediately approved of the Southern Pacific Railway. From the moment I heard Gustavo talk about the *enganchador* and the passes I was ready for a long ride on a train, having no idea of what one was like. Thus far I had learned from Gustavo that it was pulled by a locomotive that had a whistle and a bell. My mother's questions were mostly about the family in Jalco—how to bring them to Tepic and from there to Santiago and whether they could use the passes, too. She must also have been thinking that José would be safe from the draft and less likely to run away into the mountains to join the guerillas.

After withdrawing our savings we sorted out the coin bags and made out the budget—so much for the expenses, this for Gustavo and José, that for the savings. Our share was deposited in the cedar box. Gustavo and José, who had already signed up with the *enganchador,* wrapped their coins in cloth belts with pockets which they called "rattlesnakes," because they tinkled musically when they were full. The safest place to carry your money on a journey was in a *víbora* tied around your waist under the belt.

Doña Henriqueta wrote a long letter from Tepic that night. She lowered the candil on the wire a few inches above the top of the sewing machine. Sent to bed, I watched her take some sheets of paper out of the cedar chest and the indelible pencil which I was forbidden to use because I liked to wet it with my tongue and tattoo purple spots on my hands. She wrote for a long time. I fell asleep. The next morning there was a sealed envelope on top of the Ajax. It was handed to the *varillero,* with some money for delivery on his next trip through Jalco.

Gustavo and José were at supper with us one night and gone the next morning. Before the day was over I told the whole *vecindad* that they had gone with the *enganchador,* that they would be building trains, that we would get a pass and that we were going to live in Mazatlán. In my imagination, the future always happened immediately with considerable improvement.

My mother's sewing and mending continued, along with my lessons, until a letter came from Santiago. It was from Gustavo, who was now the lead man of the family moving north, step by step. The letter said we were to move to Acaponeta, and gave the name and address of the family we were to look for there.

There were days of much running around in Tepic, saying good-bye to our cousin, telling customers that we would not be sewing for them any longer, and talking to the man in charge of the *arrieros* who took freight from Tepic to northern cities. A drover came to our apartment, packed the Ajax, and took it off on the back of a mule. We stood by the *zaguán* as they went down the street with our most prized possession. "It is going to Mazatlán. Doña Florencia will take care of it for us."

It was a gift my mother had, explaining things in such a way that our life seemed only to be taking a different shape, not coming apart. Wherever Mazatlán was— far away and unknown—our sewing machine would be waiting there. It was like the feeling I had whenever I saw the rainbow sarape come out of the cedar box for an airing. We, the sarape and I, had been together in Jalco. Doña Esther, Jesús, and Catarino, Coronel and Nerón were part of it. Even the smell of the cedar box was exactly the same in Tepic as it had been in Jalco—the powerful whiff of the camphor marbles my mother kept in the bottom under the sarape.

We spent the last afternoon at the *vecindad* cleaning our room, as we had already done with the one that Gustavo and José had vacated. We scrubbed the straw mats with soap and water and doused the table with suds. I cleaned out the ashes of our *pretil* in the community kitchen and brushed the bricks in the corridor in front of our apartment. My mother polished the *candil* and filled it with kerosene. Together we turned over the planks of my bed and swabbed them until the wood smelled soapy and damp. With the big straw broom that was kept by the wash tubs we swept our quarters, leaving them tidy for the next occupant.

After these chores and with nothing to do except prepare our bedrolls and wrap the cedar box, we had our supper with the landlady. When we finished, my mother put some coins on the table and we both said good night and goodbye. I was told that we would be leaving at daybreak and sent to bed. A stagecoach was to take us to Acaponeta.

Before daylight we were up and preparing to set off. Our bedroll was tied and the cedar box wrapped in a blanket. Odds and ends were put in two straw shopping bags and in a *chiquihuite* my mother packed our food for the trip. The landlady's errand boy unbarred the *postigo* and we stepped into the twilight of the street, the boy shouldering the bedroll and the cedar box, my mother carrying the *chiquihuite* and the large bag, and I carrying the small one.

We walked across the city to the *mesón*, the combination motel for mule trains and terminal of the stagecoaches that traveled east to Guadalajara and north to Acaponeta. Standing in front of the *mesón* was our overland clipper, the like of which I had never seen before. It was the shape of a huge wooden tub with a bottom rounded front and back and a flat top with a low iron railing. In the back a canvas flap hung from the railing and on each side there were two windows and a door. Up front there was a double seat higher than the iron railing. Four mules were already hitched to the coach, the reins gathered and tied in a knot to one side of the seat. On the roof deck of the enormous rig there were bundles and sacks and boxes secured to the railing with ropes. In a socket next to the driver's seat there was a whip, a short club with a long strip of braided rawhide. This was the famous *chicote*, about which every boy in Mexico knew. Some families kept junior-size whips of this kind on hand for educational purposes. It was far worse than having your ear pulled to hear your father or mother say: "I am going to get the *chicote*."

Around the *diligencia* there was a stir of barefoot men and boys, the *mozos* who carried and loaded the baggage. They were bossed by a tall man in tight pants and boots whose voice snapped like a *chicote*. One of the *mozos* took our things, pulled up the canvas flap, and tied them in the luggage compartment. At my mother's insistence the cedar box was not lashed to the jumble of hand trunks and crates but placed under a seat inside the *diligencia*. Someone gave us a lift up the step to the door and we took the back seat facing forward, my mother on the outside and I in the middle.

The other passengers boarded. Next to me a man in a topcoat and a long beard sat down. He wore glasses, little rectangular lenses in a brass frame that sat on his fat nose. Immediately he began to squeeze me, his wide bottom taking up more space than I and my mother together. In the middle seat with their backs to us, a lady and a gentleman sat down, dressed like the people in Tepic who owned carriages and elegant homes. Two other men sat down on the front seat facing us. As they got in, the passengers said good-morning to one another and wriggled themselves in as comfortably as they could, keeping their legs sorted in the narrow space between the seats.

Outside a young man ran by and jumped up to the stirrup by the driver's seat. The driver hoisted himself to his perch high above us all. There was a waving of hands by people who had come to see their friends and relatives off, everybody saying "Adios" to everyone. We didn't know anyone but we waved "adios" anyway. There was a crack of the *chicote*, the driver yelled "Arre," and we were trotting out of Tepic. The wheels stopped clacking when we left the cobbled streets and began rolling on the dirt road of the open country.

Cooped between the fat man and my mother, I tried to see as much as I could through the windows. They framed moving pictures of woods and distant mountains, pastures with cattle and fields smoking with burning brush, racing by on the level stretches of the road. On the upgrades the mules slowed to a walk that made the driver mad, as we could tell from his cursing and the snapping of the *chicote*. Going downhill we jerked from side to side, back and forward, making our heads bob together this way and that.

At first I thought it was fun to see all the passengers joggle together when our lumbering tub slid off a rock or snapped up on its springs. The fat man was constantly pushing his glasses back to the top of his nose. When the *diligencia* hit a rut, the lady in front whispered "Ay, Dios," and when it yawed around a curve she said, "Ave María Purísima." I knew that the Hail Pure Mary was something women said when they didn't have more than a second to pray. My mother held on to the window frame with one hand and to my shoulder with the other. She whispered that I was not to lean on the fat man and annoy him. The more room I gave him the more he squeezed.

On top of these discomforts I began to feel sick. I wished I could move up to ride with the driver and then I wished we had never got into the *diligencia*. I felt like throwing up, but my breakfast of a cup of coffee and a couple of tortillas wasn't very much to dispose of. When I awakened, my head was on my mother's lap and the fat man was leaning the other way thumping his head gently against the frame of the window. He was asleep.

With stops to let the passengers get down, stretch, and rest from the weariness of the long ride, and to water and feed the mules, we traveled until dark. We stopped for the night at a *posada*, a sort of *diligencia* motel. It was an adobe brick building with a large corral in the back and a gateway for the coach to drive through. Inside the corral the mules were unhitched; the next day a fresh team would take their places. The *posada* served us supper at a long table lighted with candles. The passengers, who had not said much during the day's drive except "Ay Dios" and "Ave María Purísima," talked like chatterboxes, mostly about *diligencias* that had been held up by bandits and passengers who had been kidnapped. My mother and I said nothing to the company and they said nothing to us. The driver and the whip boy ate in the kitchen.

For sleeping, some straw mats were spread for us between two thatch partitions in a long hall open on one side to the corral. We untied the bedroll and slept under our own sarapes.

As usual, I was awakened while it was still dark. We rolled our sarapes, had breakfast with the other passengers inside the *posada*, and trotted away to the snapping of the *chicote*, which I now knew was the job of the *sota*, the whip boy. He and the driver knew the same tricks as the *arrieros* to keep their mules moving—"Arre, mulas," "f-z-z-t" and the needle-sharp whistles the mules seemed to understand. The driver did not swear as much as the *arrieros*, from whom I had learned words I had to keep to myself.

Through the second day I was thoroughly bored by the *diligencia*. The motion pictures coming through the windows were now familiar and dull. Nothing short of a holdup or a kidnapping would have made the stagecoach exciting again. I kept asking my mother when we would arrive, but her answer, "Soon," was hopeless. I dangled my legs, wished I had the abacus and the slate, and slept on and off.

In the late afternoon we came to the edge of a river and turned to follow its course on a wide rocky beach. The crunching of the wheels over the stones and the lurching of the coach gave us the worst shaking of the trip. When the driver found the ford he reined the mules into it and they began to pull slowly through the smooth shallow water. Feeling their way, they breasted the current until it reached above the hubs of the wheels, as I could see by craning my neck out of the window. When it lapped at the floor of the compartment, the lady whispered, "Ave María Purísima." With the deepest part of the ford behind us, we drew toward the opposite shore until the mules began to pull up the slope on the other side. At the top of the bank the *sota* whipped the team into a trot which we kept up until we stopped in front of a square adobe house with a tin-roofed porch.

It was getting dark. Our bundles were handed down and stacked in one corner of the porch. My mother searched in her bag and fished out a piece of paper. She showed it to a man who pointed down the street. One of the *mozos* attending the coach walked us a block to the house we were looking for. It was the home of the family with whom Gustavo had arranged for our stay in Acaponeta. We had supper with them sitting under a thatch lean-to, the *pretil* glowing and the familiar oil lamp sputtering over our heads, hanging from a wire. Behind the curtain that divided the only room of the house we made our beds on two army cots that squeaked when we braced them with the two cross pieces that stretched the canvas tight.

In the morning our hosts explained how matters had been arranged. The cottage they occupied was next to an orchard surrounded on the four sides of the block by an adobe wall. There were several cottages along one side of the orchard, all of them built into the wall. The only way to get inside the orchard was to walk through one of the cottages. The one in the middle of the block was to be our temporary home. Like the others it was an adobe building of one room, with a back porch covered by thatch, no windows, and two doors, front and back.

We settled down to live in luxury, with an orchard for our back yard that we shared with the other tenants. The *pretil* was in a corner of the room, next to the back door. In the front corners were two bedsteads with raw-hide springs standing on short legs. Near the *pretil* there was a long shelf above a row of pegs for pots, pans, tools, and clothes. Our table was made of short planks standing on four logs, and our two chairs were stools made of the same rough stuff. The dirt floor was smooth and hard.

Close to the back door an enormous mango branched over the roof of our cottage, the most elegant tree among the palms, walnuts, and bananas that grew in the block. The well was beyond the mango enclosed by a low adobe wall. The opening was covered with planks, and above them a smooth log mounted on two posts and turned by a handle. A bucket was tied to the end of the rope coiled around the windlass. Some of the tenants culti-vated vegetables next to their cottages. Except for these patches, the estate was shared by all of us, although it belonged to none of us.

In Acaponeta families that had no well walked to the fountain near the plaza to fill their jars, buckets, and cans. Our well was only a few steps away. From it the paths to each cottage curved around the trees and bushes to all the kitchen doors, like crooked spokes. Only the men and women and older boys could turn the windlass; I caught the bucket when it cleared the planks and poured the water into our pail. The handle squeaked like saddle leather on the horse we rode from Jalco.

For the boys of my age on the block the orchard had everything. When mangos were to be picked we were hoisted to the lowest branches, from which we worked our way up, down, and through the tree pulling the fruit and lobbing it into the aprons of the women below, or into a blanket they held by the corners. Away from the cottages we had ample space for playing war, perched in the trees as sharpshooters or defending barricades of broken adobe bricks and fallen branches.

The orchard also had a mystery. Across from the well and surrounded by a clump of tall grass there was a depression in the ground several feet across. The shallow hole sloped toward the center a foot or more below the level of the ground. It was well known in Jalco that a depression of that kind was a sign of buried treasure. Usually a famous bandit was said to have dug a pit to stash his loot, killed a captive, and thrown the body in with the gold and the jewels so that his ghost would guard the treasure. The bandit then filled the hole and leveled the dirt. But the rains packed it down little by little until it settled and made the tell-tale circle. A treasure was certainly there, for some of the neighbors had seen charcoal glowing in the pit on certain nights, another sure sign of buried riches. The question was: who would dare to dig? Before the treasure could be reached a skeleton would have to be pitched out; and it was well known also that anyone who touched a single bone would be cursed for the rest of his life.

I repeated the story to my mother, who no doubt had heard it many times before. I assured her that I had seen the pit burn. She said perhaps there was a treasure, perhaps there wasn't. I was not to do any digging without the permission of the owner of the orchard, wherever he lived and whoever he was. If there was a treasure it belonged to him. Perhaps, if I promised to uncover it myself, he would share it with me. After this conversation she began to dump the suds from the laundry wash into the pit. I protested, unable to make out whether the answers were serious or comical. The suds, she said, would put out the fire, soften the earth, and make digging easier for anybody who would like to try. Perhaps the ghost was thirsty and needed a drink. I never dug for the treasure.

Within the four walls of the orchard we were welcomed into the life of the small community of half a dozen families. We helped the caretaker gather and burn the brush that fell from the trees and patch the cracks in the adobes. When the vegetables needed water, whoever they belonged to, we carried bucket after bucket from the well to the ditches. Some of the men worked at their crafts in the cottages, mending, repairing, or manufacturing, with the boys as apprentices. In the evening, people sat under the thatch lean-to's back of the cottages and talked. Each family rooster watched over his own flock of hens wandering about the orchard pecking for insects and looking for places to lay their eggs. In the early mornings the grove came alive with bird songs, of which to me the most familiar was the call of the mourning dove because my mother sang a song about it, "La Paloma."

From our cottage the main points of the compass were the river, the market, and the railroad station.

On Sunday afternoons the riverbank was our grandstand to look on the free show of the countryside and its people. The river ran smooth and shallow at our feet, and beyond it a wide sandy beach sloped upward gently to the edge of the forest, against which the rocks shone as white as weathered bones. The red soil bank on our side of the river, the silver sheet of water in front of us, the wet browns and greys of the sandbars, the whitewashed ramp of rocks on the opposite shore, the green forest front and the pale purple of the Sierra Madre were like stripes of water colors. Across them strings of mules and donkeys moved with their loads, fording the river with their bellies awash. The drivers followed, their white *calzones* rolled above their thighs and the water up to their waists, carrying their belongings in bundles on top of their heads to keep them dry. We could see women washing clothes among the boulders and children splashing in the pools.

The time of the day we liked best was the evening twilight. Halfway between our cottage and the river the view opened on pastures covered with knee-high grass. As the twilight deepened, the fireflies started to blink here and there—so few at first we could spot and count them. The darker it became the more numerous the pinpoints of light, until they thickened into a shimmering blue carpet suspended above the grass. "Los cucuyos," my mother said to herself, to me, and to the gathering night, always with the same wonder and surprise as when she said to me, "Listen, the mourning dove."

Our new *mercado* was not in the same class with the one in Tepic. The stalls or *puestos* were a jumble of square patches of awning stretched over rickety wooden frames. Each was a tiny shop with a single item of merchandise—mangos, peanuts, cornhusks, leather belts, clay pots, caramel bars, jerked meat, live hens, huaraches, ribbons, pictures of Our Lady of Guadalupe, bamboo flutes, peppers, pin wheels, shawls, straw hats, coconut chips, jumping beans, little pointed heaps of glazed brown clay that were supposed to look like where a person had just gone to the toilet on the ground, and a thousand other wares. With a basket over her arm, my mother wound us this way and that among the *puestos*. The shopkeepers sat on the ground on mats or on stools, some begging the "dear customer"—the *marchantita*—to approach and buy, others reading from a paperback novel, too absorbed to bother about business. The way home from the *mercado* was by the plaza where we nearly always bought and shared a caramel or a chip of coconut.

The railway station was to me the most important and fascinating place in Acaponeta. We explored it promptly after our arrival in the town. It was two blocks away from the orchard, at the end of a wide dusty street. Side-stepping the carts and mules that hauled freight to and from the depot, we hurried there the first time we heard a locomotive whistle: The station was a squat building with long extensions, roofed with corrugated iron, the tracks alongside the passenger platform. We stood well back as the locomotives clanked and wheezed to a halt, pulling a string of boxcars, flats, gondolas, and cabooses.

With the crowd of admiring spectators we ran to the spot where the locomotive stopped and examined the marvelous monster. It belched great puffs of smoke from a stack adorned with a polished headlight. The main part of the black giant looked like a barrel with two humps on top. From inside the boiler there came clanking noises and now and then a deep, sad cough. The boiler rested on four large iron wheels and eight small ones. Just back of the cowcatcher a cylinder spit long feathers of live steam, as if the locomotive were hissing at the people to keep away. Behind the engine cab there was the tender, piled with firewood and coal. As the fireman shoveled fuel into the back end of the boiler we could see his face in the orange glare of the open fire box. On the side of the tender there were huge white letters which my mother read to me: *Sur Pacífico de México*, and the number of the locomotive below.

The engineer came down from the cab on a narrow ladder of iron steps. He was dressed in striped overalls with the bib high up on his chest, a blue shirt, the sleeves buttoned tight to his wrists and garters above the el-bows, a knotted scarf around his neck. His hat was of the same striped stuff as the overalls, round and high with a visor. The engineer moved alongside the locomotive, tipping an oil can with a brass handle and a long beak into the bearings of the wheels. He looked and acted like someone as important as the *Autoridades*, for it was he who pushed and pulled the levers that moved the enormous train. His assistant, the fireman, pulled the rope that made the brass bell behind the stack tip and swing and clang.

The locomotive, despite its terrifying noises, made me want to be near it, to climb up the iron ladder. Had I not been holding my mother's hand all the while, I might have run back inside the walls of our orchard. As I became less and less frightened of locomotives I began to feel a family connection between us and the Sur Pacífico de México. My uncles were working with the *enganchador* of the railway. They had been transferred somewhere near Mazatlán and might even be making locomotives themselves, the difference between that and laying tracks not being very clear to me. I felt like an important part of the departure of every train that stopped at Acaponeta. Standing near the station, well away from the tracks, I watched the fireman blow a blast from the whistle and clang the brass bell as the train moved out. I stood by until the caboose was only a red dot between the tracks, chasing the cloud of smoke.

After the trains left we usually toured the depot, tried the benches in the waiting room, and watched the telegraph operator through a grilled window. The tac-tac of the brass key he wiggled between his fingers was a letter he was sending, my mother explained to my consternation. The letters, she said, moved through the black wires strung on the poles alongside the tracks. They went to Tepic and to Mazatlán where another dispatcher listened to the tac-tac and wrote down the words. Out of all these sights and sounds I concluded that whipping a team of mules on a *diligencia* was as nothing compared to commanding a locomotive, or jiggling a brass castanet in the telegraph office with a green shade over your eyes.

We found out that the railway station was not only an exciting place in Acaponeta but more importantly the center of the revolution. Sometimes a freight train went by carrying people on the roofs of the boxcars and soldiers in uniform armed with rifles. One afternoon I watched from across the road as soldiers climbed down from the boxcars and out of the gondolas with the high iron sides. They made little tepees with their rifles as they stacked them, and began unloading boxes and guns. A troop of horsemen came up the road, raising a cloud of dust. They dismounted at the depot and spread up and down the track. Some had sabers and all of them wore bandoliers packed with ammunition criss-crossed over their chests and backs. Later the soldiers formed into a column and marched down the street by our house toward the plaza. We often heard the bugles from the barracks on the other side of town.

The street from the depot turned toward the river and passed in front of our orchard. Some days we saw bands of men in huaraches, straw hats, and peasant clothes straggle by, carrying rifles slantwise or flat across their shoulders as they trudged along. At night we heard them shuffle by, and in the morning we would see them cooking or warming themselves by the camp fires near the station. The soldiers in uniform, those who rode horses and wore stars and chevrons, came and went among the shifting crowds of the infantry. They were quiet and businesslike.

The fighters in huaraches and peasant clothes sometimes traveled in the revolution with their wives. The women cooked for their soldier husbands, carried their rifles, toted the bedrolls, and cared for the children as they moved here and there. Whenever the troops camped near the station the women scattered through the neighborhood, stopping at the cottages to ask for a stick of pine kindling to start their fires or for a pot of water. When they knocked on our door, Doña Henriqueta invited them to help themselves at the well. She always offered a pinch of salt or a pepper or a small lump of corn dough for tortillas. Behind our closed door, after we barred it at night, my mother explained the ever changing scenes of the revolution that passed along our street. The *soldaderas*, as she called them, often sat outside our door, nursing their babies, the way the women did in Jalco.

One evening, out of the traffic of marchers, *soldaderas*, and horsemen, the revolution stepped into our cottage. We were at the table after supper doing a lesson on the slate when there was a knock on the door.

"Who is it?" my mother called.

"Good persons," a man's voice answered. *Gente buena* was the password if your intentions were friendly.

"Who are good persons?" My mother was asking for the second part of the password.

"An officer of the first battalion who comes in peace," said the voice. There was nothing to do but unbar the door and open it.

By the light of the candle I saw a tall figure in a jacket with metal buttons, riding pants, and leather puttees. He wore a neck scarf with a ring above the knot, and around the waist two belts, one for his pants and the other for the holster and pistol. His hair was black and rumpled, as black as the droopy mustache over his lips. In one hand he held the bridle of his horse, standing behind him in the shadows; in the other, a heavy peaked hat.

In the dim light and the dusty uniform he was a tired, slouching *revolucionario*.

"If you will pardon the trouble," he was saying to my mother, "I would be very grateful to you if you could provide me with a little aliment."

"Please do the favor to come in," she said. Doña Henriqueta was cool and wary.

She opened the door wide and propped the bar against it. The officer hooked the reins of his horse to the hinge of the door.

"Will you be good enough to be seated?" she said.

He stepped to the table, hitched a stool around so he could sit with his face to the door, sat down, and said as he propped his hat against his leg, "Señora, excuse the trouble." He caught me staring at him and smiled.

"It is no trouble," my mother said.

She stirred the ashes in the *pretil*, blew on the coals, and presently was laying tortillas on the *comal*. She placed a pot of beans in one corner of the fire pit and took down from the shelf some cheese wrapped in a napkin. In another pot she made fresh coffee.

Standing in the corner behind the *pretil* I spied on our visitor, pretending I was watching the fire. I had already decided that he was a captain for no reason other than that I had often heard the soldiers address their officers as *mi capitán*. He sat slumping a little, looking at the flame of the candle or through the doorway at his horse. His holster dangled below the seat of the stool, the brim of his hat resting against his knee.

My mother served him a plate of hot beans and kept bringing fresh tortillas. He spread the beans over them and rolled them into tacos. The coffee was served steaming from the coals. As he ate, my mother stood silent and watchful by the back door. On the pretense of bringing more charcoal from the porch, she had unbarred it, leaving it wide open like the front one.

The captain finished. The plate was clean, the coffee pot was drained, and the last tortilla had been eaten.

"A little water, if you will do me the favor."

She placed on the table a bowl filled from the pail by the stove. The captain stood up, drank from the bowl, and stepped to the door. He gargled several times, rinsed his mouth, and spit into the street.

As he turned back into the room he seemed revived by the meal. Picking up his hat and holding it in his hand he stood, formidable, against the frame of the door. "Señora, may God pay you," he said. With that he unhooked the reins and disappeared in the dark, leading his horse.

We closed the doors and barred them. I sat at the table where the captain had dined while my mother washed things. When she had finished we sat for a while. "Que susto," she said, so I realized for the first time that she, too, had been frightened.

"Was that the revolution?" I asked.

"That was a *revolucionario*."

"Was he a captain?"

"Perhaps." She went on to tell me about captains, sergeants, lieutenants, and generals.

From the way my mother explained matters, I concluded that the revolution was far more important than the train, and the career of a revolutionary captain was something to consider. I went to bed wondering whether we would ever see the captain again.

What I was gathering, from watching the foot soldiers, *soldaderas*, and captains and listening to what my mother said about them, was that they were brave people. In Tepic I had heard ladies and gentlemen talk about them as *pelados*, which always made José's temper come to a boil and my mother look angry. It seemed about time for me to join a *bola*, so I could have the chance to show courage like theirs.

The fact that I wasn't ready for a career in *la revolución* was proved soon after the captain came to supper.

A neighbor who lived at the other end of the block, across from the orchard, came to our cottage in distress. There was a sick person at their house and help was needed. It was a situation in which I would clearly be in the way. My mother did something unusual; she decided to leave me alone in the cottage. She would be nearby. There would be people in the houses on our side of the block.

She warmed my supper and braced the front door. I was given my instructions: the front door was not to be unbarred under any circumstances. If she was not back by dark I was to go to bed. She would ask one of the neighbors to let her into the orchard and she would come in by our back door, which was to be left open. I was not for any reason whatever to make a light.

While the twilight lasted I had no problems. I sat by the back door facing the orchard, thinking of many things, alert for the footsteps of Doña Henriqueta. But as night fell and the darkness deepened I decided that since I was taking care of the house I might as well be inside of it. Sitting on the bed looking at nothing but inky space made me notice every sound and remember the treasure hole and the skeleton, Captain Espanto on his ghost horse and the murdered passengers of *diligencias*. Noises seemed to be coming up to the back door, going away and coming back, as if trying to make up their minds to come in.

My mother had said that if I felt sleepy I was to get into bed. That would have been very well if she had been there and it was still light outside. Now it was certainly the wrong thing to do. The back door would be open and

I might be caught asleep on top of the bed by a ghost or a kidnapper.

I crawled under the bed wrapped in my sarape and wedged myself on the floor as close to the door as possible. I intended to stay awake and crawl out as soon as my mother was home.

I was awakened by voices in the room. By the candlelight I could see feet wearing huaraches shuffling by me. People were calling my name. I heard my mother say: "The well. Please look in the well again."

I wormed my way from under the bed, stuck out my head, and said, "Here I am."

What happened next was confusing. It took me a few days to make sense of it. I could not understand why a mother should not be overjoyed to find that her son had not fallen into the well and drowned but had only been asleep under the bed. She wanted to know since when I had become a disobedient child; and since when I had forgotten that I was to answer instantly when I was called.

"But how can I answer when I am asleep?" We argued. As her fright lessened, the scolding was over. Besides the reprimand and the jokes of the neighbors about my appearance from under the bed, I had reason enough to feel badly: I wasn't enough of a *revolucionario* to sit alone in pitch darkness and watch the house.

Doña Henriqueta had other reasons to be worried. One night we were awakened by gunfire. She told me to get up and dress. In the dark we listened to the shots, far away. Some troops moved past the house, as we could tell from the muffled tramp of the soldiers going by. We sat up most of the night, listening.

The next morning our neighbors gathered by the well to exchange rumors. This was the way news passed from house to house and from block to block. I listened. Someone who had just come from the plaza said that two men had been captured and shot and that their bodies were being hauled around Acaponeta in an open cart for everyone to see.

The neighbors scattered to spread the report. We walked back to our house. My mother wrote two letters that afternoon, one to my uncles and another to the family in Jalco. Now, when we went for the *mandado*, we walked faster, taking a roundabout way to avoid the plaza.

Since we arrived from Tepic my mother had been in the habit of reading the family letters to me. We picked them up at the town post office, a small shop that looked like a corner grocery store. On the wall next to a long table there was always a sheet of paper with a column of names on it. This was, my mother explained, the *lista de correo*, the general delivery of Acaponeta. She read the list, running her finger down line by line. If our name was on it, we approached a man dressed in a black jacket who always peered at us under his glasses, lifting his chin and looking down his nose. We gave him our name and asked for the letter.

Back at our cottage, the flap of the envelope was lifted carefully with a knife. Next the letter was opened. It always came in a neat packet, folded in squares and triangles, the corners of the sheets tucked into the folds. When the letter was spread out on the table and smoothed, the creases made a pattern of diagonal lines and right angles, diamond shapes and squares.

An important letter we received from Gustavo, like all the others, was read to me after Doña Henriqueta had first read it to herself. It said:

"My dear sister—I write you these few lines to tell you that José and I are both well, thanks to God, and to say that I hope you and Ernesto are well, too, and to inform you that we are working in Urías with the Southern Pacific not far from Mazatlán. I will tell you also that we are sending money to Esther in Jalcocotán which will be for their transportation to Tepic and after to Urías and that you and Ernesto should transport yourselves to Urías where we work, and to inform you that we can live in the camp of the company here for which reason we are sending you a postal money order for you and Ernesto to transport yourselves from Acaponeta as soon as possible, inasmuch as you can arrange with the station master at Acaponeta for your transportation. I will close these few lines with an embrace for you and Ernesto. Your brother, Gustavo."

The money order, a paper with scrawls and stamps on one side, was wrapped in the letter. We examined it carefully and folded it back into the envelope, which was placed under a loose brick of the *pretil* for safe deposit.

In the days following we went to the post office to cash the money order, interviewed the station master, and called on our neighbors to tell them of our plans. The day before we were to leave we went through the familiar routine of cleaning the house. I gave the street a heavy drenching with buckets of water from the well, sprinkled in such a way as to settle the dust but not make mud.

On our last evening in Acaponeta nothing was unusual except my excitement. The cedar box was wrapped, the shopping bags packed, and everything prepared for an early start.

"Tomorrow," my mother told me, "we will leave for Urías. We are going on the train." When I went to bed she was at the table, writing a letter by the light of the candle.

When I awakened, she seemed not to have slept. The candle was still burning. Breakfast was served off the *pretil* and the coals put out. We tied our bedrolls and barred the front door. A neighbor let us out into the street through her cottage and helped us with our impedimenta to the railway station.

People were milling about on the dark platform, in a great confusion. A brakeman strode through the crowd, swinging a lantern by a wire hoop. The lamp made his legs cast two huge shadows on the pavement, opening and closing like enormous scissors. The passengers were calling out to one another; trying to find the first, second, and third-class coaches. We passed by the locomotive, hissing and thumping, its headlight boring a cone of light through the darkness. At the other end of the train the tail signal of the caboose glowed like a ruby star on the horizon.

We found the third-class coach and boarded with our bedroll, bags, and cedar box. A passenger ahead of us was carrying, besides his luggage, a *huacal* with some hens. Another boarded with a suckling pig in his arms. The overhead racks and the space under the seats were stuffed with parcels, rolls of grass mats, large pots and baskets with food for the journey. The seats in the third-class coaches were plain benches on which the passengers sat back to back. On the window end there was at least the wall of the coach to lean on; on the other there were no arm rests to keep a passenger from sliding off into the aisle. My mother appropriated the first empty bench we came to, pointing me to the window seat. Everything we were taking with us was packed over our heads or at our feet.

A couple were already sitting facing us. They were dressed like peasants—plain cotton clothing, huaraches and sarape and blue shawl. They were barefooted. She held a wicker basket on her lap covered with a white cloth. They murmured "buenos dias" as we sat down.

Outside I saw the brakeman swing his lantern in circles above his head to signal the engineer. From the platform the conductor bawled "Vámonos." The couplings of the coaches clanked as we jerked into motion. The station building moved slowly by my window and disappeared.

When I awakened, the morning sun was coming through on my side of the coach from over the crest of the Sierra Madre. I could see the length of the coach, the passengers swaying together to the rhythm of the train, the racks and the aisles crammed with goods, and children of all ages tucked in among the baggage, asleep. The coach smelled from being crowded and some of the passengers had opened windows for fresh air. Through them came the cinders and the smoke from the locomotive. They got into my eyes and sifted down my neck. Watching the telephone poles that rushed past along the track going backward made me dizzy. It was more pleasant when the train slowed down to cross a wooden trestle over a river bed, dry and rocky like the desert all around. Passing a village our locomotive gave two long hoots and two short ones like a greeting to the people who stood outside their huts waving good-bye. When the train stopped to take on fuel and water we were allowed to get down and walk for a few minutes. We watched the crew pitch chunks of firewood into the tender and observed the feed line of the water tower poke its canvas spout over the locomotive. There was a scramble by the passengers at the warning call, "Vámonos," and the train began to move slowly.

The conductor came through our coach collecting the tickets, followed by a brakeman stepping over the bundles in the aisle and standing beside us, his legs wide apart to keep his balance. To me he was an astonishing figure on account of his blue uniform with metal buttons, the chevrons on his sleeves and a gold chain crossing his vest, and the cap with brass letters above the visor.

The couple in front of us said nothing, but toward the middle of the afternoon the woman uncovered the basket and began sorting out tacos and fruit. She looked at my mother and said: "Ustedes gustan?" which was acknowledged with the customary "Thank you, and good appetite." My mother reached under the seat and brought out the *chiquihuite* with our dinner of beans and rice and meat rolled in cold tortillas.

By kneeling on the seat I could look out through the windows on the other side of the coach. The country beyond was flat with patches of water that rushed toward the train as we passed and rushed away again. "Swamps," said my mother to my question. "Out there is the Pacific Ocean." When she was a girl she had lived by the sea, in San Blas. The blue haze on the horizon which I took to be the ocean looked unexciting. The journey had reached the point where there was nothing to do but sit still and dangle my legs.

It was dark when we arrived in Mazatlán. The jolts of the train awakened me and I could see by looking closely at the lights outside my window that we were moving backward. There was a stir in the coach when the brakeman looked in through the door and called out "Mazatlán." While people all around us tugged at their baskets and packages and their children to make their way out we sat and waited. We were nearly the last to leave, hurrying to get our belongings safely to the waiting room, my main worry being not to be separated from Doña Henriqueta. We piled our luggage under an electric light on the platform and waited. José and Gustavo found us there.

"How are you, boys?" "How are you, sister?" They were smiling but not excited. Tired from the jouncing on the wooden seat I looked at them and felt happy, too, but I remained collapsed on the bedroll.

Gustavo lifted me to his shoulders and hooked the bedroll with his free arm. José and my mother gathered the rest of our things and we started walking down the track. I looked back half asleep, at the lights of the station moving farther and farther away, and felt the regular one-two thumps of my uncle's steps on the railway ties.

The next morning I awakened lying on blankets spread on the wooden floor of a tent.

"Get up, lazy one." I saw my mother, looking in through the flap.

Wrapped in a sarape, I stood by her looking about.

She was pointing out things. "This is our camp. That is Casa Redonda, where your uncles work. Those are the railway tracks that come from Acaponeta. Look, over there. That is Mazatlán."

The two of us spent the morning settling down and tidying up the tent that was to be our home, cleaning and sweeping. With a broom my mother beat the dust off the sides of the tent. By noon the four army cots were in place and neatly made up, one in each corner of the tent. Near the door there was a table with wooden boxes for chairs; the boxes, turned over on their sides at night, served as benches and shelves. There were large nails on the central pole of the tent on which we hung our clothes. Over each bed there was a drape of mosquito netting held by safety pins to cords that stretched from the pole to the corners. During the day the nets were lifted and folded over the cords. At night they were spread, tent-like, around the cots, to keep out the mosquitoes that buzzed hungrily in search of warm human blood.

When the side flaps of the tent were rolled up and tied, a new world took shape around me. Stretched on my cot I could look on the flat swamp country, the woods behind us and the purple crest of the mountains beyond. Through the open sides the salty breeze of the sea came in, gentle and fresh. Altogether life in Tepic had never been so good.

At the Casa Redonda everything was regulated by the steam whistle of the roundhouse. When it blew for lunch I trotted between the kitchen and the table moving on the double in order to have the meal hot and on time. Covered with smudge and grease spots my uncles came in, washed, and sat down at once to eat, saying little. I stood by to wait on them wondering whether there would be enough food left for me. There always was, but I always wondered. Fifteen minutes later the men rushed off, walking up the tracks toward the roundhouse. They had barely disappeared beyond a bend in the tracks when the whistle blew again.

My mother explained matters. Gustavo and José left for work early. They had half an hour for lunch. They would be home at six o'clock. We were to eat our meals after them except for supper.

Every afternoon we went on walks, and in a few days the lay of the land around us was clearly in my mind.

Our tent was next to the last in a row of several others just like it—a square of brown canvas curtains with a roof sloped like a pyramid, held up by a pole that peeped through a vent at the top. The plank floors of the tents were set up on bricks, the ends of the timbers sticking out in front, making a shelf which we used for a porch. The roof was held down by ropes staked down at the four corners and along the sides. Between the tents there were lean-to's where the women cooked and washed clothes in iron tubs, heating the water over stone fire pits. The swamp came up close in back, and in front spilled into a ditch, making a moat that separated the camp from the tracks just beyond. Over this ditch there was a catwalk of planks leading to the tracks, the main street of the neighborhood.

Besides the tents, there were several weather-beaten, dilapidated boxcars on a siding. Families lived inside and under them. With pieces of canvas and sacks they curtained off bedrooms between the tracks. Wooden steps from the ground to side door made the boxcar itself the second floor of the apartment. Families who had lived a long while in these battered relics had landscaped them with pots of herbs and flowers.

Night and day the switch engines and freights rumbled up and down the tracks in front of the camp, the couplings clanking and the wheels clicking. When the freights passed by, the earth quivered under my feet.

The roundhouse where my uncles worked was a short distance from camp, next to the repair shops where boxcars, flats, gondolas, cabooses, and locomotives were taken apart and put together again. Locomotives went in and out of the roundhouse through a wide gate guarded by a policeman who checked everyone entering and leaving. Somewhere in the midst of the smoke that always hung over the shops there was the steam whistle with a sound between a croak and a shriek. In the mornings the whistle gave several warning hoots to get people out of bed and report for work, which started with one long blast that could be heard for miles around.

Gustavo was a handyman in the parts department of the shops and José cleaned out the fireboxes, wiped the mucky grease off the engines, washed them, and polished the brass. Both of them now dressed in blue overalls with bibs, and canvas caps with visors, the uniform which made us a genuine railroad family.

I came to know the roundhouse better after Doña Henriqueta began preparing hot lunches for some of the men who did not have families in the camp. These I delivered before the noon whistle in white enameled saucers with a blue rim and nested in a metal frame with a handle. In each saucer there was a hot dish, tortillas packed in one and coffee in the tin cup on top. I picked up the empty lunch kits at the guardhouse and stayed a while to talk with the watchman. Doña Henriqueta helped me make friends with him by sending now and then, with her *saludos*, a piece of fresh cheese or a nip of preserves. Whoever the *patrón* of the Southern Pacific Railway might be, I regarded the policeman as the most important person in that formidable place. Even the engineers had to stop at the gate when he signaled them.

The roundhouse and the shops, as I viewed them from the guardhouse, were remarkable. I watched a crane lift huge chunks of metal, swing them aloft, and drop them with a crash. Men in khakis speeded along the tracks on gasoline runabouts with tin roofs. Everyone seemed to be pushing or lifting or dragging or carrying tools or hammering on something. On lucky days I could watch a locomotive move slowly into the yard and on the turntable, an enormous circular platform with a single track down the center. The track was maneuvered so as to stop flush with the rails on which the engine moved in. Once the engine was in position, the turntable circled no faster than a snail until the track was locked into the rails that pointed to the stall into which the locomotive was to be moved. The place was called La Casa Redonda because around the turntable there was a semi circular building divided into stalls, each with a track. When the overhaul was finished, the locomotive was backed onto the turntable and switched out of the yard to the main line.

The superintendent of the yard was a tall, slim gringo who always dressed in tight riding pants and leather puttees. He joked with the men about the dirty words in Spanish that they taught him in exchange for the dirty words in English he told them. When he gave orders he made himself understood in a mix of both languages, practicing his funny Spanish and laughing at himself with the men.

It was from him that Gustavo picked up phrases he brought home to show off before the family.

"Do you know what the superintendent wears instead of *zapatos*?" Gustavo asked. "He wears chews! Ernesto, say *zapatos* in English."

"Chews."

"Correct."

"When he means *sombrero* he says "hett." Ernesto, say *sombrero* in English."

"Hett."

"Correct." So my lessons proceeded with "chairt" for shirt, "pa-eep" for pipe, "huatine-ees" for what time is it, "tenks yu" for thank you, "hau-mochee" for how much, "wan" for one, and "por pleeze" when asking a favor.

Gustavo chuckled over the gringo's difficulties with Spanish: "What is so hard about saying tortilla? All he can say is "tar-teela." He likes frijoles so much and he calls them "free-holes," he laughed. Between lessons my mother and I practiced "chairt" and "chews" and the rest of our growing vocabulary which Gustavo brought directly from our gringo professor.

To us the superintendent, like all the other Americans, was either a gringo or a *bolillo*. What gringo meant nobody was very sure of; but *bolillo* was simple. It came from the fact that most Americans preferred, instead of tortillas, the small baker's loaves with a nipple on each end and a curl of crust between. Two remarkable things about the American *bolillos* were the way their necks turned red with sunburn, and their freckles, both good reasons why no Mexican could ever become an American, or would want to. Keeping to an ancient Mexican custom, we had nicknames for some of them, like the clerk we called the Golden Tooth, from the fillings he flashed when he smiled, and *El Zopilote*, the brakeman who flailed his arms like one when he signaled.

Taking long walks was our chief entertainment: to the salt flats to flush out sandpipers and ducks and herons; to a cove where we watched the fishermen drag dead sharks over the sand from their boats; past the Casa Redonda, exploring the narrow streets of a village backed against the walls of the cemetery.

Around the tent I invented suitable amusements. Under one corner of the plank floor I started a collection of nuts, screws, bolts, and other scraps from the trackside. It was the beginning of what I planned as my own roundhouse where Gustavo would be superintendent, José the man at the whistle, and I would be the guard, flagging down my own locomotives. When trains went by I waved to the crew in the engine cab and the brakemen in the caboose. They waved back and shouted words I couldn't hear.

The first time we saw soldiers on the trains my mother asked Gustavo what it meant. Such things were always brought up after supper when we were sitting on the plank apron in front of the tent, talking in the twilight, slapping mosquitoes, waiting for bedtime.

The men always gave us bad or disturbing news reluctantly, but Doña Henriqueta pressed them. In any case sooner or later the other women in the camp would talk.

"Some fighting up north," Gustavo finally answered, without concern. "The superintendent said there was a bridge out and the telegraph was cut."

My family could think over news like that for a half hour without saying a word. I could tell they were worried, because no more was said.

When a military train went by, headed north, my mother questioned the men about the rumors in the

Casa Redonda, where the telegraph brought news from all over the country. They heard scraps of conversation in the shops. Our neighbors, eager to listen on our grapevine, dropped in to ask what we had heard. I didn't miss much of the gossip, which was all about the revolution. It seemed to be happening here and there, not all at once, but always near the railroad. José, who mixed with the arriving train crews, passed on to us what they told him. The revolutionary *bolas* had attacked this town or that one, Don Francisco Madero was gathering an army, President Díaz had resigned.

But the revolution came closer to us one afternoon. José was sent by the superintendent to take some tools to a crew that was working on the line north of us. Whenever I wanted to go on one of these short trips he could usually get permission from the superintendent to take me.

He stopped the handcar in front of our tent.

"Henriqueta," he called to my mother, "the superintendent says that Ernesto can come with me. Are you coming, Neto?" With her permission, in two hops and a jump I was across the catwalk and on the car. José started to pump on one side of the double bar and we were off. I sat to the side close up against the steel uprights, where I was safe from getting my head bumped. The time I tried to help José pump at the opposite handle, I only succeeded in being lifted into the air and set down hard on the floor. The two bars rocked like a see-saw as José pumped powerfully on one end.

On the way out we crossed a wooden trestle that passed over a tree-covered gulch. The treetops were even with the deck of the trestle and we could look down the trunks to the sandy bottom. The black crossties, the shiny lines of the rails, the racket of the rods and gears and the green crowns of the trees viewed from such a dizzy height, made me feel like a genuine railroad man.

It was dusk when we started back. José was pumping steadily when we rolled onto the trestle, the gulch a dark shadow below us. From below came a challenge: "Quién vive?" the way I had heard the patrols in Tepic call for the pass word.

José yelled back happily: "Viva Madero." Instantly a rifle shot cracked in the woods beneath us. José barked at me "Flop," and began pumping furiously. On my belly, I flattened myself on the floor of the handcar. More shots sounded below before we reached the end of the trestle and the solid roadbed beyond. The handcar flew as José whipped up and down at the bar. We did not slow down until we passed the signal tower. A short distance from our camp he stopped the car. I sat up. José was panting and drenched with sweat. Looking scared and grim, he said: "Don't tell your mother what happened." José was more afraid of a scolding from her than of being shot at. I looked at him and saw a brave *revolucionario* who would shout defiantly "Viva Madero" in the face of the enemy.

He dropped me by the tent and went on to deliver the hand car.

At supper my mother asked, "Well, how was your trip?"

José was eating quietly and so was I.

"Nothing much." He kept looking at his plate. "We were just pumping along when we heard some shots way over by the beach—way over. We came home as fast as we could minding our own business."

"Shots. What kind of shots?"

"Oh, shots like hunters. Duck hunters maybe."

But the next morning, against my resolve that we *maderistas*, José and I, would guard our secret, my mother got the whole story from me. As José and I figured it out later, it couldn't be helped. A track hand told the story in the camp about a couple of dynamiters who had tried to blow up the trestle and had been fired on by guards. They had cheered "Viva Madero" and had escaped on a handcar toward Mazatlán at about the time we were riding home. It was my last ride on a handcar.

In the next weeks there was no longer any doubt about it. The revolution was coming to Casa Redonda. People were drifting in from the villages and towns stopping to ask for work and camping by the tracks. One night the family in the next tent left without a word to any one. The tenants of the boxcars moved their cots upstairs and pulled the doors shut at night.

Then the worst news came. My uncles were laid off at the shops and given the choice of moving up north to another job, doing maintenance work on the line. On the following evenings I listened to the conversation closely, as if I was helping to make important decisions. The talk was more than serious; it was solemn.

We had planned for the family in Jalco to come to Casa Redonda, but now they must wait. Gustavo would accept the job up north; José would stay with us for the time being. The three of us would leave the tent and find a place to live in Mazatlán. Later, when things settled down, Don Catarino, my aunt and the boys would join us, and Gustavo would return, by which time we would all have work. All these important matters were decided mainly by Doña Henriqueta and Gustavo. José, I was sure, wanted to stay and wait for a chance to join the next *bola*. I never had the courage to ask whether I could go with him.

As before, when drastic decisions had been made, the most important thing was to count our money. Little bundles of coins tied in handkerchiefs were brought out from under one of the planks. The *víboras*, filled with silver, came out of their hiding places. We arranged the coins in stacks of heavy pesos and *tostones*, the half-dollar pieces that gave a musical ping when I flipped them off my thumbnail. With our savings we could get settled in Mazatlán and provide for Gustavo's journey.

One morning Gustavo took a northbound freight that was picking up men along the way. We said good-bye at the trackside. It was a lonesome parting for us, watching the train until it was out of sight down the track beyond the signal tower.

A short time later the three of us walked miles over a dusty road to Mazatlán. We went to Doña Florencia's, the cousin who had left San Blas as a young girl and married the merchant. Around the corner from their house there was a room for rent, of which her husband was the land-lord. The down payment on the rent was made and José went back to Casa Redonda for our things. He returned with them in a pushcart and we moved into our single room on the Calle Leandro Valle, Mazatlán, Sinaloa, an address that sounded more important to me than Jalco or Casa Redonda because it took longer to say it.

We called it our house even though it was only one room, like all the places I had ever lived in. Our side of the block was a row of such rooms, with about as much space as the tent at Casa Redonda. It was a brick row, with fronts painted in pastel colors and red tile roofs laid at differ-ent angles. Each dwelling had a front window with bars reaching nearly from the sidewalk to the roof. In Jalco there were no windows of any kind; in Tepic they were only for the rich; now in Mazatlán we had one of our own. Inside the bars two heavy shutters swung into the room. The grill was rusty here and there and the shutter panels were cracked and unpainted. The important thing was that, as we said, "it gave on the street." People passed so close on the narrow sidewalk we could have reached through the bars and touched them. Better still, since the bars extended beyond the wall a few inches, we could look up and down the street sitting indoors on the window sill.

The floor was of large square bricks worn smooth and ridges of grey mortar between. The ceiling was the underside of the tile resting on beams that pointed from back to front. Families who had lived there before had left a helter-skelter of nails, bolts, and pegs driven into the walls. The kerosene lamp hung from a hook on the center beam.

A step down from the front room was our kitchen, with the brick stove and two benches to serve as shelves. José brought three steel bars and a short piece of lead pipe from a scrap heap somewhere. The bars were niched into the center fire pit to make a grate, and we used the pipe as a blower to take the place of the old-fashioned grass fan. In place of the clay *comal* José produced a piece of sheet iron that was propped on top of the *pretil* against the wall and lowered over the coals when needed. The wooden chocolate beater we bought at the market, with its carved rings and inlaid ivory dots, hung on a nail in the showiest spot.

The three cots we brought from Casa Redonda were set in the breeziest corners of our room which we carpeted with grass mats. As usual the cedar box was wrapped and slipped under my mother's bed. My uncle laid a plank on two pegs in the wall and the space beneath was curtained for our closet. Because we didn't have chests of drawers we put things away in the space under the cots.

After the floor was scrubbed and the walls washed down, an empty five-gallon tin can was set on the windowsill. It was gradually filled with soil, which the neighbors contributed along with slips of geranium. Our window garden grew into a small bush of scalloped leaves and crimson blooms like the ones we had in Jalcocotán.

Our tiny kitchen was also a balcony. A low brick wall topped the stairwell down to the back yard, connecting with the huge central patio which was the common courtyard for every family in the block. Most of it was paved with cobblestones, the center of it occupied by washtubs that drained by a ditch to one corner of the court. Since our block was on a slope the families on the high side of Leandro Valle had balconies like ours. My mother called it our "palco"—a loge—from which we could see the happenings of the *vecindad* as in a theater.

In the rainy season the patio was also the community shower for children of my age and younger. Before the thunderheads broke over the city we were called in and prepared for our toilette. As soon as the rain was pelting the court we rushed out, ran back dripping wet, soaped ourselves, and dashed back into the storm to wash off the suds. Since the showers were usually short, in a few minutes it was all over, including the rubdown. Boys of my age wore underpants while showering. The younger children took their showers naked, teetering on the tips of their toes and squealing to one another. The stately coconut palm in one corner of the patio, bowing before the wind, thrashed its fronds high over the dripping brownies bouncing on the cobbles.

Leandro Valle crowned one of the highest knolls in the city. In places the sidewalks were nearly level with the street; in others they left the grade and went on by themselves, making terraces that ended abruptly six or seven feet in the air. Since nobody ever risked a broken neck using the walks, the neighbors fenced them off and used them for front porches. Being high and breezy they were good places to sit on hot nights. From them we could look out over the roofs of the city to the spires of the cathedral, the lighthouse rock, and the palm grove of Coconut Island beyond the brewery.

But the people who lived on Leandro Valle had not moved there because of the view. They were workers, mechanics, tradesmen, and artisans who could not afford to pay rents of more than four or five pesos a month, and who had to be within walking distance of the factories, the stores, the waterfront warehouses where they worked.

There were home workshops all around our house. One of our neighbors, the grayhaired cigar maker, sat stooped all day at a low table by the window, cutting tobacco leaves with a rounded knife, rolling and shaping the *puros*, putting gold paper rings around them, and stacking them in neat piles on the bench. A couple who lived in the next block down the street made candles, pouring melted tallow into molds, and hanging them to cool in clusters over the doorway to advertise the business. On the corner of Rosales and our street the only family we knew that had two rooms used one for a cabinet shop. Several families made candy of various kinds, boiling the syrups over stone pits in the court or in their kitchens. The skyrocket maker poured powder into small cardboard tubes, which he sealed and attached to thin reeds about a yard long. We bought sweetbread from the neighborhood baker, who allowed his customers to watch him mixing dough, stripped to the waist and sweating in front of the oven, shaping the *chilindrinas*, *chamucos*, *pambazos*, and *bolillos*. When he was not too busy and he was in good humor he shaped bull horns, boats, donkeys, and clowns, sprinkled them with white sugar, studding them with raisins and shoving them into the oven on a wooden spatula with a long handle for a quick baking.

You could tell with your nose as well as with your eyes whose shop you were walking by. I could smell cured tobacco, burning molasses, firecracker powder, rancid tallow, wood shavings, turpentine, leather, and practically everything else the people of Leandro Valle used to earn a living.

What our neighbors didn't make, tradesmen brought us from other parts of the city, other workers' *barrios* like ours. Because of the steep grade, the milkman and the charcoal vendors left their donkeys at the bottom of the hill and bawled out their wares, walking up and down the block. Housewives went down the hill with pots and bags to buy. A young man came around with a large basket on his shoulders, calling out "Hot, crisp finger nail noise," by which he meant that he had roasted peanuts for sale. If something made of metal needed repairing, the welder sat on the sidewalk with his portable furnace like a Japanese hibachi, tiny anvil, and soldering irons. For shoes, people went to the *maestro* up Rosales, who measured your feet and made wooden lasts, one set for each customer. Bringing their wares from every part of Mazatlán the street merchants whistled, hooted, yelled, bugled, and yodeled up and down our street.

Many of our neighbors did not work for themselves but for wages. At the foot of our hill was one of the largest employers, La Cervecería del Pacifico, which produced beer for all of Mexico. Not far from the brewery the steamers and sailing ships unloaded at the wharves. The cigarette factory hired men, women, and children. Instead of trucks there were porters, who delivered goods on their backs—heavy wooden boxes, a mound of hay, sacks filled with grain, pagodas of crates crammed with chickens, steel rods, and every sort of material that was bought and sold in the city.

It was out of jobs like these that José began to make enough of a living for us to stretch the pesos that Gustavo sent us now and then. A job didn't last more than a few days so that he soon became a jack-of-all-trades. I saw him help unload a ship, wearing a sack folded down the middle in a way that made a peaked hood over his head and a cape down his back. For a while he substituted as a driver on the streetcars pulled by mules that trotted along the Calle de la Constitución. After a heavy shower José stationed himself at a flooded street crossing and carried ladies across for five centavos. When they were young ladies he came home with salty stories about how he had tickled them, pretending he had stumbled on a cobble in the deep water. If there was nothing else to do, he coiled a rope around his shoulder and set off for the market, thus becoming a *mozo de cordel* for the day. To get a job he pretended he was an apprentice in everything, so that he managed to learn about forging iron grills, mixing concrete, painting houses, and setting bricks.

This was what he and Doña Henriqueta called *hacerle la lucha*. Every morning was a new round in the match between us and the city. If he came back with a tostón or a peso we won the round. If not, we lost. If we won, we could tell as he walked up the hill, whistling his favorite tune, "Adios Mamá Carlota." The story of that tune he told me many times: the Empress Carlota who went completely daffy because she was unable to persuade President Benito Juárez to pardon her husband, the Emperor Maximilian, who was shot by a firing squad. José's whistling celebrated not so much the tragedy of Carlota, although he contended that she should have had better sense than to marry such a scoundrel, the invader of our country. He whistled the just deserts of Maximilian as a sign to the family that we, too, had overcome, at least for that day.

On bad days José just walked in and sat down on the back stairs. "How did it go, brother?" my mother always said, knowing well that it had gone badly, but to make conversation. He always answered: "Like being kicked before breakfast." Good or bad news, our supper talk was always about the chances of the next day. If he had brought wages home he took a few cents and walked to the plaza for a beer. If he had not, my mother offered the money but he did not take it. Instead he went to bed.

José didn't carry by himself the burden of keeping us in shelter and food very long. Every day I was sent to Doña Florencia's, our landlady, to ask whether the Ajax had come, and one day I ran home to announce that we could call for it at the railroad terminal. That afternoon José brought it home in a pushcart.

He set the sewing machine in the middle of the room and the three of us removed the wrapping of straw mats, rags, and blankets, carefully, like doctors afraid of finding a broken bone. When the machine stood clear my mother tested it, bobbin, treadle, belt and all. "Thanks to God," she said gratefully. The *arrieros*, the mules, the *mozos*, the train and everyone who had anything to do with the safe delivery of the Ajax had performed, in her opinion, a service of the Lord.

The Ajax was placed next to the window where Doña Henriqueta sat, day in and day out, bending over the sewing she did for pay. On the windowsill next to the geranium she laid out doilies, blouses, and handkerchiefs so that passersby would see them and spread the word that on Leandro Valle there was a seamstress who did beautiful work. The big pieces, like bedsheets, fell from the machine crumpled on a straw floor mat which we scrubbed every day.

As Ajax assistant production and maintenance man I picked up where we had left off in Tepic. Like a regular engineer I squeezed golden drops of oil from a thimble-sized can into the bearings of the treadle, the transmission, and the balance wheel. When we ran out of thread I went on the double to the corner store of El Chino, half a block down the street. I helped pick up the sheets from the mat and fold them for ironing. Everything from the table top up was dusted and polished by my mother; everything below the deck, by me.

Now I heard again above the bustle of the Ajax, the songs she hummed or sang softly, like the one about the seagulls fluttering their wings far over the ocean, as if they were waving handkerchiefs to say good-bye, forever.

We had a problem with the sewing in that I balked at my chores if the front door was not kept shut. Sewing was a girl's work, and my pals in the *barrio* never let me forget it if they saw me folding sheets or holding a hem. Running for thread and oiling the machinery were dignified things for a boy to do, but not fooling around with stitches. My mother pointed out that the best tailors in the world were men and they all sewed on Ajaxes. The trouble was that Perico and Corchos and the rest of the gang didn't know or appreciate this. She agreed to my point and we kept the door closed during sewing hours.

By a lucky break I found a job myself that put me on a par with José and my mother as breadwinners. An elderly woman who lived two blocks down Rosales from our street needed a boy to help on Friday afternoons. The woman was a *pozolera* and her business a sidewalk restaurant which specialized in *pozole*, a chowder made of boiled garbanzo grains, and chopped meat or pig's knuckles served steaming hot. La Pozolera set up a long table in the street in front of her house, and on the side-walk the portable charcoal stove, the pots, sauces, and tortilla pan. Sitting on the sidewalk in the midst of her kitchen gear, she served the customers on a wooden table opposite her.

My job consisted of throwing buckets of water on the street to settle the dust, helping to put the table and bench in place, carrying the big *ollas* outdoors, and fill-ing the charcoal basket that she kept handy under the table. Hot *pozole* was served from late afternoon until after dark, when the restaurant closed and the equip-ment was moved indoors.

My pay was ten centavos a week, a meal for myself and a pot of *pozole* for the family. Friday nights I stuffed myself with seconds and thirds of the chowder and all the tacos I could eat. I reported for work on my way from school, but at night I walked home with José. Our customers were the people of the *barrio* coming home from work, stopping to treat themselves with our Fri-day night special. They ate by the light of two kerosene lamps standing high on the table mounted on tin cans. The lamps made everything flicker; even La Pozolera seemed to bounce lightly to their rhythm as she sat on the sidewalk.

When the diners finished and paid for the meal, they shuffled into the night as silently as they had eaten. José and I helped clean up and the two of us walked home, José carrying the pot of *pozole* which was part of my wages. By adding onions and water my mother usually stretched the portion over Sundays.

My employer paid me in centavos—ten of them, copper coins as big as beer bottle tops. They were im-pressive wages to me because the coppers jingled in my pocket and made ten separate plunks when I dropped them into the pig bank. They also made the pig, which was kept under my bed against the wall, feel heavier sooner. When the bowels of the pig were too stuffed to jingle, I could tell that it was time to break it, count my hoard, and work out a shopping plan for our next trip to the *mercado*. Like all the money that came in, a part of my earnings was saved.

Along with discovering the profits in *pozole*, José and I explored the tidewater salt flats north of the harbor. It was a day's walk there and back from Leandro Valle, past Icehouse Hill. José had fished and combed the beaches of San Blas as a boy so he knew about tidal pools, how to pick up a crab, and where to dig for clams. We splashed about, looking for seafood, wading knee-deep along the green margins. On the other side of the sand bar the combers of the Pacific Ocean swished and collapsed in a simmer of foam and bubbles the length of the beach. From a dune we could see the masts of sailing ships riding at anchor, waiting their turn to enter the harbor.

If we had no luck finding fish or clams, we stopped on the way home to help fishermen clean their catch, of which they gave us enough for our Sunday supper. We never took home from these beach excursions more than we could eat ourselves and give to the neighbors. We had no refrigerator.

Once the ocean brought us a windfall. A sailing ship was wrecked off Lighthouse Hill and the sea scattered its cargo up and down the beaches. José haunted them for days, avoiding the customs guards. Among his booty there was a bolt of linen, a German beer mug with figurines sculptured in bright blues and yellows, and a small jewel case with purple felt lining. All the men in our *barrio* were searching for treasures like these. They were considered salvage if you found them, but only if the guards didn't see you. My mother thought that everything should be returned to the poor ship's factors to whom the cargo belonged, but she lost the argument with José. The guards, he said, only wanted the loot for themselves. The factors were rich anyway, and the storm was nobody's fault; it was just a way God had arranged so the poor could have some of the good things of the rich. My mother refused to make garments out of the cloth, so José sold it in the black market, black market, was called *el chueco*.

But the lifesaver of our budget, when sewing was scarce and José found little work, was the gold ring that was kept wrapped in tissue paper in the bottom of the cedar box. Several times it went to the pawnshop to pay the rent or keep our credit good with El Chino, the grocer. When the ring was in hock, in its place in the cedar box there was deposited the cardboard receipt that the money lender gave us. When it was redeemed, we celebrated, putting it on this finger and that, polishing it on our sleeves and returning it to its secret place. Our neighbors went to the money lender regularly to pawn their belongings as security for the repayment of loans. Banks were for the rich, like carriages and townhouses with charming patios.

It was the Chinese grocer, El Chino, as much as the pawnbroker who helped us over the hard times. We traded with him in cash, but when we didn't have it, he jotted the debits in a notebook with our name on one of the pages. Don Juan-Chon, as my mother preferred to call him because she said "El Chino" sounded disrespectful, used a large abacus to total up our charges. He laid it on the counter, running his fingers over the wooden beads as if he were plucking a guitar. I always went when we paid up, mainly because Juan-Chon always gave me a piece of candy—the *pilón*, or bonus—to celebrate the deal.

After the *pilón* and the abacus, my interest in our grocer centered on his queue. He always wore a black skullcap over the top of the braid, and I could not figure out whether the braid hung from his scalp or from the cap. It was a long one, reaching to the hem of his black jacket.

He was nearly as plump as La Pozolera, of a pale complexion like wax candles. The front of his shop was curtained, separating from the store front the back room where he lived. If I could, I sneaked in quietly to listen to his conversation in Chinese behind the curtain with friends who visited him. When he caught me eavesdropping, he scolded me in Chinese, which I pretended I understood.

Doña Florencia, our landlady, and Juan-Chon were the two anchors of our budget. We were used to jobs stopping without notice, but we were certain that other work would be found. My own credit with Juan-Chon, was solid, I suppose, because he knew that I worked for La Pozolera down the street from his store.

We worked, as I well knew, first of all to pay the rent every Saturday. Less urgent was the *gasto*, the money set aside each day for food. The shopping expenses were like the ballast of a ship; unlike the rent, they could be made heavier or lighter to balance the daily intake of wages. If there was more than enough for the groceries, it was spent on a bar of Castile soap that smelled like orange blossoms, or on a wedge of the famous preserves from Celaya, or on the aromatic raisins we bought at the plaza.

The most important thing was to avoid sickness. We had no credit with doctors or dentists or druggists, so when I wakened one morning with a swollen jaw, José was dispatched to find a certain practitioner who pulled teeth for fifty centavos. My mother walked me to his place that afternoon. A heavyset man in a white apron was reading a newspaper in a barber's chair when we entered. He took me outside, ordered me to open my mouth as I faced the sun, and asked: "Where does it hurt you?" I pointed vaguely to my throbbing gums. Without a word, he sat me in the chair, took some tools out of a drawer, and began to work his big fingers between my jaws. When he pressed the abscess I yelled and fought him off. "Madam," he said huffily, "if your boy does not cooperate I can do nothing for him." She pinned my arms to the chair and commanded me to behave like a man. After a minute of grinding torture, he pulled out a molar with his pliers. It was washed and put away in her purse, wrapped in a handerchief.

Spitting blood all the way home, I was put to bed with a hot compress on the swelling and the assurance that in the morning the pain would be gone.

But it was not. The inflammation stayed and the pain became worse. There was nothing to do but ask Doña Florencia what to do. She loaned us two pesos to pay a dentist she recommended. With my jaw in a sling we walked across town again, found the address, and I was soon in a real dentist's chair. He tipped my head back, looked me over carefully, and without a word went to work. He yanked with something bright and hard and cold, and for the second time in twenty-four hours I was minus a tooth.

As I rested and rinsed my mouth with medicine my mother unwrapped the first tooth and showed it to the dentist. He turned it in the palm of his hand. "Madam," he said, "this is a perfectly good molar." He took our two pesos and showed us to the door.

"But, Ernesto, why did you point to a good tooth?" my mother asked the next day, when I could move my jaw again. José came to my rescue. "He was just telling that blacksmith that the pain was in his head and not in his feet." We put the good tooth away in the cedar box, with the intention, I thought, of having it put back some day. The one with the cavity was disposed of with ceremony. José instructed me to stand in the middle of the court, throw it over my shoulder as far as I could, and say: "A molar for the devil." What he meant, Doña Henriqueta would not tell me. "They are inventions of your uncle," and she laughed.

The people of our *barrio* dreaded the expense more than the pain of sickness. Short of an infection or scarlet fever or whooping cough they avoided the *consultorios*, relying on the herbs, the powders, the compresses and the ointments that as neighbors they recommended to one another. It was in this way that my mother found out about Wampole, the emulsion for people with thin blood, which she thought accounted for my staying skinny. Wampole came in a tall square bottle. The stuff inside was a thick red syrup, by far the best medicine I ever had. My dose was a tablespoon morning and night, and I could not persuade my mother that doubling the dose would soon make me a heavyweight.

But she did not believe in the *merolico*. I complained of a persistent pain below the stomach and a lady up the street suggested that we go to the market for a prescription from the patent medicine man. Like the one in Tepic, he had a poster-sized picture in colors of everything inside of a human being. In his patter the *merolico* described pains and pointed to the various organs and what ailed them and how they could be relieved by the marvelous cure-all he was selling for a ridiculously small price. The miraculous liquid was in small bottles lined up on the portable table in front of him. I stared at the chart and knew exactly where my pain was—on the right-hand side, above the crotch and just below where the guts curled and went the other way. We never bought the medication. Instead I was put on a diet of cod liver oil, lemon tea, *yerba buena*, bean juice, and strained *pozole*. The pain stopped.

Nor did we see the doctor for colds. Our prescription was inexpensive: a cube of white sugar soaked in diluted turpentine to be sucked slowly and lemon rinds chewed thoroughly. For gas pains on my stomach, I was laid out flat on the bed. Warm wax was rubbed on my skin and a stub of candle was set in the wax to hold it upright. The candle was lighted and a water glass was put over it, upside down, pressed snugly against the skin. The candle flame went down little by little, raising a round welt around the rim of the glass. When the glass had cooled, a spoon handle was pushed between the glass and the skin. There was a quick suck of air and the glass came off. Why it worked I never found out, but it did. It saved the cost of an operation, and, as José explained, avoided the risk of having the wrong gut taken out.

What was remarkable to me was that whenever we had to borrow two pesos for an emergency, Doña Florencia could provide them. More remarkable still was the fact that she loaned pesos to the other neighbors who rented on our block. It was Theresa who told me this and who also led me to the explanation. The pesos came from the treasure of Don Delfino.

Don Delfino, Doña Florencia, and Theresa were the most distinguished family on our block. They owned it, at least so we believed, because we paid our rent to them. He was a fair skinned, bald, middle-aged, plump man, and blind, the reason he was never seen outside his house. Doña Florencia was a tall handsome woman who wore her hair in braids coiled like a coronet. She smiled at people not so much with joy as with patience and a touch of sadness. As her husband's business manager, she was around and about a good deal. Theresa, the young daughter, was as plump as I was skinny, and bossy. The three of them lived at the low corner of our block, on Rosales. The house was unusual; it had several barred windows instead of one. Their sidewalk jutted high above the street at the corner, leveling off into ramps by which you reached the house, which from below looked like a fortress. It was the only corner on the block that had a street lamp.

I played with Theresa when my mother went to talk to Doña Florencia about sewing or to pay the rent or to hold one of their long *pláticas* about San Blas and their relatives. Usually Don Delfino sat in the room back of the parlor, his hands crossed over the gold handle of his cane. The windows to this room were always barred and darkened. To one side there was a large heavy table with carved legs. One wall was covered with book cases, the other with shelves and cabinets. On the table there was a large book with blue canvas covers, and a pair of scales with bronze weights lined up along the front. We were not allowed in this room; but when we heard Don Delfino tap his way to the back of the house, and the *plática* became so interesting that we were ignored, Theresa whispered the signal and we sneaked into the office, for that is what it was.

It was on one of those sneak days that Theresa led me to the treasure. We were on the tile floor, crawling about on hands and knees. She whispered: "Let's go in." She parted the drapes that hung from the top of the table and crept into the dark closet below. I followed her. "Feel," she said. Taking my hands in hers she moved them along the rounded sides, the neck and the top of two huge jars, like the red clay ones I had seen so often in the market and which stood shoulder high to me. Snuggled against me, Theresa whispered "Silver" which everybody in Mexico knew meant not just silver but also gold and jewels and riches of all sorts. "Really?" I said, whispering back. "My word," Theresa answered.

Squeezed in the black hideaway against the cool clay of the *jarrones* we realized that we had committed a terrible transgression. She had given away a family secret and I had violated the strict orders of the household, which both Doña Florencia and my mother had laid down many times. We held hands, in fear most of all that Don Delfino would tap his way into the room and discover us.

"Theresa, Ernesto, where are you?" Doña Florencia was calling from the parlor. About to be caught, Theresa showed what stuff she was made of. She yanked me out as she crawled furiously from under the table, dragged me to the door, opened it, and presented us both for inspection looking like two children who had been playing in the back yard.

"Theresa, where were you?" Doña Florencia asked again.

Speaking for both of us she answered: "We were in the kitchen playing hide-and-seek." Since half of the answer was true and half was not, I knew we were in trouble if there were any more questions.

It was my mother who saved us. "Ernesto, say goodbye to Theresita and to Doña Florencia. We must leave."

I kept the secret of Don Delfino's treasure until long after we had left Mazatlán. A slip on my part and the whole *barrio* would have known it. Bandits would attack the house, Don Delfino would be killed, Doña Florencia would be locked up in a closet, and Theresa would be kidnapped. Their house would be haunted forever after. This is what always happened in the treasure stories that Doña Eduvijes had told us in Jalcocotán and in my mother's novels.

By now Leandro Valle seemed a comfortable and familiar place. I could count on certain things to happen, and certain places to be there and certain people to trust. Juan-Chon never forgot to give me the *pilón* I expected when we bought forty or fifty centavos worth from him, even though it was only two jelly beans or a caramel marble. The milkman passed by early in the morning, the charcoal man late in the afternoon. The night watchman walked by our house after dark on his way to the upper corner of the block, where he set his lamp down in the middle of the street and blew a long beep on his whistle. On the sidewalk terrace across from us, higher than our window, our neighbor watered her pots and cans of geranium, carnations, and herbs. We were friends with one of the richest men in Mazatlán, and I knew where his treasure was stashed. Everybody had heard that my mother was a first-class seamstress, that my uncle José drove a mule-drawn streetcar, and that I could speak English, things like "how-mochee" and "whatine-ees." There were many *arrimados* in the *barrio*, poor families who were temporarily unable to pay rent and who moved in with relatives. Among the *arrimados* I made new friends. At the foot of the hill was the enormous building of the Cerveceriá del Pacífico with a stack that sailors said they could see ten leagues off shore.

The neighborhood as a place where we felt we belonged became even more of a home base after I was admitted as a junior member of the gang. The four blocks on our hill, including the *cervecería*, was the *Barrio* of the Brewery, and we were the brewery boys who guarded it. The foreigners, who took chances if they crossed our turf without permission, were the boys of the *Barrio* of the Lonesome Palm, the *Barrio* of the Slaughterhouse, the *Barrio* of Icebox Hill and the *Barrio* of the Breakers. We were *cerveceros*, *mazatlecos*, and Mexicans, in that order; Mazatlán belonged to the Authorities and Mexico belonged to Don Porfirio Díaz. It was only in the *barrio* that we could make something belong to us, not the way houses and stores belonged to people but the way friends belong to one another.

The leader of the gang when we moved to Leandro Valle was a boy we called El Perico, who talked endlessly, like a parrot, and whose faintly curving nose also suggested his nickname. He was about three years older than I, a fast runner, a marksman with rocks, and a reputation for getting the worst beatings of any boy on the hill. Perico was the boss and the protector of about a dozen of us. We included Corchos, who was always chewing pieces of cork; El Chato of the pug nose; and Colilla, the cigarette butt collector and smoker. My nickname was El Huilo, for skinny, and sometimes I was called El Wampole, which I didn't like as well.

I didn't become a *cervecero* by merely moving to Leandro Valle. My credentials came one by one. I doused a boy from another *barrio* when he made fun of me while I was watering down the street for La Pozolera. I caught a king-sized crab on the salt flats by myself. When Perico sneaked a bottle of tequila from his house and offered us all a swig, I took mine without a blink. It was well known, because I told it, that I had fought crocodiles in the arroyo in Jalcocotán and that I rode a horse once over a razorback called the Devil's Spine.

My final initiation, however, was an encounter with Perico himself. Once too many times he tried pushing me off the sidewalk. As I fell into the street I reached for a rock, got up, and heaved it at my tormentor. He doubled up with the rock in his midriff, but he, too, came up with ammunition. I ducked the first stone. He heaved again and the next thing I knew I was lying in bed, my head bandaged and my mother putting compresses on the wound. Perico had spotted me on the forehead just above the nose.

A policeman came to our house as I lay dying, but neither Doña Henriqueta nor José would sign a complaint against Perico. José argued that, while my condition was deplorable, it had been a man-to-man encounter. Rock throwing was outlawed on Leandro Valle and we were both guilty. The *barrio* itself would take care of both of us. I was sentenced to house arrest for several days by Doña Henriqueta, and Perico, so he later told us, got the worst beating of his life. Thus, wearing a small scar in the middle of my forehead, I became El Huilo, alias Wampole, junior member of the Brewery Boys.

To the adults on Leandro Valle we were not so much a gang as a *palomilla*, a harmless swarm of young nuisances who had to be swatted now and then. There was no way for us to get lost or to mix with older *barrio* boys to learn about pilfering, smoking weeds, or accosting girls with dirty words. El Perico knew the most in these matters; he pictured to us the deeds we might do some day in true macho style, but neither he nor the rest of us could shake the surveillance of parents, relatives, *arrimados*, and *compadres* that surrounded us. It was law and order without policemen. Everybody knew that we drank, but it was only from empty bottles we picked up in the beer garden, from which we drained the last drops of rancid brew. Nobody ever bothered to find out whether the bottle tops we collected were new or used. The used ones we gleaned on the street. The new ones we traded in our own black market supplied by bootleggers. They were more valuable because they were not dented by bottle openers.

All together, we enjoyed the inside privileges and the outside hatreds of our *barrio* club. As insiders, we received lessons from El Perico on how to spin a top, how to throw a rock, how to kick and trip an opponent. We met every night, except when it rained, under the street lamp in front of Don Delfino's house to listen to El Perico describe his imagined affairs with girls, always in some other *barrio*. We crushed under foot the moths and cockroaches that crawled within the circle of light at our feet. It was at these meetings that we divided the gang into *maderistas* and *guchos* to fight with rocks the next time we had a chance. We gambled with bottle tops flipping them in a heads-or-tails toss we called *corcho-o-lata*. Our "tails" was the cork lining of the cap, "lata" the tin top. If anyone had a cigarette butt it was produced and Perico demonstrated the *golpe* technique of deep inhaling.

When we ran out of club business and no one could think of new riddles, we discussed the grapevine news from the other *barrios*. The news did not have to be true but it had to be exciting such as that the waterfront boys had stolen the captain's sword from a ship in the harbor, or the slaughterhouse gang had kidnapped a *gucho*, dressed him, and sold him for fresh meat in the market. El Perico rehearsed our own favorite plot: how to capture the brewery and run off with the millions of freshly minted *corcholatas* that we knew were stored there.

But even this was not the peak of our plotting. Most of all we were determined to kidnap one of the *niños* from the *Barrio* de las Olas Altas, the aristocratic quarter of Mazatlán. The *niños* were the sons of the rich, of the familias with carriages and servants, and who called us *la pobretería*. They wore patent leather shoes to school, shirts with wide lace collars, and embroidered handkerchiefs tucked in their silk shirt pockets. Worse, they were escorted to school by uniformed servants. We yelled insults at the *niños* whenever our paths crossed, and only the servants could hear us. Our idea of humiliating them was to dunk one of them in a flood of muddy water some stormy day.

Without the brewery boys my life in Mazatlán would have been without these touches that gave me a feeling of social importance. At home, José explained about *maderistas* and their reactionary enemies, the *guchos*, and the progress of the revolution. My mother's distaste for the airs of our high society was more subdued than José's, but even when she spoke of them with her gentle sarcasm I could feel something in common between our gang and our family. The difference mainly was that at home Doña Henriqueta made it clear that in many ways my manners needed as much improvement as those of the rich.

I was taught all the ceremonies of *respeto*—the proper greetings for delivering messages to the neighbors; to press myself against the walls to allow adults to pass me on the narrow sidewalks; to speak only when addressed and not to put my spoon into adult conversation; never to show that I was bored with the questions adults asked me when we were visiting; never under any circumstances to ask for anything to eat; to enter the house with my cap in my hand; to answer instantly when called; to address everyone as señor or señora; and to talk quietly in conversation. Breaches of these rules of *respeto* fell somewhere between a sin and a crime. Not to know them thoroughly and to observe them unfailingly showed more than anything else that you were *muy mal educado*. In my mother's book, to be well instructed was to know how to read, write, and count; to be well educated was to show deference to persons older than yourself. The older they were, the more *respeto* they were entitled to.

In addition to all these rules there were the proverbs and folk sayings my mother and José used frequently in their conversation. Something strange, something funny, something sad was put into a familiar phrase that not only explained matters but also gave you a safe rule to go by. If someone, often myself, was caught in a lie, it only proved, as my mother said, "sooner a man will fall who lies than one who limps." A man of truth and conviction, she said, was like a rooster who can crow from the top of a trash heap as well as from the top of a castle. Prudence is never trying to wear a shirt with eleven-yard sleeves. More important than one's word of honor or the word of an Englishman was the word of Ernesto, and once I gave it, I had to keep it, regardless of how much it hurt. As to *vergüenza*, I learned by a hundred examples what it was to have it or not have it. Doña Henriqueta wrapped all hypocrites and deceivers in one of her sayings: "They are born naked, which they can't help; and they die without *vergüenza*, which they can."

What with the workshops of the neighborhood, the brewery gang, my job with La Pozolera, the lectures on manners, and José's enthusiastic reports on the progress of Don Francisco Madero's revolution, my education was well started when I was enrolled in the first grade of the Escuela Municipal de Varones Número Tres. Dressed in a cotton suit of knee pants and jacket, long black stockings held up by rubber bands, high-buttoned shoes with nailed soles, and a flat-topped straw hat, I trotted with my mother to the school to be registered.

It was a two-story building formerly used as a factory and warehouse, remodeled for the instruction of boys from the *barrios*. In a small office on the first floor, we presented ourselves to Don Salvador, the *Director* or principal. After listening to a recital of my studies at home with the slate and the abacus and asking me some questions, the Director ushered my mother to the front of the school. As she walked away he kept me on the front portico of the school, chatting about where we had lived, what I liked best about Mazatlán, and whether I could identify the steeples and cupolas we could see from where we stood. Holding me by the hand he walked me to the second floor and assigned me to Señorita Bustamante, with sixty boys looking on. I overcame a slight sense of panic, knowing that I could certainly run to my old friend, the Director.

Señorita Profesora Catalina Bustamante was tall and stately in a high-collared white blouse with puffed sleeves, tight belt cinching her waist, and floor-length skirts. The slim, towering palm tree in the courtyard at Leandro Valle did not sway as gracefully as she. Standing at her table in the front of the room she commanded five files of boys sitting on wooden benches, each with double seats. I was assigned a seat midway in the center file, next to a boy about my size. With light provided only by the windows on the street side, the room was dim and stuffy. The high beams of the open ceiling were twice as high as in our house. There was a blackboard on two uprights near the table and a faded colored print nailed high up on one wall of the father of our country, Don Miguel Hidalgo y Costilla. The teacher regulated the class with a bronze handbell that she tinkled for attention, and a ruler that she used when she didn't get it.

The lesson changed from one subject to another when she jiggled the bell and directed us to close the notepad for civics and open the one for spelling. The notebooks were our texts. In them we put down as best we could whatever she dictated or wrote on the blackboard. Three monitors, boys from the upper grades, walked up and down the aisles checking our notations and making corrections. Only when the Señorita Profesora left the room did the head monitor have the authority to whack us with the ruler. Otherwise they let us have their contempt in whispered comments she could not hear as they leaned over our workbooks—"mule," "stupid," "rock head."

The Señorita sang out the lessons slowly and precisely. The review of the lesson was a series of questions by her and a chorus of answers by us. "Who was the father of our country?" "Don Miguel Hidalgo y Costilla," we sang back loud enough to be heard around the block. "Who was the Illustrious Son of the Americas?" "Don Benito Juárez," we chanted. "Five and five?" We made the dust fall from the beams with a shout: "Ten." "The Capital of Jalisco?" "Guadalajara." So we listened and memorized and recited, five days of the week and half a day on Saturdays.

I was soon bored by the humdrum of the dictation and the chanting of things I had already learned at home. I kept taking my slate and pencil to school, hoping I would be allowed to use it instead of the bulky notepads. On the notebooks it was hard to erase mistakes, you had to bring three or four lead pencils from home. You could not play at killing Frenchmen with tiny cannon and a quick stroke, as I could on the slate. When I wasn't scribbling on the notebooks, I drew on the *pizarra*.

At recess the street gate of the playground remained closed, but through the iron grill we could buy caramels, peanuts, and other snacks. There were no bars or rings or basketball courts for team play. During the breaks we simply chased one another or climbed the grain sacks that were still stacked in the part of the warehouse that had not been converted into classrooms. Where the sacks reached nearly to the ceiling we stretched ourselves and poked holes in them, pinching grains of corn or wheat to crunch. Climbing the piles was frowned on. Pinching them was an offense for which you could be locked up in the *calabozo* until Don Salvador could attend to you.

For me the curriculum soon divided itself in two parts—the monotonous singsong of words and numbers, and the exciting stories of National History and

Civic Instruction. We followed our Señorita phrase by phrase through the national anthem until we knew it so well we could make the old building tremble with patriotic song. "Mexicans, hear the call to war" it began, thundering on to the part I liked best, where it said that when Mexican cannon fired the very center of the earth trembled.

Don Salvador took over the class to give us lectures in history. They were more like dramatic recitals than lectures: about Hidalgo, the tragic fighting priest; Galeana, the general who chased Spaniards with his guerrillas; Guerrero, whose very name meant war. We learned about Pipila, the Indian boy who strapped a slab of rock to his back and thus armored crawled on all fours through a rain of Spanish bullets and set fire to their fortress that had withstood the whole patriot army. The Director was a dark-complexioned, sturdy gentleman with an alert moustache and vivid black eyes. As he talked he strode back and forth in front of the class, as if he were marching with Guerrero or charging with Galeana.

One day the Director's subject was the battle of Puebla and the forthcoming celebration of its anniversary, the *Cinco de Mayo*, the next to the most important national holiday. He announced that our school would stage a military drill and mock defeat of the French in one of the city's theaters, and that the students from each class would be selected to form the assault battalion.

I was picked with several others to defend the military honor of the first grade. For weeks we drilled at recess and after class hours on the playground, commanded by the Director himself. While he was whipping our outfit into shape, our families were making the uniforms designed by the teachers and sketched on a paper which we took home. The older boys fashioned the wooden rifles with which we were to be armed.

Doña Henriqueta was determined to make me the best uniformed Mexican soldier of the school. Off the Ajax came my bell-bottomed white cotton pants, the first long ones I ever wore, creased as sharp as a bayonet. My jacket front was studded with brass buttons. A shiny band of black imitation leather crossed me front and back like a bandolier, sewed to a belt of the same material. The shako was like a section of stove pipe complete with visor, chin strap, and plume. José made my knapsack, the *mochila*, a large cigar box padded with rolled newspapers in the shape of a *U*, with the ends hanging and the whole thing covered with the sarape of many colors we had brought from Jalcocotán.

Of course it was known up and down Leandro Valle that I had been honorably appointed to the service of our country for the celebration of the *Cinco de Mayo*. José knew the manual of arms and we drilled in our room— I with the pipe length we kept to blow on the kitchen coals, José with the broom. When it was finished my uniform was pinned to a cord strung from wall to wall, my shako on a nail and my new shoes on the window sill.

It was late in the afternoon when the three of us set out for the downtown theater where the celebration was to be held, José carrying the musket and my mother the *mochila*. I walked between them in my starched splendor so as not to spoil the crease.

They left me backstage, where the troops were mustered for final instructions. It was dark outside. We heard the rockets exploding on the street and the band in the pit playing an overture. There were dances and songs on the program ahead of us, and a reading of the official battle report of General Zaragoza to the president of Mexico that he had vanquished the French army.

While all this was going on we waited backstage, crowded and hot. I was pushed and elbowed by the bigger boys into a corner, where I waited my turn for the sergeant to harness my *mochila*. When he finally got to me he was cross and impatient. He spun me around, cinched me, and went off totally disgusted with first grade soldiers.

Leaning wearily against the wall, I was thirsty and wishing that the Emperor Maximilian and his French army had stayed home. The audience was clapping and shouting its approval of the dancers and the mariachi, who took repeated curtain calls and obliged with more encores than was necessary, considering that we were suffocating in the wings.

Finally our cues sounded—a bugler blaring "to arms" and the snare drums rattling a double-quick. El General and the sergeant placed us in single file, the taller boys in the lead, the short ones bringing up the rear. I was the last one in the line.

To a fanfare of bugles and drums El General barked, "Forward, h'arch" and we advanced onstage, the green, white, and red colors at the head of the column. As I stepped from the wings I looked over the footlights. The theater was packed and the crowd was giving us a rousing welcome. Somewhere in the jam of people were my mother and José, neighbors from Leandro Valle, and some of the Brewery Boys. It felt as if every eye in that crowd was on me alone; for now I noticed that the *mochilas* of the others were the mouse gray or canvas brown of ordinary blankets. My knapsack, in startling contrast, was a roll of purples, yellows, blues, and crimsons, hanging like a limp rainbow on my back. Someone in the audience called out gleefully: "The one with the fantastic *mochila*."

The fantastic *mochila* and I were not doing very well. As El General put us through close formations on the small stage I was whipped this way and that. "In column of twos—h'arch," and I had to skip to close the gap between me and the rank ahead. "In column of fours—h'arch," and the line snapped me around like the end man in a snake dance. Halfway through the drill it was plain to me that the whole strategy of my war against the French was simply to keep up. I knew it and the crowd did, too, for every time I was left behind someone would yell: "Hurry up, little soldier with the butterfly knapsack."

Not a shot had been fired and I was already feeling utterly weary and ready for an armistice. My heart was thumping faster than the snare drums and I couldn't get my breath below the collar bone. The bandoliers were sagging and the *mochila* kept hitching to one side.

In this condition I heard the order, "As skirmishers—deploy." I found myself standing at attention at the foot of a single line facing the audience. "As skirmishers—sound off." We barked our numbers "one, two, three" down to the end of the line. I was a number three. "As skirmishers—ready," commanded El General, his tin sabre glinting above the footlights. "Numbers one—post," and one third of the battalion took three steps back to remain standing at the ready. "Numbers two—post," and the second third of the line positioned themselves on one knee. "Numbers three—post."

That was for me and the last third of the battalion. We had been drilled on the martial approach to the prone firing position—knee, elbow, chest down, spread. But I was so glad to have a rest that I simply lurched to the floor of the stage and wriggled myself into a relaxed stretch. The bandolier snapped and the *mochila* slid well up over my neck. Coming apart but comfortable I heard the command: "Prepare arms-aim-fire."

The brass and the snare drums went into a pandemonium of bangs and booms that everybody knew was the fire of our attack. We aimed our wooden rifles point blank at the audience, who drowned out El General's orders with shouts. "Aim a little higher." "That one was a blank." "You got me." Out there the spectators were turning the show into an *alboroto*, a small riot of joyful participation.

The bugles sounded "To the colors" and the battalion, without a single casualty, reformed in single line. For me it would have been better if a French bullet had left me flat on the stage, unconscious if not dead. I picked myself up and somehow made it to the foot of the line. "Halfturn to the right—h'arch" and the tall end of the battalion began to lockstep into the wings.

As the anchor man I was halfway across the stage when the *mochila* dropped to the floor. I turned back and bent to pick it up. The bandolier snapped and hung from my belt, more to the purpose of pulling my pants down than to hold them up. I dropped the musket and yanked on the belt. My shako came loose and teetered. By this time the *alboroto* in the audience had become a cheering, stamping, whistling mob. "*Viva* the little soldier with the butterfly *mochila*." "*Viva* the little Mexican with the wooden gun."

I looked for the battalion. The next to the last man was already exiting. Taking a chance with my pants, I gathered *mochila*, shako, and gun from the floor and retreated off stage.

The curtain came down. The house was shaking with cheers and *Viva's*. "The little soldier. We want the little soldier." But the *soldadito* was sitting in the wings on the floor, choked with *vergüenza*.

The battalion took no curtain calls, fortunately for me. Instead El General was now front stage, delivering the closing oration. The crowd interrupted him, cheering and shouting.

"Compatriots : Two score and ten years ago a valiant Mexican army under the indomitable General Ignacio Zaragoza defeated the perfidious invader in the glorious battle of Puebla. (*Viva El General Zaragoza.*) Offering their lives in a holocaust of sacrificial patriotism the heroes of Puebla gave notice to the entire universe that the Mexicans will never bend the neck to a foreign yoke. (*Death to the foreigners.*) Not in the East, not in the West, not in the South, nay, not even in the North, is there a power capable of subjugating our national destiny or staining our national honor. (*Death to the gringos.*) As in the centuries gone by so in the centuries to come Mexico will never lack patriots to follow in the steps of the victorious of Puebla. (*Vivan los patriotas.*) You have seen upon this stage that the mold of heroes has not been broken. (*Vivan los heroes.*) Should our country call it may be that from the ranks of the First Battalion of the *Escuela Municipal de Varones Número Tres* of this noble city of Mazatlán will come the saviours of our Republic. (*Viva la republica. Viva el Batallón. Viva la Escuela Municipal de Varones Número Tres.*)
Compatriots: The national anthem."

The band struck up "Mexicans, hear the call to war." Knowing my duty I hoisted myself up from the floor and stood at attention. The curtain went down, the theater emptied and the Director was among us, beaming with approval. "Dismissed," ordered El General; but by that time I was already at the stage door, my impedimenta dragging, looking for my folks.

They were there, waiting for me. I was relieved of everything but my *vergüenza* and we walked home through the night up the hill to Leandro Valle. Not a word had been said. We had sweet bread dunked in hot chocolate, foamy and spiced with cinnamon. From the talk of Doña Henriqueta and José I gathered that the maneuvers had been brilliant, the battle heroic, and my rear guard action a model of soldierliness. Why the bandolier snapped or the *mochila* collapsed was easily explained: the stupid sergeant had made a mess of my trim. The following morning a neighbor dropped in to offer her felicitations to my mother for my performance, about which everybody was talking. My *vergüenza* was melting away. It was generally agreed that under heavy fire from the enemy my gallantry had been a credit to the *barrio* of Leandro Valle.

The gun was returned to the school arsenal; the bell-bottoms were cut off my military pants and remodeled into knee britches, the jacket was turned inside out, and the shako was hung on a nail as a souvenir.

With my stage success my reputation among the Brewery Boys was now solid; beyond the school and the *barrio* the city began to take shape as my home town, with places and people I began to know well.

The Plaza de Armas of the city was a mile from our home, downhill straight on Leandro Valle and two blocks west. It was like a showcase of the city. The most expensive shops were all around it—Las Fábricas de Francia, La Torre de Babel, La Perla del Pacífico. In the center of the one-block park was the grandstand—a *kiosko* with iron scrolls and slender steel columns holding up a peaked cupola donated to the city by the German merchants—the Melchers, the Claussens, the Jeckers.

Boys in ragged clothes and bare feet ran about with their shoeshine gear—homemade boxes studded with brass nails—asking the gentlemen sitting on the iron benches around the *kiosko*, softly and pleadingly: "*Bola, señor?"* On the street and snug against the high terrace of the plaza, pushcarts lined themselves, selling candy, gum, colored juices, and knick-knacks. At dusk the strings of electric lights running from the *kiosko* to the lamp posts and looped around the laurel trees were turned on.

On certain evenings the regimental band quartered in Mazatlán gave concerts in the plaza. People from the rich *barrio* of Las Olas Altas drove slowly by in their carriages. On the broad cement walk of the plaza that enclosed the bandstand, young men in sharp clothes walked arm in arm three or four abreast, round and round in one direction, and young women in chic dresses walked arm in arm, three or four abreast in the opposite direction. The idea was to look and smile at your boy or girl friend each time you passed. With the girls' parents watching from the benches or the carriages, this was as close as you could approach your beloved. People without carriages and fine clothes stood across the street from the plaza, in the shadow of the Palacio Municipal or the cathedral, or the arcades of the shops.

It was at these concerts that I heard "El Niño Perdido" and decided to become a clarinet player. This was a musical piece about an instrument that strayed from the band and got lost, and how it was found one concert night crying on a balcony. The piece, a wailing melody in slow tempo, turned into a duet between the band in the *kiosko* and a clarinet player standing on a balcony of the second story of the Palacio Municipal across the street. The band pleaded and the clarinet wept until the stray child strode happily across the street, up to the bandstand, and took his seat in a finale of joyful reunion. If the "Niño Perdido" was not on the program, to me the concert was dull; if it was, I walked home wondering where I could get a clarinet, who would teach me to play the part on the balcony, and where I could join a band. My mother thought no concert was complete without the famous waltz, "Over the Waves," while José would suffer through a concert of classical music only if the band played "Adios Mamá Carlota."

It was also at the plaza that I saw the captain of the *rurales* swagger, his blouse tied in a knot in front over his belly, his spurs jingling on the cement and his saber dragging. Across the street, pasted to the wall of the Palacio, was a large poster with a picture of the president of the Republic, Don Porfirio Díaz. With a chestful of medals, a bulldog jaw and a crew cut, he had an iron look that watched the captain of the *rurales*, as the captain was certainly watching us.

José took me to see the burning of Judas at the plaza. High above the street, from a cable strung between two buildings, dangled a scarecrow with a horribly painted face, his twisted arms and legs stuffed with straw and spangled with firecrackers. This was Judas, the betrayer of Our Lord. He was set on fire during Lent, spewing his straw guts over the crowd below as the powder exploded. As usual I questioned my uncle. He told me the whole miserable story of the kiss and the betrayal. Later, on the way home, he said that not all the Judases were dead yet, and that someday the people would take the captain of the *rurales*, stuff him with torpedos, hang him over the plaza, and fire him. With the smell of powder in my nose and my uncle's strong, warm hand in mine, I agreed completely. If it ever happened, José promised grimly, we would be there to help.

Occasionally, the three of us had supper at the street restaurant by the corner of the market. For twelve centavos we shared a dinner of enchiladas and beans, browned to a sizzle. Opposite the restaurant there was the ice cream stall, by far the gem of the market to me.

On ordinary days, if I begged hard enough, we would buy one serving of *nieve de leche*—smooth, aromatic, and creamy, of one color. On special days I would be treated to a serving of two colors. Rarely was I allowed a helping of *nieve* in three colors—chocolate, vanilla, and strawberry. My uncle called the ice cream lady Doña Eructa, from the fact that she gave out continuously with tremendous belches. These sonorous outbreaks of Doña Eructa were a source of wonder to me, since I could seldom bring up a noticeable belch myself. My mother warned me never to mention the matter in the lady's presence.

In the middle of the block, between the restaurant and the ice cream stand, was the tortilla shop where I went every day for our daily supply during my two-hour school noon break. I didn't mind waiting my turn at the counter, watching the women pat the small buns of cornmeal into round disks, flipping them skillfully on the hot *comales*, and making neat stacks from which the customers were supplied. The clapping of a dozen *tortilleras*, each one to her own rhythm, made a soft patter, like raindrops plopping on wet ground. We talked across the counter without paying attention to the boss. "How does it go with you, Ernesto?" "Well, señora." "How is the little soldier?" "Very well, señora." "My greetings to Doña Henriqueta." "Thank you, señora." I trotted home, nibbling on a hot tortilla.

My uncle and I gambled in the market only by special permission of Doña Henriqueta. Some centavos were set aside for the purpose and we went off to the lottery tent that did a brisk business not far from Doña Eructa's. We selected two cards with colored pictures of animals, with which we were given a dozen red beans to spot on the cards. In the center of the tent a man whirled a bicycle wheel with a wooden tire and a nail on the rim.

Around the wheel were pictures of the same animals as on the cards. When the wheel stopped, the man called out "The Cow," "The Bull," or "The Snake." If the picture was on our card we placed a bean on it. In order to win, the card had to have a bean on each of the six squares. The prizes were on a shelf above the wheel—an alarm clock with a tin bell on top, a black and red painting of a bull. We never won anything.

Where we bought school supplies at a bookstore near the plaza, the display of paperbacks on the racks was a reading lesson for me. On the covers were sensational colored drawings of murders, holdups, and stagecoaches crashing down mountain sides. The titles were read to me over again until I learned them myself, browsing among my favorite bandits.

Our family library began in that shop. My mother bought a paperback novel called *The Countess with the Black Gloves* and for me my first book, *The Tales of Uncle Tonche*, who seemed to have lived everywhere and knew all sorts of people, including, as I found to my delight, Pipila. Tio Tonche added some details about his single-handed attack on the Spanish fortress that Don Salvador had omitted. When I mentioned these details at school my classmates allowed me some modest recognition as an historian.

Tio Tonche's tales were read to me until I memorized them and I could guess and imagine and spell my way through them myself, reading aloud to whoever would listen. Between readings, Tio Tonche was kept in the cedar box, along with the *Countess with the Black Gloves* and the *Cocinera Poblana*.

I began to understand what our neighbor the carpenter was doing when he sat in his doorway looking at a paperback with dog-eared pages, paying no attention to anyone. Now and then I tried it myself. I sat cross-legged at our door, reading Tio Tonche where people could see that I did not want to be disturbed.

From my door a new world of letters spread over Mazatlán. The signs over the shops where we traded were read to me until I could read them back. We didn't buy the town newspaper, the *Correo de la Tarde*, but I began to make something of the headlines on the newsstands. I stopped and listened when I saw a group of people standing by a telephone pole as someone read aloud from a white paper tacked on it. Most remarkable of all was my discovery of stone writing, like the sign chiseled on a sidewalk in front of a shop that said "Mercería Alemana," and of the iron writing on the statue of a famous man in one of the parks. Before I finished the first grade I was able to read, more or less, and write somewhat.

Besides literary discoveries, Mazatlán offered me opportunities to become a traveler of sorts. We rode the spiders and the mini-train. The spiders were carriages with two wheels taller than a man. Two passengers sat in the single seat next to the driver under a black top with a fringe. People in our *barrio* saved for a holiday turn in one of the *arañas* around the plaza or out to the ocean front. The crackle of the iron rims of the wheels on the cobbles, the hula-hula of the rig, the black beads of the fringe bouncing like raindrops, and the plume bobbing on the head of the trotting nag gave us, once or twice a year, a feeling of class. We passed the rich people in their four-wheeled, two-horse carriages with uniformed coachmen and we could look them level in the eye.

The mini-train was not so aristocratic but still only for holidays, because of the fare of ten centavos per round trip. It was a narrow-gauge imitation of real trains, running on a single track around the city to the beer garden of the Cervecería del Pacífico. A steam locomotive with a brass bell, beep whistle, and two flags before the stack pulled a half-dozen roller coaster cars. The engineer sat high on the tender, his feet stuck into the cab, looking altogether like the most important man in Mazatlán. When the toy locomotive stalled, all the passengers got out and helped the engineer heave and push to start it again.

The finances for these train excursions were carefully planned. We could walk to the downtown starting point of the ride, pay for one way, walk back up the hill to Leandro Valle and share one beer between us at the garden. Or we could take the full round trip and have no beer. Or we could walk to the garden, watch the train come and go, buy a bottle of beer for each of us and walk back home. The choice was left to me.

On foot, we explored the city in all directions. South from Leandro Valle we walked to the harbor to watch the longshoremen load the steamers, the sailing ships, boats, mule trains, wagons, and carts. West we walked to the Paseo de las Olas Altas, a promenade built by the rich people of the town facing the rocky beach where the waves came in high and broke in spindrift against the sea wall. North on the other side of Little Icebox Hill we walked to the truck farms, tilled by Chinese who bargained with us in sign language and trotted up and down the fields, swinging their pigtails and carrying vegetables in baskets slung on a pole across their shoulders. East were the salt flats and the fishermen's shacks and beyond them Coconut Island, where the *zopilotes* perched.

These were the familiar scenes of the Mazatlán I began to know. In the *barrio* of Las Olas Altas gentlemen in black suits and derbies tipped their hats to one another from their carriages. A German merchant rode a magnificent black horse, sitting stiffly like a general on parade, dressed in high laced boots, white breeches, velvet jacket, and checkered cap. On the waterfront I watched barefoot men stripped to the waist carrying enormous loads on their backs, skipping down gangplanks that bent and bounced under them. Along the beach I saw fishermen ripping open the bellies of dead sharks and pulling their guts out with bare hands. In the plaza old blind men with white eyes walked about in rags, leaning on crooked canes and led by children who held their hands out and begged. Juan-Chon stayed in his gloomy corner store, counting the beads on his abacus and talking in Chinese with his friends in the back room. Don Delfino sat in his den, staring out of bright blue eyes that saw nothing and with a treasure at his feet.

But the differences between rich and poor were impressed upon me more dramatically at the Christmas party.

A rich lady who lived in a mansion announced in the *Correo de la Tarde* that she would entertain the children of the poor barrios on the feast day of the Three Wise Men. Wealthy persons in Mazatlán often gave such parties. Their purpose was to do something for *la pobretería*, as we were called. Several from Leandro Valle went to the party, escorted by one of the mothers of the neighborhood.

We walked across town to the palatial house of the Lady Bountiful. There was a small crowd of children at the front gate. Inside the iron picket fence that surrounded the residence servants and ladies were walking about. Outside at the gate, a lady and a man in uniform were inspecting the children one by one before letting them in. My turn came. The man in uniform handed me to the lady. She looked me up and down and said: "Not this boy. He is not poor. He is wearing shoes." Another boy from our *barrio* was turned away because he was wearing a pressed cotton suit and new sandals. There was an argument between our chaperone and the guards. They were adamant: we were not poor and we could not go in.

All the Leandro Valle children were marched back to the *barrio*, and news of our rebuff spread until it got to Doña Florencia. She promptly organized a fiesta of our own. Our party was a day late but it came off, complete with Wise Men and *piñata*.

There was another red-letter event for me that Christmas season. I saw my first motion picture.

Mazatlán was becoming a modern town. We had electricity at the plaza and on the streets. For a penny you could buy electric shocks from a man who handed you two copper tubes wired to a small brown box with a handle which he turned faster and faster until you could not let go of the tubes. On the salt flats where the bicycle races were held, a new game was being played in which a player threw a small white ball at another who hit it with a stick and ran. José, who was up-to-date on all these matters, found out about the cinema.

The show was in a large hall somewhere near the market. High up on one wall there was a white screen facing a wooden tower from which a brilliant purple light shone through a small square hole. When we entered, the lights were on. Because there were no seats, the audience was standing. We pushed our way to one corner, where I was hoisted to a windowsill so I could look over the heads of the crowd.

The lights dimmed. There was a whir from the top of the tower and pictures began to flicker on the screen. A murmur of surprise and wonder rose from the audience.

Now it was pitch dark in the hall except for the beam of light from the tower and the moving pictures above us. Words and the pictures took turns on the screen and the story began to unfold. It was a tragedy at sea, the sinking of a great ship and the drowning of many people.

All went well during the shore scenes. Suddenly the ship was on the ocean in stormy weather. As the waves broke over the prow someone yelled: "The ocean! Watch out! Run!" The audience turned into a panicky mob. Jammed against the door of the hall they burst it open and poured into the street.

The lights went on and a man climbed up the tower. He harangued the few spectators who remained near the door until he convinced them that the ocean on the screen was make-believe. He climbed down, found a ladder somewhere, and propped it against the screen. The pictures went on again and he touched the waves, holding his hand out to show that it was absolutely dry. Little by little the crowd came back and the film was finished.

On the way home José had much to say about the difference between motion picture water and the real thing. Now that it was all over I could understand how ridiculous it had all been. But I had felt like running myself.

Apart from the excitements of movies and mini-trains and the problems of making a living, there was always the big project, the hope of bringing all the family together again. My Aunt Esther and the boys were still in Jalco. My Uncle Gus was now writing from a place called Nogales, far away to the north, near the United States. We were in between.

The letters we received, which my mother read aloud many times by the light of the oil lamp after supper, brought us skimpy news, all of it bad. Around Tepic the stagecoaches were not getting through and the mule trains had stopped. Some of the older boys had disappeared into the mountains to join the guerrillas. Madero's agents were stirring up the villages. Gustavo wrote that bridges had been burned and railway tracks torn up to stop President Díaz's troops. The Southern

Pacific line was becoming more dangerous every day. The revolution, he reported, was spreading to the south, which meant us, in Mazatlán.

The family letters, the gossip in the courtyard among the women, and the talk of the *barrio* gang kept me informed on the drift of things in the city. Country families were moving into our neighborhood from places like Rosario, La Noria, and Cosalá. From them we heard of General Osuna, General Tirado, and General Carrasco, who were gathering volunteers and getting ready to fight. El Perico picked up the news at the plaza from the shoeshine boys that General Díaz had been defeated at El Quelite by General Osuna.

It was José who scouted the city for firsthand information of the gathering troubles. Our family talks after supper were now about nothing but the revolution. José spoke with a mule driver who had been at Guamuchil when General Leyva's men held up and looted a train. He heard an orator in the plaza and the people shout "Viva Madero." Somebody had ripped the picture of President Porfirio Díaz from the wall of the Palacio Municipal. He brought home a paper which had been handed out at the waterfront and which said the revolution was for the public liberties and against President Díaz being reelected over and over again.

By this time I was a 100 percent *maderista*, though I had no idea why Señor Madero was against reelection or what he meant by public liberties. In the gang, the rock fights stopped because no one would take a turn at being a detestable *gucho*, a partisan of the government. El Perico told us that the shoeshine boys at the plaza were painting *maderista* slogans on their boxes. We went down to see and it was true.

In the *barrio* there was no question that something important and dangerous was happening. In addition to the night watchmen with their lanterns and tinny whistles there were now the army patrols. They chased us away from the corner lamp post and the gang meetings under the street light stopped. Up and down Leandro Valle our neighbors took in relatives who felt safer in Mazatlán and who needed a place to sleep while they found a room of their own. El Perico's brother disappeared and the word was out that he had run away to join Carrasco's men. La Pozolera stopped serving Friday night suppers on the street and I lost my job. Juan-Chon closed his store, the only one where we could charge groceries when our money was low. Corchos, my fellow gang member, reported one day that there was a government gunboat in the harbor. We ran across the city to look, and saw it riding at anchor, off shore from Las Olas Altas. Worst of all, soldiers armed with rifles and bayonets were posted around the brewery, the heart and center of our *barrio*. Loitering around the beer garden and the warehouse was now forbidden. We watched the guards from the top of the hill, hated them and President Díaz and wished with all our might for the revolution.

It came to Mazatlán soon enough, without any help from the Brewery Boys.

One night we heard rifle fire from the direction of Casa Redonda. José went out for news. He came back to tell us that the *revolucionarios* were moving in from the north along the railway line and that all roads leading out of the city had been cut. We were besieged.

The siege lasted many weeks. There was gunfire in some part of the town every night. Shoppers going to and from the market walked close to the walls of the houses and ran across the streets. Food and water became scarce. I scurried across the courtyard on errands to exchange food with our neighbors. School closed and there was no sewing for my mother to do. With the mail service disrupted Gustavo could not get through to us, nor we to the family in Jalcocotán. On days when José found work and came home after dark my mother and I sat on the windowsill, peering in the darkness down the street until we heard him coming, whistling "Adios Mamá Carlota." At all other times the window shutter was kept barred, like the front door.

When José was absent, we feared that the shots we heard now and then had killed my uncle. Almost as much we feared the searchlight of the gunboat. Night after night it swept over the town trying to spot revolutionary troops. The huge yellow beam often swung around to the back of our apartment, lighting up the kitchen. Or it would lift and shine on the front of our neighbor's house across the street, which stood higher than ours. The boom of the navy guns was familiar to us and we knew that they were shelling the revolutionary positions around the city; but the attackers were moving in, the searchlight might catch them prowling along Leandro Valle, and we might get a shell right in our kitchen.

Since the top of our hill overlooked the strategic Cervecria and the west end of the harbor beyond, it was a favorite spot for the patrols that were guarding that part of the city. A few nights before the end of the siege there was a skirmish between one of these patrols and the attackers. Somewhere toward the harbor we heard the shooting. The line of fire was straight up the hill, toward our house.

The safest corner in our apartment was in the kitchen, between the *pretil* and the stairwell. Doña Henriqueta and I sat there throughout the night. Crouching in the dark I heard the rifle shots of the revolution, something like "whee-oo," swift and short, like the snap of a *chicote*.

For me it was not a night of terror, since I did not understand the danger in each of those musical zings.

Doña Henriqueta had the situation under control, as usual. I was wedged between her and the wall, attentive, when I wasn't asleep, to the explanations of the noises I was hearing for the first time. "Those are bullets. Sharpshooters. . . . That was the gunboat. They are shooting over the city, not at us. . . . That's the patrol going down the hill."

It was bright and sunny on the street the next morning when José knocked on the door. He had spent the night in the cemetery near Casa Redonda, pinned down by the shooting. People were moving about on Leandro Valle. We sat down to breakfast and I heard the talk between Doña Henriqueta and José, somber talk about the revolution all around us.

There was a stir on the sidewalk. José opened the door and we looked out. Two stretcher bearers were passing by, carrying a body dressed in soiled cotton clothes. The man's feet were bare and he had a thin moustache and coal black hair.

"A dead man," José said. "Here, take these," he added, as he handed me three brass rifle shells—shiny and cool and smelling of burnt powder. I kept them in my pocket, feeling them and rubbing them together, until my mother persuaded me to put them away in the cedar box, along with Tio Tonche and the butterfly sarape.

We knew almost before anyone else on our street that the siege was over. José, on one of his job hunts, had seen the advance units of the revolution by the cemetery and had found out that they would take the city in force the next morning.

Everyone in the *barrio* came out to watch the entry of the victorious troops. They went by on foot and on horseback, old men and young men in work clothes, shoes or huaraches or boots or in bare feet. Some wore bandoliers and others ammunition belts, carrying their rifles this way and that on their shoulders or resting them across their saddles. Many wore pieces of green-white-and-red ribbons stuck in their hats. We joined the mob and followed it to the plaza where a revolutionary general spoke from a balcony. At the end of the speech the men raised their rifles and fired into the air, yelling "Viva Don Francisco Madero" and a lot of other *viva's* I couldn't make out. Standing in the doorway of a shop facing the plaza we cheered as the revolution took possession of Mazatlán. I never saw the captain of the *rurales* again, or the picture of Don Porfirio Díaz.

But this great event was not the end of the hard times. José told us that shops and factories that hired people were closing. Ships were not putting into port as usual, which meant that the jobs we had depended on—loading, warehousing, and delivering—were scarce. My mother had pawned the ring and we were waiting for the mails to start again, sure that Gustavo would send us enough to get by. From all the rumors that José gathered and that the neighbors picked up about town, there seemed as much trouble ahead as there had been behind.

José came with good news one evening. He had been hired with another young man to build stone markers around a mining claim in the mountains. The owner of the claim was a businessman of Mazatlán for whom José had worked before. Once more, as many times before, we sat around the supper table the night before José left, counting our savings, dividing them between his expenses and what we would need while he was away.

The next morning he was gone before I awakened.

Many days passed. Late one night there was a knock on the door. "It's José, sister."

My mother got up, lit the oil lamp, wrapped a blanket around her and opened the door.

My uncle came in, a bedroll over his shoulders, a stick in his hand.

"How did it go with you, brother?" she asked.

"Sit down, I'll tell you."

But my mother replied. "No. Eat first." While she was warming food in the kitchen José threw himself on the cot and was silent. He didn't joke with me. I knew there was trouble.

"Come, the two of you," she said.

At the table José ate in silence. When he had finished we waited for the story.

The two men had walked two days to the place where they were to work. Together they had built four markers of the kind called *mojoneras*, hauling the stones from a quarry. They started to walk back to Mazatlán to report to the *patrón* and collect their wages—one peso a day for each man for two weeks' work. Late in the afternoon of the first day they were shot at as they were tramping through a stretch of brush. José and his companion dived into the bushes. My uncle recognized one of the attackers as the foreman of the *patrón*.

José told the story with a quiet rage that made his lips quiver, as if he were ready to cry, and I was already old enough to know the signs of terror and anger in my mother—a slow shaking of the head and a slight tremor, as if she felt a chill.

"Why?" she asked José.

"So they wouldn't have to pay us the wages."

Then he added: "Tomorrow I am going to kill the *patrón*."

The two of them must have talked most of the night. I went to sleep lying on the cot, listening to the recital of the strange story and Doña Henriqueta's argument against taking revenge. Was José right? Was my mother wrong? Should not all three of us go the next day and kill the *patrón*?

We three did go, but not to kill him. My mother in the lead we walked into his office, the front room of a residence across town.

We stood during the brief encounter. My mother looked the *patrón* level in the eye and said: "The wages— that is all—the wages." I was afraid. The *patrón's* face was red with anger and perhaps fear. He called a clerk who counted out fifteen pesos to José.

"Thank you, and may you have a good afternoon," my mother said as she gave us our cue to leave. But José, with the stack of pesos in his hands, said a different sort of goodbye.

"The next time you want to kill a man for his wages, you should come and do it yourself, if you are that much of a man."

"José!" It was a sharp command from my mother, and we left.

"He knows we know," she said to José on the way home. "It is better that we leave Mazatlán."

One evening at supper I asked why we had to leave Mazatlán.

"It is better," was all she said, and everything after that showed that that was the way it was going to be.

There were no more trips on the mini-train or visits to the beer garden. My mother was out a good deal more looking for sewing to do, with the help of Doña Florencia. José left every morning before I was awake and returned late at night, leaving nothing to luck. There were letters back and forth between Gustavo, my Aunt Esther, and ourselves. From all the conversation and the letters one thing became clear to me: we were going to try to get the family together not in Mazatlán but in the United States.

José went to the pawnshop and redeemed the gold ring. I was sent to Doña Florencia with some coins tied in a handkerchief and a note. It was for Juan-Chon, in case he came back, and the money was for what we owed him. We packed the Ajax and José carried it on his back across the street and up the steep ramp of the sidewalk into our neighbor's house. She was to keep it until we sent for it from the United States. On our last morning the three cots and kitchen things were sold. We said good-bye to some neighbors. In a pushcart José trundled our two straw bags, bedrolls, and carefully wrapped cedar box. In it were the family letters, my report card from school, the sarape, the three rifle shells, some fine embroidery of my mother's, and our books. José carried a money belt around his waist, under his pants, with part of our money. The rest was in a pouch sewed inside Doña Henriqueta's blouse where she also tucked away an envelope with the railway pass for the two of us which Gustavo had sent.

We walked behind José and his cart to the railway station

Part Three

NORTH FROM MEXICO

AT THE STATION I was deposited in a corner of the waiting room sitting on the heap of our belongings while José and my mother took care of the business of the trip. He was working his way on the train as helper on the locomotive tender. The pass had to be presented at the ticket window and part of the fare paid. My mother returned with a supply of food for the journey. José produced a small trunk covered with tin squares hammered into colored designs of flowers and birds. The humped lid, like the rest of the box, was held together with metal straps, black and shiny. Into the trunk went our cedar box and other things we would not be using on the way. The trunk was locked and José carted it off.

We followed José through the crowd and walked along the tracks. The train was a *mixto*, passenger coaches and an assortment of freight cars, boxcars, flats, gondolas, and tanks. The people bustling to get aboard, too, were a mixed lot. There were families from villages and ranches, in country dress, blue shawls, and straw hats. Men, women, and children carried their goods in crates, sacks, and blankets in fat bundles tied at the corners.

There were ladies and gentlemen; by their dress, and the silk umbrellas and canes they carried, we knew that they were not people who had lived in our *barrio*.

With José in the lead we bumped and shoved our way to a coach, climbed in, and took possession of one of the wooden seats. While those about us scrambled for places and argued over them, we had our final instructions from José—to stay in our places and to wait at every station stop until he could get back from the tender. There were soldiers up front on the locomotive and back in the caboose. If they came by it was nothing to worry about. They were carrying rifles and bayonets to guard the train. In case there was shooting we were to fall flat on the floor of the coach, between the seats. "And don't look out of the windows," he cautioned us.

He hopped off and ran forward along the tracks. The locomotive bell was clanging. The station platform was crowded with people, some of them waving good-bye, others reaching up to touch hands with those who were leaving. The conductor was waving both hands, signaling the engineer and bawling; "Vámonos." The couplings slammed, and with a jerk and a rattle of chains and rods we were moving.

The last I saw of Mazatlán were the salt flats west of us. It was near sunset and I watched from my window seat as the miles of brush became a dark blur with patches of water here and there. I sat looking out, like all the other silent people in the coach, until the stars came out. On a sarape laid out under our seat, I went to sleep.

It was light when I awakened, hungry and cramped. I walked to the forward end of the coach for a drink from the water barrel. Waiting in line I nudged a fat man sitting next to the aisle.

"Dispénseme," I said, turning to the man.

It was Juan-Chon, our grocer.

His face looked as joyful as I felt at the sight of it.

"Huilo," he called me by my gang name. "Doña Henriqueta? José? They are on the train?"

"Yes, sir," I answered nodding toward our seat. As he turned his head I was dumbfounded. He had cut off his braid. Now, this was exactly the situation in which, as I had been taught, you said nothing and pretended you saw nothing.

He got up. I filled my cup and walked back with him to our seat. It was a courtesy visit, very short and ceremonious. I waited until I saw him sit down at his place. With the cup still in my hands, I whispered: "He cut off his braid."

"Ssh-sh. I saw it. You are not to speak of it." As my mother dipped a handkerchief in the cup and began to give my face and hands a cat wash, I asked, "Why?"

"Don Juan-Chon has sentiment, just like everyone. Only children with a bad education hurt people's sentiments." I knew what she meant by sentiment—a deep feeling of dignity and self-respect—that puzzling, powerful Mexican word, *sentimiento*.

At noon, before we had our lunch I was sent up forward with two tacos for Juan-Chon.

"My mother sends greetings and she hopes you will like them." I handed Juan-Chon the tacos, as if I had been delivering a gift and a message in the *barrio*.

He received the offering with a nod, put it on his lap, and told me to wait. Out of a bag at his feet he dug out a brown sugar bar, the *caramelo* that always made me drool.

"Give my salutations to Doña Henriqueta and tell her I hope you will do me the favor of enjoying this." He was wrapping it in a piece of paper. But before he handed it over Juan-Chon stared at me and finally said, in a low voice: "Have you noticed? I cut off my braid."

If the train had jerked to a stop and thrown me to the floor I would not have been more shocked. I looked at the nearest passengers. They had not heard. I leaned close to Juan-Chon and whispered: "Ssh-h-h. I am not supposed to talk about it." My friend opened his eyes wide, pressed his lips, and nodded slowly. His face, I thought, was puffed with mirth over a secret that of all the people on the train only the three of us knew.

The train moved slowly and stopped often. In the middle of the lonesome plains we waited for hours, not knowing why. The soldiers walked up and down the track, keeping people from getting off. As a member of the train crew José was able to run back and forth, to report how things looked up ahead: a piece of track was being repaired or a patrol had stopped us.

We laid over at Culiacán to replenish our food. The long journey was already wearing us out. Inside the coach it began to smell. Children cried all day long and some passengers were spitting on bits of dry leaves and sticking them on their temples to cure their headaches. In a cup, my mother ground some herbs we had brought and gave them to the lady ahead of us who kept her head out of the window, vomiting.

Just who broke out with the measles first, we didn't know, but the word spread up and down the train: "Sarampión." The conductor and a brakeman came by, looking closely at every child. José came back with the report: there was an epidemic on board. We were moving toward El Nanchi, where every family with children would be held up for medical inspection.

EI Nanchi was a clearing in the forest near the railway tracks where soldiers were stationed to guard the line. They put up extra tents for those who had to lay over in quarantine. I broke out with the measles the day after we arrived in the camp. Along with every other sick child I was moved to a large tent in the middle of the camp and put to bed on an army cot over which drapes of mosquito netting were hung.

I lay stark naked on my cot for several days, living on sips of ice water and corn gruel. Now and then a nurse parted the drapes and looked at me. The rest of the time my mother watched over me when she wasn't helping to care for the other children.

After the misery of the fever was over, my chief problem was to keep from scratching the red pimples all over me, which broke and scabbed and itched. During the day the heat inside the tent was suffocating. At night the moths buzzed around the lamp that spluttered next to the center pole.

When I was over the bout, I was allowed to sit up on the cot, but I could not dress until all the scabs had cleared up. The nurse looked me over, scrubbed me with warm water and suds, and I was released.

We waited for days, sitting by the track, going for short walks in the woods, and watching the people at El Nanchi. Many of the soldiers lived there with their wives and children. They cooked outside their tents, sitting round the fires in the dark. We exchanged food with them and they welcomed us to their family circles. There were dogs all around us. People threw scraps to them, starting fights among the skinny, starved mongrels that sneaked past with their tails between their legs.

Around the family campfires I heard the songs the men of the revolution were singing. I learned snatches of "La Valentina," about the lover who would just as soon die today as tomorrow, fighting the devil himself; "Adelita," the flirt; "La Cucaracha," the comical cockroach who wouldn't walk unless he had a cigarette of marijuana. But my favorite of these evening sing-ins was "El Quelite," a simple love song to a small town with its plaza and friends who had been left behind. The stanza I learned and remembered went like this :

Al pie de un encino roble
me dio sueño y me dormí.
Me despertó un gallito
cantando qui-qui-ri-qui.

which in English would have sounded something like:

I went and I fell asleep
under an apple tree.
A little rooster awoke me
crowing kee-kee-ree-kee.

On Saturday nights the music in El Nanchi turned rowdy. At the edge of the village a low wooden platform about the size of a boxing ring was set up. To one side there was a table where tequila and *aguardiente* were sold. Next to the bar the mariachi played. The musicians, in huaraches, plain country dress and conical hats played all night on double basses, violins, harps, trumpets, and guitars. Lanterns stuck on poles at each corner of the platform lighted the weird scene. We watched it from a distance listening to the thumping dances of the men and the shouts of the drunks. As the mariachi played, the couples swirled in folk dances, looking furious and happy in the lamplight. The music sounded melancholy and distant, appropriate for the stars above and the fireflies blinking in the dark pastures all around.

We were beginning to think the revolution had pinned us down to El Nanchi, we had waited so long, when José brought word to pack up and get ready. We broke camp and said good-bye to our soldier friends and their families. Lined up along the track we watched as our train pulled in. A *mixto* also, but this one with more freight cars than coaches, which were already filled with passengers. Most of the boxcars were occupied by families, some of them inside, some on the roofs.

There was a scramble for places. We found a space in the center of a flatcar with families who made room for us. Between the stakes along the sides of the platform they had strung wires and ropes to which they tied strips of canvas, sacks, and anything else that would provide a roof. It was our shelter for the rest of the journey.

We traveled slowly and only by day. We soon found out why.

Not long after we had left El Nanchi the train came to a jerking halt with a series of short blasts from the locomotive whistle. A brakeman and some soldiers trotted by, coming up from the caboose. The people on top of the boxcars ahead of us could see better but they, too, could only guess what had happened. The usual explanations were passed around: we had run over a cow; a telephone pole had fallen over the tracks; the locomotive had blown a signal torpedo on the tracks.

The brakeman came back, calling out that it would be a long stop and we could get off for a change. It was like an invitation to a picnic. Down the sides of the boxcars, off the flats and out of the coaches the passengers scrambled to the ground. They formed a parade on both sides of the train. We fell in with the others and joined the crowd around the locomotive to find out why we had stopped.

Just ahead of us there was a trestle over a sandy gulch. Halfway across, the trestle had collapsed into a tangle of crossties, twisted rails, and fallen piles. There had been a fire and some of the piles were still smoking. A lady holding a parasol next to us said out loud: "Thanks to God that it was daylight." The gentleman with the lady was fanning himself with a flat-topped straw hat and pointing with his cane to the debris. "Dynamite," I heard him explain to the lady. "They intended to blow us up as we crossed," he said out loud so everyone could hear him.

In the bottom of the gulch, the engineer, the fireman of the train and the officer of the military guard were looking at the damage. At the other end of the trestle there was a gasoline runabout on the tracks. A man in leather boots and khakis and some workmen were standing on the far side of the break in the trestle.

Everyone went back to his quarters. Like them we did not know whether we would have to wait one night or one month before we could get across the gulch.

That night meals were cooked on the edge of the desert over camp fires that glimmered ruby red along the track. We had supper with our fellow travelers, gathering wood with them and sharing the food. José brought a pail of water from the tender.

When supper was over it was pitch dark. The stars were thick—white, blue, and purple specks like pinholes in the inky sky. Huddled near the fire and surrounded by the vast shadow of the desert the adults talked of revolutionaries hiding out there, waiting to blow up the train and kill us all. We sat wrapped in blankets and shawls because of the chill of the evening. One by one we got up, the men walked a short way into the bushes and came back, the women and children went in couples. I went to bed on our flatcar, where I could hear the comforting conversation nearby. Now and then I heard the sentry pass, crunching gravel under his feet. José slept under our flat on a bed of branches and straw that he made between the tracks. I listened to the silence of the desert as long as I could stay awake, wondering what you do when you are blown up by dynamite. Besides, I had heard that we were in the middle of the country of the fearsome Yaqui Indians who hated strangers and were formidable fighters.

But there was no dynamiting and no shooting that night. In the morning we walked to the back end of the train and saw the guards far down the track. Up front we watched workmen unloading tools and timber from a flatcar coupled to a locomotive across the trestle. Others were already at work down in the gulch repairing the damage. During the heat of the day I moved down to José's bunk and swapped stories with another boy about our lives and adventures. My own most famous story was about the crocodiles I hunted in the arroyo back in Jalcocotán, to which I had now added one about our battle against the *porfiristas* in Mazatlán, right up to our front door, and how we captured the plaza and hanged the *guchos*. I had three rifle shells to prove it.

We wished, my pal and I, that the train would never move and ruin our bunk. The rails were far enough apart so we could stretch ourselves comfortably between them. The trucks and wheels made an ideal fort in case we were attacked by the Yaquis. It was breezy and cool under the deck of the flatcar. We could look down the slope of the roadbed and watch the women cooking and the sentries going by. Beyond them there was nothing but the gray, blazing desert and the dim purple rim of the Sierra Madre, the whole countryside looking like we felt—lazy.

On the second day all passengers were ordered off the train. We lined up along the track and saw it move forward inching along until the caboose passed, followed by the guards on foot. When the caboose had cleared the far end of the trestle, safe on the roadbed beyond the gulch, the whistle signaled us to come across and get aboard. Some walked the ties straight across the trestle, others went down one side of the gulch and up the other. The fireman was giving us a performance on the bell, a kind of celebration and a warning we would be left behind if we didn't hurry. A guard in a white uniform with a rifle slung over his shoulder walked up and down helping the stragglers. We climbed on the flat and watched the brakemen waving their arms, signaling the locomotive crew.

We moved steadily through the kind of country we had looked on for days, miles and miles of brush on both sides of the line, sandy patches and rock piles and cactus trees pointing their fingers, green and prickly, at the pale blue sky. I wondered what had happened to Juan-Chon and where The North really was, the place we were all supposed to be going to, and that seemed to keep moving away as fast as we moved up.

At dusk of the last day of our long trip from Mazatlán we finally approached the North. During the afternoon dark clouds had piled up over us, rolling over the desert from the mountains. At sunset the first drops fell on our canvas roof. The rain picked up and the train slowed down. It was pouring when we began to pass the adobe huts of a town. We passed another train standing on a siding, the deck of our flatcar flooded and the awnings above us sagging with rainwater and leaking. It was night.

The train stopped. Out of the darkness a man in uniform with a rubber cape over his shoulders climbed our flat. He picked his way down the platform, swinging his lantern and holding it high, looking us over.

"Ladies and gentlemen," he said, "This is Nogales. All passengers will debark immediately and assemble in the waiting room of the station." The passengers in boxcars and the coaches stayed on board until we had been detrained.

We broke camp in a heavy rain, dragging the soggy bundles of our belongings and sorting ourselves out, waiting our turn to get down at the ends of the flat.

While we were waiting, two men carrying lanterns and wearing slickers walked up alongside. They put the lanterns on the deck at our feet. By the light I could see the jacket, collar, and flat-brimmed hat of an American soldier, such as I had seen in pictures. The one in front of me had long droopy moustaches. The brim of his hat was dripping.

He motioned to me to drop into his arms. I shrank back for he was certainly a gringo, and a gringo soldier besides, the kind Don Salvador had taught us were the mortal enemies of our country.

My mother's hands were on my shoulders. The other soldier was motioning to her. She understood the signals. Pulling our bundles to the edge of the platform, she said to me: "Do not be afraid. Go." She pushed me gently as I sat down and rolled over into the arms of the American soldier, who looped one arm around me, pulled the slicker over my shoulders so that only my head showed, and with the other hand gripped one of our bundles. He did not move until my mother had been helped down. She swung her legs overside, held out her arms, and sprang to the ground beside us. We scurried through the storm across the tracks and into the waiting room. My gringo, smiling and saying something I could not understand, put me down next to our baggage. My mother thanked them with smiles and bows and Spanish words and they went off to unload other rain-soaked refugees off the flatcars.

In the waiting room there were several kerosene stoves placed about to warm the shivering crowd. The stoves were small black chimneys with nickel handles. We stood around them rubbing hands and watching our clothes steam. An American lady, in a slicker, like the men, and rubber boots up to her knees kept bringing bowls of soup and shiny tin cups with hot coffee. Whatever she said to us and whatever we said to her neither understood, but she was talking the language of hot soup and coffee and kindness and there was perfect communication.

José found us. He came in with a gunnysack folded over his head and shoulders, looking like a monk, his pants legs rolled up and barefooted. He came to take us to a *mesón* nearby, a place two blocks from the station where we could sleep. He was carrying the green tin trunk with the humped back. For himself José had already set up his bunk in a corner of a boxcar. Until the train returned south he would be working as helper on the tender.

That night we shared a small room at the *mesón* with two ladies and their children. There was little space for anything besides the army cots lined up in two rows. There were no windows in the adobe room and the only light came from the kitchen. In the dark corner next to my cot I stripped and wrapped myself in a blanket. Our wet clothes and shoes were arranged near the stove to dry.

In the sunny morning of the next day we walked back to the station. Our train was still there, the flats and boxcars and coaches deserted, Mexican and American soldiers walking back and forth. "Look, the American flag," my mother said. It was flying over a building near us. Down the street, beyond the depot, there was a Mexican flag on a staff. "We are in the United States. Mexico is over there."

It took further explaining to clear up certain points to my satisfaction. The North was the same place as the United States, and we had finally arrived. The Americans never drew an eagle on their flag. The red and the white were the same as on ours but why they liked blue better than green was just one of those peculiar things about Americans. Where did Mexico begin? Just beyond the railway station. How far did it go? "A long way," said

Doña Henriqueta, "far down the track, farther than Jalcocotán." It was the closest thing we did to saying good-bye to our country.

That evening at the *mesón*, José and my mother and I reread Gustavo's letter, the last we had received in Mazatlán. José was to work his way on the railroad to a place called Sacramento. My mother and I were to go to another city called Tucson and wait there until another pass and money could be obtained.

José then explained a remarkable thing about our money. Mexican centavos and tostones and pesos were good for nothing in the United States. He had already exchanged some of our Mexican currency for dollars. "Listen carefully," he told us. "You have to give two pesos for one dollar. For one tostón you get one quarter. For ten centavos you get one nickel." On the table he laid out the coins, in rows two for one.

He turned to me.

"Now, Ernesto, you are the man of the family. You will take care of your mother until we are together in Sacramento. How do you say *por favor*?"

"Plees."

"Right, how do you say *cuánto es*?"

"Hau-mochee."

"How do you say *qué hora es, par favor*?"

"Hua-tinees, plees."

"Correct."

"Now say the numbers."

"Huan, too, tree."

"Correct. If you don't know the other numbers, hold up your fingers and count in Spanish."

In Nogales we sold the extra blankets. José bought us two cardboard suitcases and one for himself, and an alarm clock like the one we used to try to win in the lottery tent in Mazatlán. With our new luggage and the tin trunk, we set off for Tucson, saying good-bye to José. In one of the suitcases there was a brown folder tied with a blue tape. In it were the pass, the letters from Gustavo with certain names and addresses, and the instructions for our arrival in Sacramento. The suitcase with its precious papers was never out of our sight, and the American paper money that José had exchanged. Gustavo's forwarding address was puzzling. The best we could make out it was a General Delibri. It sounded as if generals were in charge of the mail in the United States, nothing like our *lista del correo* in Acaponeta.

In Tucson we found our way to the address Gustavo had sent. It was a small hotel where the clerk spoke Spanish. He took us down a long, dark hall to a room, where I immediately began to explore the remarkable inventions of the Americans.

Hanging from a cord attached to the middle of the ceiling there was an electric bulb, low enough for an adult to reach and turn the black switch. I realized that this was our own electric light for us to turn on and off as we pleased. I pushed a chair under it and after some instruction from my mother proceeded to create lightning in the room by turning the switch as fast as I could.

Next I discovered the bedsprings. When I sat on the bed it sank deliciously. Jumping on it in my stocking feet, I held my balance dangerously as I made the bed creak and the mattress bounce. The head and foot of the bed were made of iron scrollwork in loops and rosettes painted white. On each of the four posts there was a large brass knob that unscrewed. I took one off, deciding to take it with us since it matched the three cartridges in the cedar box. My plan didn't work. Doña Henriqueta ordered me to screw it back.

My next stop was the toilet, which came to my attention in the ordinary course of going to bed. It was down the hall, in a closet with a plate on the door, white with blue letters. Not knowing what they meant we asked the clerk, who explained that when the sign said M-E-N it was for me. Suspecting something, he added: "When you are finished, don't forget to pull the chain. See. That's what the sign says." And, to be sure, there was a paper with writing tacked to the wall, next to an aluminum up-and-down pipe.

I was left alone in the room for M-E-N. I examined it with great care—the smooth enamel bowl with water in the bottom, the wooden lid with a large hole that looked like a horse collar, the small brown box up near the ceiling, the chain hanging from it. Pressed for time I finally decided it was safe enough to try. I buttoned up and looked at the sign, remembering what the clerk had said, making it sound very important. I grabbed the chain with both hands and pulled. A small torrent of water gushed into the bowl, swirling and disappearing down the drain with a deep, sonorous gargle. I waited a few minutes and pulled the chain again.

That night I got up several times to go to the toilet, until I was ordered to go to sleep.

We stayed only one day at the hotel, long enough for me to become acquainted with the bathtub, located in another closet next to the toilet. A rope of water twisted and whirled from a brass faucet, filling the tub. I sat in the cold water up to my neck and discovered that I could slide down the back of the tub and hit the bottom with a great splash. When my water party was interrupted, both the bathroom and I got a scrubbing.

With the help of the hotel clerk we located the family with whom we were to stay, an elderly couple who took in boarders and rented a spare room. They lived in a muddy alley with narrow board sidewalks and rickety planks connecting the walks with the droopy unpainted porches. The whole scene was in two colors—the mud-brown of the alley, the empty lots between the houses, the plank fences propped from behind to keep them from falling; and the dirty gray of everything else—like the fronts of the houses and the winter sky.

Our temporary home was halfway down the alley between two streets. Our landlady was plump, quiet, slow-moving, and wore her greying hair in two thick braids. The husband, a fat man with sad eyes who talked even less than his wife, did odd jobs around town.

Our front room had two small beds. Mine swayed and squeaked when I got into it. There was a dresser between the two windows with a washbowl and a white pitcher on the marble top. The blinds were ragged at the bottom and were kept down all the time because there were no curtains. I discovered the blinds could snap and roll up with a whir and a clap if I jerked them, but Doña Henriqueta immediately stopped my game.

Because there was nothing to do outside but get wet and muddy we spent the first days helping with the housework and looking at the people who sloshed by. All of them were Mexicans, *barrio* people. The empty lot next door was a sump of drainage from the alley, littered with tin cans and empty bottles that had become stuck in the gumbo. We had to walk alongside this swamp of garbage to get to the toilet, an outhouse connected to the back porch by planks raised on bricks.

Since the kitchen was the only heated room, we spent our evenings there, feeding the fire one stick at a time, the adults talking as I listened. The oil cloth on the kitchen table was covered with a design of huge red roses. In the center, the oil lamp, its glass belly full of amber kerosene, burned in a yellow crown of flames. The old couple told us about Tucson and my mother told them of Jalco, of the siege of Mazatlán, the revolution, and our mishaps on the way to Nogales. Privately we called the old couple *los abuelitos*, and our visit with them gave me some idea of what it was like to have a grandfather and grandmother in the house. They were not our kinfolk but the *respeto* I felt for them, after Doña Henriqueta's lectures, was genuinely Mexican.

Except for the quiet company of the *abuelitos*, we were locked in the alley, my mother with no work and I with no friends. The Mexican boys who lived in the other row houses had no place to play where we could become acquainted. The one time I ventured out of the alley and down the street I was chased back by three American boys who yelled something I could not understand but which didn't sound friendly. And when I was on an errand to the grocery store and was caught in the middle of a fight between white and black boys, I was convinced that I should stay in the alley.

Regularly we went to the hotel to ask for mail from Gustavo. Almost always there was a letter with money, but it was many weeks before we received the most important one of all, the one that had the pass and the instructions for the trip. We were to take the train to Sacramento, go to the Hotel Español and stay there until Gustavo and José came for us.

The *abuelitos* walked us to the railroad station, helping us with our tin trunk and suitcases. As if we had lived together all our lives everybody embraced everybody and the old couple waited to wave good-bye as our train pulled out of the station.

As soon as we were in the coach I knew we were riding first-class. The seat was a green felt cushion, plump and comfortable. The packages and suitcases were placed on the racks and under the seats, not in the aisles, so I could walk up and down when I felt stiff or when I wanted a drink of ice water which came out of a silver faucet. By watching, we determined that the closet up front was for M-E-N and the one in the back was for the ladies. I found the men's room as surprising as the one at the hotel. You stepped on a lever instead of pulling a chain. Sitting there, I was rocked from side to side, swaying deliciously above the roar of the tracks and hanging onto the washbowl in front of me for fear of falling through.

When the conductor came by to check tickets, he punched two colored tabs and slipped them through a metal frame on the seat in front of us. I discovered to my delight that the brass letters on his cap were exactly like those of the conductor in Mazatlán. I spelled them out silently as I watched him—c-o-n, con, d-u-c,-, duc, t-o-r, tor, conductor. In a whispered conversation with my mother over the subject, we agreed that a gringo conductor would not be wearing Mexican letters on his cap, and that *conductor* in Spanish was the same as conductor in English. This started a guessing game that kept us amused the rest of the trip. Some words worked out neatly in both languages, like *conductor*, others failed to match by a syllable or a letter, in which case we thought English spelling idiotic.

I had never moved as fast as on this train which sped along faster even than the *diligencia*. The telephone poles whizzed by, making me dizzy if I watched them, and around the curves the coach leaned a little.

We began to notice the eating habits of the gringos. The man with the large tray strapped to his shoulders did not have tortillas or tacos or meat snacks with pepper sauce. He sold slices of white bread cut in triangles with mushy stuff between the slices. After one bite I wrapped mine in a napkin and didn't touch it again until I realized that it was either sandwiches or starvation. Once a day we bought peanuts and fruit, which we selected by pointing to the tray. To pay the vendor I held out on the palm of my hand an assortment of nickels and dimes and quarters. It was not even necessary for me to ask "hau·mochee." At the station stops, hawkers did not rush up to the coach windows to sell us food. In the middle of the train there was a car where you could eat a meal sitting at a table, but we never went there.

I asked the conductor several times while we were on the long journey, "hua-tinees, plees." One conductor pulled the watch out of his vest pocket, flipped open the gold lid and read the time to us, which meant nothing at all since we didn't know the numbers in English. Another, after looking us over and guessing our difficulty, snapped his watch open and held the face up for us to read.

Not seeing any soldiers with rifles and bayonets I asked my mother if the Americans were not having a revolution. "No," and when I asked why, she only said, "People are different."

And from what I saw in the coach on that long ride, the Americans were indeed different. They ate the repulsive sandwiches with relish. They put their feet, shoes and all, on the seats in front of them. When the men laughed it seemed more like a roar, and if they were close by it scared me. Doña Henriqueta frowned and admonished me. "Be careful I never hear you braying like that." Many of them kept their hats on as if they didn't know that the inside of a coach was like the inside of a house, and wearing your hat in either a sure sign of being *mal educado*. On the station platforms gentlemen in bowler hats, suits, and shiny boots blew their noses first with their fingers and then with their handkerchiefs. "What a thing," my mother said. "Asquerosos."

It was late in the afternoon after countless hours from Tucson that the conductor stopped by our seat, picked up our stubs and pointing to us, said, "Sacramento." With the greatest of ease I said "Tanks yoo" and felt again the excitement of arriving somewhere. We looked out at the countryside to be sure we didn't miss the first sights of the city with the Mexican name where we were going to live. As far as I could see there were rows on rows of bushes, some standing by themselves, some leaning on wires and posts, all of them without leaves. "Vineyards," my mother said. I always wanted to know the number or quantity of things. "How many?" I asked. "A heap," she answered, not just *un montón*, but *un montonal*, which meant more than you could count, nobody really knows, sky-high, infinity, millions.

We left the vineyards behind, passing by orchards and pastures with cattle. At the crossroads, our locomotive hooted a salute to droves of cattle, automobiles and horse-drawn buggies with school children waiting to cross.

Our train began to make a great circle, slowing down. The roadbed carried the train higher than the roof tops, giving us a panorama of the city. Track crews standing by with the familiar brown faces of Mexicans waved to us. I looked hard for Gustavo and José, for the last we had heard they were working on the Southern Pacific, making tracks or locomotives. Through the window we could see long buildings with stacks belching smoke like a dozen Casas Redondas, boxcars, flatcars, coaches, gondolas, cabooses, and locomotives dismantled or waiting for repairs.

A brakeman opened the door at the front of the coach and called, "Sack-men-ah," by which we knew he meant Sa-cra-men-to, for we had passed a large sign with the name in black and white at the entrance to the corporation yard.

Unlike the Mexicans, the Americans were not in a great hurry to leave the coach. We were the last, carrying our luggage.

We stepped down into a frightening scene, a huge barn filled with smoke and noise and the smell of burnt oil. This was the station, nearly as long as the train and with a sooty roof twice as high as the *mercado* in Mazatlán. Our locomotive was still belching black clouds from the stack. Men were hurrying along pulling four-wheeled carts loaded with baggage, jerking hoses close to the train and thrusting the nozzles into holes here and there, washing windows with brushes on long sticks, opening the axle boxes with hammers and banging them shut.

We dashed through the confusion over the tracks and into the waiting room, myself dragging one of the shopping bags. The depot was a gloomy, dangerous place. We sat watching the crowd thin out. Our train departed, headed in the same direction, and I felt that we were being left behind.

Out of the bag my mother pulled the small envelope with the address of the Hotel Español. She handed me the paper. Holding it I watched the men in uniforms and green visors who passed by us and the clerks behind the ticket counters. Taking a chance I stopped one and thrust the paper at him. I said, "Plees" and waited, pinching one corner of the envelope while he read it. Like the conductor, the man guessed our problem. He smiled, and held up a forefinger, crooking and straightening it while he looked at us. I had no idea what he meant, for in Mexico you signaled people to follow you by holding up your hand and closing all the fingers over the palm with a snap a few times. But Doña Henriqueta knew instantly and he guided us under an arch and out of the station. Handing back the envelope he pointed down the street and smiled us on.

One more stop to ask our way with another "plees" and we were at the Hotel Español.

Part Four

LIFE IN THE LOWER PART OF TOWN

IN A CORNER of the musty lobby of the Hotel Español, we waited until it was our turn to talk with the manager. The place was filled with people stacking and moving luggage, some talking in Spanish, others in English and other strange tongues. The manager wore a long white apron and a blue beret and spoke *gachupín* like the Spaniards of Mazatlán. He led us to a back room, took our baggage claim check, showed us the dining room and returned later with our tin trunk.

The hotel was a prison, even more confining than the alley in Tucson. We were frightened by the traffic of mule teams, wagons, and the honking automobiles that passed by continuously. From our view in the lobby the street was a jumble. Up and down from the doorway of the hotel all we could see were shops and stores, warehouses and saloons, hotels and restaurants, few ladies and no children. Sacramento, I decided, was an ugly place, not like the vineyards and the eucalyptus trees with pastel colored trunks we had seen from the train.

For breakfast in the hotel kitchen we drank coffee with buttered hard rolls. Lunch was not served and since we were afraid to venture into the street, we did not eat. Supper was served in a room without windows, at a long table crowded with people who lived in the hotel and outsiders who came for meals. It was served by the manager, who was also the cook. Up and down both sides of the table he poured boiling soup out of a kettle into our plates, forked out pieces of meat, sawed thick chunks of bread from loaves as long as my arm, and poured wine. It was a noisy table, with loud talk and the clatter of dishes and the burly *gachupines* slurping soup. But it was a show to us, funny and very un-Mexican.

In the corner of the lobby nearest the street window we sat for hours on a wooden bench, watching the pedestrians closely. At last we saw the two we were waiting for. Gustavo and José passed by the window, looked in, and stepped inside. With a shout I charged them and wedged myself between their legs, where I held tight. The three exchanged greetings.

"How are you, sister?"

"Very well. How have things been with you?"

After a little weeping by Doña Henriqueta we stood and looked at one another. My uncles were dressed in blue bib overalls and work jackets of the same stuff with brass buttons, and caps. Gustavo was the shorter of the two, chunky and thick-shouldered. José was thin all over-neck, arms, fingers, and face.

They paid our hotel bill and we gathered our things. We stepped into the cold drizzly street, my uncles carrying the suitcases and tin trunk and holding me by the hands. With the two of them on either side and Doña Henriqueta behind me I trotted confidently through the scurrying crowd on the sidewalks, the rumbling drays and the honking automobiles. I was beginning to lose my fear of Sacramento.

It was a short walk from the hotel to the house where we turned in, the tallest I had ever seen. A wide wooden stairway went up from the sidewalk to a porch on the second story, and above that another floor, and still higher a gable as wide as the house decorated with carvings and fretwork. The porch balustrade was in the same gingerbread style of lattice work and the wooden imitation of a fringe between the round pillars. We walked up the stairway and the three of us waited while José went inside.

He came back with the landlady. She was certainly a gringo lady-two heads taller than Gustavo, twice as wide as José, square-jawed, rosy-faced, a thin nose with a small bulge on the end and like all Americans, with rather large feet. She had a way of blinking when she smiled at us.

Standing as straight as the posts of the porch and holding her shoulders square and straight across she seemed to me more like a general than a lady.

Mostly with blinks and hand motions and a great many ceremonial smiles, we were introduced to Mrs. Dodson, who led us into the house, down some narrow, dark stairs and to the back of the first floor where she left us in our new apartment.

It consisted of one large room, a kitchen and a closet that had been a bathroom from which all the fixtures had been removed except the bathtub. Directly behind the kitchen was a cramped back yard enclosed on three sides by a board fence like all the other American fences I had already seen—dirty gray planks, streaked and cracked. Rising from the yard there was a steep wooden stairway resting on cement blocks. It made a right angle at the second story and turned back toward the house, continuing to the third floor. The stairway had panels on each side and a landing on each floor. From the yard the fire escape looked like a ladder into the wild blue yonder. Since people rarely used it, and the panels made private cubicles of the landings, I discovered that I could use them as private crow's nests from which I could survey the *barrio's* back yards for blocks around.

The apartment was furnished. In the living room there were three single beds, a clothes closet as high as the ceiling, an oil stove, a round dining table covered with checkered linoleum, a chest of drawers, and some chairs. In the kitchen there was a gas stove on a wooden platform, a table, a bench, and a dish closet next to the sink. A small icebox on the back porch dripped into a rubber tube to the ground through a hole in the floor. The bathtub in the big closet was covered with boards and a mattress on top of them. This was to be my room. It had no windows but an electric cord with a small bulb and a print curtain over the door connecting with the kitchen gave me quarters of my own.

We reached the front door through a long gloomy hall that opened on the street porch, from which we stepped to the sidewalk over a boardwalk. Along one side of the house there was an open corridor between the house and the fence, by which we got to the toilet and bathroom that all the tenants on the first floor used. We were enclosed from the street by a picket fence flanking the stairs, set off by a scraggly peach tree on each side. Because our rooms were dank and cheerless we sat on the porch or stood behind the picket fence, street watching, when the weather permitted. Mrs. Dodson's apartment was on the second floor back, with a door to a side porch from which she could look out over the yard and the street. This was the command post of 418 L Street, our refuge in a strange land.

Since Gustavo and José were off to work on the track early the next morning after our arrival, it was up to us to tidy the apartment and get the household into shape. As usual when we moved into a new place, we dusted and swept and scrubbed floors, doors, woodwork, windows, and every piece of furniture. Mrs. Dodson provided us with cans of a white powder that was sprinkled on everything that needed cleaning—cans with the picture of an old lady dressed in wooden shoes, a swinging skirt, and white bonnet.

The Americans, we discovered, put practically everything in cans on which they pasted fascinating labels, like *La Vieja Dotch Klen-ser*. Doña Henriqueta admired the bright colors and the delicious pictures of fruits and vegetables. We spelled and sounded out as well as we could the names of unfamiliar foods, like corn flakes and Karo syrup. On the kitchen shelf we arranged and rearranged the boxes and tins, with their displays of ingenious designs and colors, grateful that the Americans used pictures we knew to explain words that we didn't.

Once the routine of the family was well started, my mother and I began to take short walks to get our bearings. It was half a block in one direction to the lumber yard and the grocery store; half a block in the other to the saloon and the Japanese motion picture theater. In between were the tent and awning shop, a Chinese restaurant, a secondhand store, and several houses like our own. We noted by the numbers on the posts at the corners that we lived between 4th and 5th streets on L.

Once we could fix a course from these signs up and down and across town we explored farther. On Sixth near K there was the Lyric Theater with a sign that we easily translated into Lírico. It was next to a handsome red stone house with high turrets, like a castle. Navigating by these key points and following the rows of towering elms along L Street, one by one we found the post office on 7th and K; the cathedral, four blocks farther east; and the state capitol with its golden dome.

It wasn't long before we ventured on walks around Capitol Park which reminded me of the charm and the serenity of the Alameda in Tepic. In some fashion Mrs. Dodson had got over to us that the capitol was the house of the government. To us it became El Capitolio or, as more formally, the Palacio de Gobierno. Through the park we walked into the building itself, staring spellbound at the marble statue of Queen Isabel and Christopher Columbus. It was awesome, standing in the presence of that gigantic admiral, the one who had discovered America and Mexico and Jalcocotán, as Doña Henriqueta assured me.

After we had thoroughly learned our way around in the daytime we found signs that did not fail us at night. From the window of the projection room of the Lyric Theater a brilliant purple light shone after dark. A snake of electric lights kept whipping round and round a sign over the Albert Elkus store. K Street on both sides was a double row of bright show windows that led up to the Land Hotel and back to Breuner's, thence down one block to the lumber yard, the grocery store, and our house. We had no fear of getting lost.

These were the boundaries of the lower part of town, for that was what everyone called the section of the city between Fifth Street and the river and from the railway yards to the Y-street levee. Nobody ever mentioned an upper part of town; at least, no one could see the difference because the whole city was built on level land. We were not lower topographically, but in other ways that distinguished between Them, the uppers, and Us, the lowers. Lower Sacramento was the quarter that people who made money moved away from. Those of us who lived in it stayed there because our problem was to make a living and not to make money. A long while back, Mr. Howard, the business agent of the union told me, there had been stores and shops, fancy residences, and smart hotels in this neighborhood. The crippled old gentleman who lived in the next room down the hall from us, explained to me that our house, like the others in the neighborhood, had been the home of rich people who had stables in the back yards, with back entrances by way of the alleys. Mr. Hansen, the Dutch carpenter, had helped build such residences. When the owners moved uptown, the back yards had been fenced off and subdivided, and small rental cottages had been built in the alleys in place of the stables. Handsome private homes were turned into flophouses for men who stayed one night, hotels for working people, and rooming houses, like ours.

Among the saloons, pool halls, lunch counters, pawn-shops, and poker parlors was skid row, where drunk men with black eyes and unshaven faces lay down in the alleys to sleep.

The lower quarter was not exclusively a Mexican *barrio* but a mix of many nationalities. Between L and N Streets two blocks from us, the Japanese had taken over. Their homes were in the alleys behind shops, which they advertised with signs covered with black scribbles. The women walked on the street in kimonos, wooden sandals, and white stockings, carrying neat black bundles on their backs and wearing their hair in puffs with long ivory needles stuck through them. When they met they bowed, walked a couple of steps, and turned and bowed again, repeating this several times. They carried babies on their backs, not in their arms, never laughed or went into the saloons. On Sundays the men sat in front of their shops, dressed in gowns, like priests.

Chinatown was on the other side of K Street, toward the Southern Pacific shops. Our houses were old, but those in which the Chinese kept stores, laundries, and restaurants were older still. In black jackets and skull-caps the older merchants smoked long pipes with a tiny brass cup on the end. In their dusty store windows there was always the same assortment of tea packages, rice bowls, saucers, and pots decorated with blue temples and dragons.

In the hotels and rooming houses scattered about the *barrio* the Filipino farm workers, riverboat stewards, and houseboys made their homes. Like the Mexicans they had their own poolhalls, which they called clubs. Hindus from the rice and fruit country north of the city stayed in the rooming houses when they were in town, keeping to themselves. The Portuguese and Italian families gathered in their own neighborhoods along Fourth and Fifth Streets southward toward the Y-street levee. The Poles, Yugo-Slavs, and Koreans, too few to take over any particular part of it, were scattered throughout the *barrio*. Black men drifted in and out of town, working the waterfront. It was a kaleidoscope of colors and languages and customs that surprised and absorbed me at every turn.

Although we, the foreigners, made up the majority of the population of that quarter of Sacramento, the Americans had by no means given it up to us. Not all of them had moved above Fifth Street as the *barrio* became more crowded. The bartenders, the rent collectors, the insurance salesmen, the mates on the river boats, the landladies, and most importantly, the police—these were all gringos. So were the craftsmen, like the barbers and printers, who did not move their shops uptown as the city grew. The teachers of our one public school were all Americans. On skid row we rarely saw a drunk wino who was not a gringo. The operators of the pawnshops and secondhand stores were white and mostly Jewish.

For the Mexicans the barrio was a colony of refugees. We came to know families from Chihuahua, Sonora, Jalisco, and Durango. Some had come to the United States even before the revolution, living in Texas before migrating to California. Like ourselves, our Mexican neighbors had come this far moving step by step, working and waiting, as if they were feeling their way up a ladder. They talked of relatives who had been left behind in Mexico, or in some far-off city like Los Angeles or San Diego. From whatever place they had come, and however short or long the time they had lived in the United States, together they formed the *colonia mexicana*. In the years between our arrival and the First World War, the *colonia* grew and spilled out from the lower part of town. Some families moved into the alley shacks east of the Southern Pacific tracks, close to the canneries and warehouses and across the river among the orchards and rice mills.

The *colonia* was like a sponge that was beginning to leak along the edges, squeezed between the levee, the railroad tracks, and the river front. But it wasn't squeezed dry, because it kept filling with newcomers who found families who took in boarders: basements, alleys, shanties, run down rooming houses and flop joints where they could live.

Crowded as it was, the *colonia* found a place for these *chicanos*, the name by which we called an unskilled worker born in Mexico and just arrived in the United States. The *chicanos* were fond of identifying themselves by saying they had just arrived from *el macizo*, by which they meant the solid Mexican homeland, the good native earth. Although they spoke of *el macizo* like homesick persons, they didn't go back. They remained, as they said of themselves, *pura raza*. So it happened that José and Gustavo would bring home for a meal and for conversation workingmen who were *chicanos* fresh from *el macizo* and like ourselves, *pura raza*. Like us, they had come straight to the *barrio* where they could order a meal, buy a pair of overalls, and look for work in Spanish. They brought us vague news about the revolution, in which many of them had fought as *villistas*, *huertistas*, *maderistas*, or *zapatistas*. As an old *maderista*, I imagined our *chicano* guests as battle-tested revolutionaries, like myself.

As poor refugees, their first concern was to find a place to sleep, then to eat and find work. In the *barrio* they were most likely to find all three, for not knowing English, they needed something that was even more urgent than a room, a meal, or a job, and that was information in a language they could understand. This information had to be picked up in bits and pieces—from families like ours, from the conversation groups in the poolrooms and the saloons.

Beds and meals, if the newcomers had no money at all, were provided—in one way or another—on trust, until the new *chicano* found a job. On trust and not on credit, for trust was something between people who had plenty of nothing, and credit was between people who had something of plenty. It was not charity or social welfare but something my mother called *asistencia*, a helping given and received on trust, to be repaid because those who had given it were themselves in need of what they had given. *Chicanos* who had found work on farms or in railroad camps came back to pay us a few dollars for *asistencia* we had provided weeks or months before.

Because the *barrio* was a grapevine of job information, the transient *chicanos* were able to find work and repay their obligations. The password of the *barrio* was *trabajo* and the community was divided in two—the many who were looking for it and the few who had it to offer. Pickers, foremen, contractors, drivers, field hands, pick and shovel men on the railroad and in construction came back to the *barrio* when work was slack, to tell one another of the places they had been, the kind of *patrón* they had, the wages paid, the food, the living quarters, and other important details. Along Second Street, labor recruiters hung blackboards on their shop fronts, scrawling in chalk offers of work. The grapevine was a mesh of rumors and gossip, and men often walked long distances or paid bus fares or a contractor's fee only to find that the work was over or all the jobs were filled. Even the chalked signs could not always be relied on. Yet the search for *trabajo*, or the *chanza*, as we also called it, went on because it had to.

We in the *barrio* considered that there were two kinds of *trabajo*. There were the seasonal jobs, some of them a hundred miles or more from Sacramento. And there were the closer *chanzas* to which you could walk or ride on a bicycle. These were the best ones, in the railway shops, the canneries, the waterfront warehouses, the lumber yards, the produce markets, the brick kilns, and the rice mills. To be able to move from the seasonal jobs to the close-in work was a step up the ladder. Men who had made it passed the word along to their relatives or their friends when there was a *chanza* of this kind.

It was all done by word of mouth, this delicate wiring of the grapevine. The exchange points of the network were the places where men gathered in small groups, apparently to loaf and chat to no purpose. One of these points was our kitchen, where my uncles and their friends sat and talked of *el macizo* and of the revolution but above all of the *chanzas* they had heard of.

There was not only the everlasting talk about *trabajo*, but also the never-ending action of the *barrio* itself. If work was action the *barrio* was where the action was. Every morning a parade of men in oily work clothes and carrying lunch buckets went up Fourth Street toward the railroad shops, and every evening they walked back, grimy and silent. Horse drawn drays with low platforms rumbled up and down our street carrying the goods the city traded in, from kegs of beer to sacks of grain. Within a few blocks of our house there were smithies, hand laundries, a macaroni factory, and all manner of places where wagons and buggies were repaired, horses stabled, bicycles fixed, chickens dressed, clothes washed and ironed, furniture repaired, candy mixed, tents sewed, wine grapes pressed, bottles washed, lumber sawed, suits fitted and tailored, watches and clocks taken apart and put together again, vegetables sorted, railroad cars unloaded, boxcars iced, barges freighted, ice cream cones molded, soda pop bottled, fish scaled, salami stuffed, corn ground for masa, and bread ovened. To those who knew where these were located in the alleys, as I did, the whole *barrio* was an open workshop. The people who worked there came to know you, let you look in at the door, made jokes, and occasionally gave you an odd job.

This was the business district of the *barrio*. Around it and through it moved a constant traffic of drays, carts, bicycles, pushcarts, trucks, and high-wheeled automobiles with black canvas tops and honking horns. On the tailgates of drays and wagons, I nipped rides when I was going home with a gunnysack full of empty beer bottles or my gleanings around the packing sheds.

Once we had work, the next most important thing was to find a place to live we could afford. Ours was a neighborhood of leftover houses. The cheapest rents were in the back quarters of the rooming houses, the basements, and the run-down clapboard rentals in the alleys. Clammy and dank as they were, they were nevertheless one level up from the barns and tents where many of our *chicano* friends lived, or the shanties and lean-to's of the migrants who squatted in the "jungles" along the levees of the Sacramento and the American rivers.

Barrio people, when they first came to town, had no furniture of their own. They rented it with their quarters or bought a piece at a time from the secondhand stores, the *segundas*, where we traded. We cut out the ends of tin cans to make collars and plates for the pipes and floor moldings where the rats had gnawed holes. Stoops and porches that sagged we propped with bricks and fat stones. To plug the drafts around the windows in winter, we cut strips of corrugated cardboard and wedged them into the frames. With squares of cheesecloth neatly cut and sewed to screen doors holes were covered and rents in the wire mesh mended. Such repairs, which landlords never paid any attention to, were made *por mientras*, for the time being or temporarily. It would have been a word equally suitable for the house itself, or for the barrio. We lived in run-down places furnished with seconds in a hand-me-down neighborhood all of which were *por mientras*.

We found the Americans as strange in their customs as they probably found us. Immediately we discovered that there were no *mercados* and that when shopping you did not put the groceries in a *chiquihuite*. Instead everything was in cans or in cardboard boxes or each item was put in a brown paper bag. There were neighborhood grocery stores at the corners and some big ones uptown, but no *mercado*. The grocers did not give children a *pilón*, they did not stand at the door and coax you to come in and buy, as they did in Mazatlán. The fruits and vegetables were displayed on counters instead of being piled up on the floor. The stores smelled of fly spray and oiled floors, not of fresh pineapple and limes.

Neither was there a plaza, only parks which had no bandstands, no concerts every Thursday, no Judases exploding on Holy Week, and no promenades of boys going one way and girls the other. There were no parks in the *barrio*; and the ones uptown were cold and rainy in winter, and in summer there was no place to sit except on the grass. When there were celebrations nobody set off rockets in the parks, much less on the street in front of your house to announce to the neighborhood that a wedding or a baptism was taking place. Sacramento did not have a *mercado* and a plaza with the cathedral to one side and the Palacio de Gobierno on another to make it obvious that there and nowhere else was the center of the town.

It was just as puzzling that the Americans did not live in *vecindades*, like our block on Leandro Valle. Even in the alleys, where people knew one another better, the houses were fenced apart, without central courts to wash clothes, talk and play with the other children. Like the city, the Sacramento *barrio* did not have a place which was the middle of things for everyone.

In more personal ways we had to get used to the Americans. They did not listen if you did not speak loudly, as they always did. In the Mexican style, people would know that you were enjoying their jokes tremendously if you merely smiled and shook a little, as if you were trying to swallow your mirth. In the American style there was little difference between a laugh and a roar, and until you got used to them you could hardly tell whether the boisterous Americans were roaring mad or roaring happy.

It was Doña Henriqueta more than Gustavo or José who talked of these oddities and classified them as agreeable or deplorable. It was she also who pointed out the pleasant surprises of the American way. When a box of rolled oats with a picture of red carnations on the side was emptied, there was a plate or a bowl or a cup with blue designs. We ate the strange stuff regularly for breakfast and we soon had a set of the beautiful dishes. Rice and beans we bought in cotton bags of colored prints. The bags were unsewed, washed, ironed, and made into gaily designed towels, napkins, and handkerchiefs. The American stores also gave small green stamps which were pasted in a book to exchange for prizes. We didn't have to run to the corner with the garbage; a collector came for it.

With remarkable fairness and never-ending wonder we kept adding to our list the pleasant and the repulsive in the ways of the Americans. It was my second acculturation.

The older people of the *barrio*, except in those things which they had to do like the Americans because they had no choice, remained Mexican. Their language at home was Spanish. They were continuously taking up collections to pay somebody's funeral expenses or to help someone who had had a serious accident. Cards were sent to you to attend a burial where you would throw a handful of dirt on top of the coffin and listen to tearful speeches at the graveside. At every baptism a new *compadre* and a new *comadre* joined the family circle. New Year greeting cards were exchanged, showing angels and cherubs in bright colors sprinkled with grains of mica so that they glistened like gold dust. At the family parties the huge pot of steaming tamales was still the center of attention, the *atole* served on the side with chunks of brown sugar for sucking and crunching. If the party lasted long enough, someone produced a guitar, the men took over and the singing of *corridos* began.

In the *barrio* there were no individuals who had official titles or who were otherwise recognized by everybody as important people. The reason must have been that there was no place in the public business of the city of Sacramento for the Mexican immigrants. We only rented a corner of the city and as long as we paid the rent on time everything else was decided at City Hall or the County Court House, where Mexicans went only when they were in trouble. Nobody from the *barrio* ever ran for mayor or city councilman. For us the most important public officials were the policemen who walked their beats, stopped fights, and hauled drunks to jail in a paddy wagon we called *La Julia*.

The one institution we had that gave the *colonia* some kind of image was the *Comisión Honorífica*, a committee picked by the Mexican Consul in San Francisco to organize the celebration of the *Cinco de Mayo* and the Sixteenth of September, the anniversaries of the battle of Puebla and the beginning of our War of Independence. These were the two events which stirred everyone in the *barrio*, for what we were celebrating was not only the heroes of Mexico but also the feeling that we were still Mexicans ourselves. On these occasions there was a dance preceded by speeches and a concert. For both the *cinco* and the sixteenth queens were elected to preside over the ceremonies.

Between celebrations neither the politicians uptown nor the *Comisión Honorífica* attended to the daily needs of the *barrio*. This was done by volunteers—the ones who knew enough English to interpret in court, on a visit to the doctor, a call at the county hospital, and who could help make out a postal money order. By the time I had finished the third grade at the Lincoln School I was one of these volunteers. My services were not professional but they were free, except for the IOU's I accumulated from families who always thanked me with "God will pay you for it."

My clients were not *pochos*, Mexicans who had grown up in California, probably had even been born in the United States. They had learned to speak English of sorts and could still speak Spanish, also of sorts. They knew much more about the Americans than we did, and much less about us. The *chicanos* and the *pochos* had certain feelings about one another. Concerning the *pochos*, the *chicanos* suspected that they considered themselves too good for the *barrio* but were not, for some reason, good enough for the Americans. Toward the *chicanos*, the *pochos* acted superior, amused at our confusions but not especially interested in explaining them to us. In our family when I forgot my manners, my mother would ask me if I was turning *pochito*.

Turning *pocho* was a half-step toward turning American. And America was all around us, in and out of the *barrio*. Abruptly we had to forget the ways of shopping in a *mercado* and learn those of shopping in a corner grocery or in a department store. The Americans paid no attention to the Sixteenth of September, but they made a great commotion about the Fourth of July. In Mazatlán Don Salvador had told us, saluting and marching as he talked to our class, that the *Cinco de Mayo* was the most glorious date in human history. The Americans had not even heard about it.

In Tucson, when I had asked my mother again if the Americans were having a revolution, the answer was: "No, but they have good schools, and you are going to one of them." We were by now settled at 418 L Street and the time had come for me to exchange a revolution for an American education.

The two of us walked south on Fifth Street one morning to the corner of Q Street and turned right. Half of the block was occupied by the Lincoln School. It was a three-story wooden building, with two wings that gave it the shape of a double-T connected by a central hall. It was a new building, painted yellow, with a shingled roof that was not like the red tile of the school in Mazatlán. I noticed other differences, none of them very reassuring.

We walked up the wide staircase hand in hand and through the door, which closed by itself. A mechanical contraption screwed to the top shut it behind us quietly.

Up to this point the adventure of enrolling me in the school had been carefully rehearsed. Mrs. Dodson had told us how to find it and we had circled it several times on our walks. Friends in the *barrio* explained that the director was called a principal, and that it was a lady and not a man. They assured us that there was always a person at the school who could speak Spanish.

Exactly as we had been told, there was a sign on the door in both Spanish and English: "Principal." We crossed the hall and entered the office of Miss Nettie Hopley.

Miss Hopley was at a roll-top desk to one side, sitting in a swivel chair that moved on wheels. There was a sofa against the opposite wall, flanked by two windows and a door that opened on a small balcony. Chairs were set around a table and framed pictures hung on the walls of a man with long white hair and another with a sad face and a black beard.

The principal half turned in the swivel chair to look at us over the pinch glasses crossed on the ridge of her nose. To do this she had to duck her head slightly as if she were about to step through a low doorway.

What Miss Hopley said to us we did not know but we saw in her eyes a warm welcome and when she took off her glasses and straightened up she smiled whole-heartedly, like Mrs. Dodson. We were, of course, saying nothing, only catching the friendliness of her voice and the sparkle in her eyes while she said words we did not understand. She signaled us to the table. Almost tiptoe-ing across the office, I maneuvered myself to keep my mother between me and the gringo lady. In a matter of seconds I had to decide whether she was a possible friend or a menace. We sat down.

Then Miss Hopley did a formidable thing. She stood up. Had she been standing when we entered she would have seemed tall. But rising from her chair she soared. And what she carried up and up with her was a buxom superstructure, firm shoulders, a straight sharp nose, full cheeks slightly molded by a curved line along the nostrils, thin lips that moved like steel springs, and a high forehead topped by hair gathered in a bun. Miss Hopley was not a giant in body but when she mobilized it to a standing position she seemed a match for giants. I decided I liked her.

She strode to a door in the far corner of the office, opened it and called a name. A boy of about ten years appeared in the doorway. He sat down at one end of the table. He was brown like us, a plump kid with shiny black hair combed straight back, neat, cool, and faintly obnoxious.

Miss Hopley joined us with a large book and some papers in her hand. She, too, sat down and the questions and answers began by way of our interpreter. My name was Ernesto. My mother's name was Henriqueta. My birth certificate was in San Blas. Here was my last report card from the Escuela Municipal Numero 3 para Varones of Mazatlán, and so forth. Miss Hopley put things down in the book and my mother signed a card.

As long as the questions continued, Doña Henri-queta could stay and I was secure. Now that they were over, Miss Hopley saw her to the door, dismissed our interpreter and without further ado took me by the hand and strode down the hall to Miss Ryan's first grade.

Miss Ryan took me to a seat at the front of the room, into which I shrank—the better to survey her. She was, to skinny, somewhat runty me, of a withering height when she patrolled the class. And when I least expected it, there she was, crouching by my desk, her blond radiant face level with mine, her voice patiently maneuvering me over the awful idiocies of the English language.

During the next few weeks Miss Ryan overcame my fears of tall, energetic teachers as she bent over my desk to help me with a word in the pre-primer. Step by step, she loosened me and my classmates from the safe anchorage of the desks for recitations at the blackboard and consultations at her desk. Frequently she burst into happy announcements to the whole class. "Ito can read a sentence," and small Japanese Ito, squint-eyed and shy, slowly read aloud while the class listened in wonder: "Come, Skipper, come. Come and run." The Korean, Portuguese, Italian, and Polish first graders had similar moments of glory, no less shining than mine the day I conquered "butterfly," which I had been persistently pronouncing in standard Spanish as boo-ter-flee. "Children," Miss Ryan called for attention. "Ernesto has learned how to pronounce *butterfly*!" And I proved it with a perfect imitation of Miss Ryan. From that celebrated success, I was soon able to match Ito's progress as a sentence reader with "Come, butterfly, come fly with me."

Like Ito and several other first graders who did not know English, I received private lessons from Miss Ryan in the closet, a narrow hall off the classroom with a door at each end. Next to one of these doors Miss Ryan placed a large chair for herself and a small one for me. Keeping an eye on the class through the open door she read with me about sheep in the meadow and a frightened chicken going to see the king, coaching me out of my phonetic ruts in words like *pasture, bow-wow-wow, hay,* and *pretty,* which to my Mexican ear and eye had so many unnecessary sounds and letters. She made me watch her lips and then close my eyes as she repeated words I found hard to read. When we came to know each other better, I tried interrupting to tell Miss Ryan how we said it in Spanish. It didn't work. She only said "oh" and went on with *pasture, bow-wow-wow,* and *pretty.* It was as if in that closet we were both discovering together the secrets of the English language and grieving together over the tragedies of Bo-Peep. The main reason I was graduated with honors from the first grade was that I had fallen in love with Miss Ryan. Her radiant, no-nonsense character made us either afraid not to love her or love her so we would not be afraid, I am not sure which. It was not only that we sensed she was with it, but also that she was with us.

Like the first grade, the rest of the Lincoln School was a sampling of the lower part of town where many races made their home. My pals in the second grade were Kazushi, whose parents spoke only Japanese; Matti, a skinny Italian boy; and Manuel, a fat Portuguese who would never get into a fight but wrestled you to the ground and just sat on you. Our assortment of nationalities included Koreans, Yugoslavs, Poles, Irish, and home-grown Americans.

Miss Hopley and her teachers never let us forget why we were at Lincoln: for those who were alien, to become good Americans; for those who were so born, to accept the rest of us. Off the school grounds we traded the same insults we heard from our elders. On the playground we were sure to be marched up to the principal's office for calling someone a wop, a chink, a dago, or a greaser. The school was not so much a melting pot as a griddle where

Miss Hopley and her helpers warmed knowledge into us and roasted racial hatreds out of us.

At Lincoln, making us into Americans did not mean scrubbing away what made us originally foreign. The teachers called us as our parents did, or as close as they could pronounce our names in Spanish or Japanese. No one was ever scolded or punished for speaking in his native tongue on the playground. Matti told the class about his mother's down quilt, which she had made in Italy with the fine feathers of a thousand geese. Encarnación acted out how boys learned to fish in the Phillipines. I astounded the third grade with the story of my travels on a stagecoach, which nobody else in the class had seen except in the museum at Sutter's Fort. After a visit to the Crocker Art Gallery and its collection of heroic paintings of the golden age of California, someone showed a silk scroll with a Chinese painting. Miss Hopley herself had a way of expressing wonder over these matters before a class, her eyes wide open until they popped slightly. It was easy for me to feel that becoming a proud American, as she said we should, did not mean feeling ashamed of being a Mexican.

The Americanization of Mexican me was no smooth matter. I had to fight one lout who made fun of my travels on the *diligencia*, and my barbaric translation of the word into "diligence." He doubled up with laughter over the word until I straightened him out with a kick. In class I made points explaining that in Mexico roosters said "qui-qui-ri-qui" and not "cock-a-doodle-doo," but after school I had to put up with the taunts of a big Yugoslav who said Mexican roosters were crazy.

But it was Homer who gave me the most lasting lesson for a future American.

Homer was a chunky Irishman who dressed as if every day was Sunday. He slicked his hair between a crew cut and a pompadour. And Homer was smart, as he clearly showed when he and I ran for president of the third grade.

Everyone understood that this was to be a demonstration of how the American people vote for president. In an election, the teacher explained, the candidates could be generous and vote for each other. We cast our ballots in a shoe box and Homer won by two votes. I polled my supporters and came to the conclusion that I had voted for Homer and so had he. After class he didn't deny it, reminding me of what the teacher had said—we could vote for each other but didn't have to.

The lower part of town was a collage of nationalities in the middle of which Miss Nettie Hopley kept school with discipline and compassion. She called assemblies in the upper hall to introduce celebrities like the police sergeant or the fire chief, to lay down the law of the school, to present awards to our athletic champions, and to make important announcements. One of these was that I had been proposed by my school and accepted as a member of the newly formed Sacramento Boys Band. "Now, isn't that a wonderful thing?" Miss Hopley asked the assembled school, all eyes on me. And everyone answered in a chorus, including myself, "Yes, Miss Hopley."

It was not only the parents who were summoned to her office and boys and girls who served sentences there who knew that Nettie Hopley meant business. The entire school witnessed her sizzling Americanism in its awful majesty one morning at flag salute.

All the grades, as usual, were lined up in the courtyard between the wings of the building, ready to march to classes after the opening bell. Miss Shand was on the balcony of the second floor off Miss Hopley's office, conducting us in our lusty singing of "My Country tiz-a-thee."

Our principal, as always, stood there like us, at attention, her right hand over her heart, joining in the song.

Halfway through the second stanza she stepped forward, held up her arm in a sign of command, and called loud and clear: "Stop the singing." Miss Shand looked flabbergasted. We were frozen with shock.

Miss Hopley was now standing at the rail of the balcony, her eyes sparking, her voice low and resonant, the words coming down to us distinctly and loaded with indignation.

"There are two gentlemen walking on the school grounds with their hats on while we are singing," she said, sweeping our ranks with her eyes. "We will remain silent until the gentlemen come to attention and remove their hats." A minute of awful silence ended when Miss Hopley, her gaze fixed on something behind us, signaled Miss Shand and we began once more the familiar hymn. That afternoon, when school was out, the word spread. The two gentlemen were the Superintendent of Schools and an important guest on an inspection.

I carne back to the Lincoln School after every summer, moving up through the grades with Miss Campbell, Miss Beakey, Mrs. Wood, Miss Applegate, and Miss Delahunty. I sat in the classroom adjoining the principal's office and had my turn answering her telephone when she was about the building repeating the message to the teacher, who made a note of it. Miss Campbell read to us during the last period of the week about King Arthur, Columbus, Buffalo Bill, and Daniel Boone, who came to life in the reverie of the class through the magic of her voice. And it was Miss Campbell who introduced me to the public library on Eye Street, where I became a regular customer.

All of Lincoln School mourned together when Eddie, the blond boy everybody liked, was killed by a freight train as he crawled across the tracks going home one day. We assembled to say good-bye to Miss Applegate, who was off to Alaska to be married. Now it was my turn to be excused from class to interpret for a parent enrolling a new student fresh from Mexico. Graduates from Lincoln came back now and then to tell us about high school. A naturalist entertained us in assembly, imitating the calls of the meadow lark, the water ouzel, the oriole, and the killdeer. I decided to become a bird man after I left Lincoln.

In the years we lived in the lower part of town, La LeenCon, as my family called it, became a benchmark in our lives, like the purple light of the Lyric Theater and the golden dome of the Palacio de Gobierno gleaming above Capitol Park.

With safer bearings of our own we were ready for another attempt at a family reunion.

One had already failed. The Lopez's had left Jalco and reached Mazatlán but had returned to the village to await better times. Now the revolution was moving south again, making travel by rail to the United States unsafe. It was agreed that they would make the journey by sea to San Francisco.

By the kitchen calendar we counted the days. On the last one Gustavo, my mother, José and I took the train for a trip that was a fiesta of smiles and anecdotes, and a great deal of reminiscing about our last days in Jalco when we had last seen our relatives. Together again we would be four men accustomed to *trabajo*, sufficient to support the women and the young.

On the waterfront we boarded a launch that took us across the bay to Angel's Island where our kinfolk were in quarantine. The boat churned up a heavy wake and seagulls swooped around us, squeaking. As she always did, my mother nodded her head this way and that, explaining the things or the people she was calling to my attention. I watched the pilot turn us smoothly alongside a wharf. A man in uniform took us through a building and out into an open courtyard from which we could see the city across the bay. A strong sea wind was blowing, cold and salty.

The Lopez family were standing at the far end of the yard: my aunt, slender and poised in long skirts and a shawl; Don Catarino, in freshly washed work clothes, a coat and a felt hat which he held clamped down with one hand; Jesús, Catarino and a younger brother wrapped in blankets. Huddled between them were two wicker baskets, each with a twin, born on the trip.

There was no laughter, no shouting for joy, no back-slapping at the reunion. The excitement was inward and it came out only in the smiles and the formal, gentle *abrazos* all around. Following the cue of the adults I merely said: "How are you, Jesús? How are you, Catarino?" And they answered, "How are you, Ernesto?"

My cousins were shy and I just stood by them, staring at my relatives, one by one. My aunt and my mother were talking. Gustavo and José were listening to Don Catarino.

The women took our hands, the men carried the cribs and together we went inside the building. After a long wait the man in uniform joined us. An interpreter was with him.

The immigration officer, through the interpreter, was explaining. The Lopez's would not be allowed to enter the United States. There were papers on the desk in front of him. He explained the rules and the laws and the orders and they all made the same point: the family would be detained for a few days on the island and would then have to return to Mexico the way they had come.

So it was hello and good-bye in one afternoon. We left them by the wharf. From the launch we waved and lost them in our wake.

The trip back to Sacramento was like returning from a funeral. My uncles exchanged puzzled questions, bitter and despairing, anger and grief in their faces, staring out of the window to avoid looking at each other.

They paid little attention to my comments, caught up in their own distress. The man in uniform had merely shown us some papers but he had not told us why. He had not even said what would have to be done to bring our family back and take them home with us. I saw him vividly in my mind, ugly and menacing, and silently called him all the names I could think of, like *gringo pendejo*. But my secret revenge did not make me feel better as I tried to guess what Gustavo meant when he had said on the launch: "Es una injusticia." Our hopes had been denied and our joy had been turned to sadness by people we were powerless even to question. My own response to injustice seemed the only way to get even. I turned to Doña Henriqueta and said : "Let us go back to Jalcocotán together." She smiled compassionately, as if there were still many things I had to learn, and said nothing.

That night Mrs. Dodson was in our kitchen, myself interpreting around the table questions and answers that were asked and discussed quietly and desperately. Were there any higher *Autoridades* who could change the orders? Where could we find a lawyer who spoke Spanish? How much would he charge? Did the *Autoridades* make a mistake, or did we? What was it? And in the following days, our landlady telephoned and talked to certain of her American friends about our plight.

The days passed, and there came a letter from Doña Esther. The Lopez's had sailed back and had made their way home. Once a month we wrote them, with a worn-out dollar greenback wrapped in the note papers. We began once more to save and to talk in the evenings in our basement home about how things had been for all of us in Jalco and how they might be someday in the *barrio*.

There were probably twenty tenants living in the apartments and rooms at 418 L Street. The room next to ours was occupied by a very old man with thin white hair who always dressed in black. His left arm was shriveled by paralysis and his legs partly so. To move about he used a metal walker, a semi-circular aluminum frame which he jerked ahead with his right hand. Except for short walks to the corner and back, the Old Gentleman, as everybody called him, spent most of the day in a stuffed chair on the basement porch.

On our floor we also had for neighbors Mr. Grover and his woman, a dark beauty with coal black hair and the true olive complexion of a Mexican. She said she was Indian. She was a foot taller than he and when she wore her wide-brimmed floppy hat with the ostrich feathers, she looked like an amazon with a captive in tow. Somewhere upstairs lived Mr. Brien, the printer, who parted his hair in the middle and had a black mole on his lower lip. He had a bushy red moustache which curved down over his lips like a fine screen. Mr. Brien was an expert spitter, as I noted with admiration. He could shoot a streak of dark brown tobacco juice under his moustache without touching a hair of it. After every spit he stroked it with the back of his hand, first right, then left, and went on chewing.

Mr. Hans was a carpenter and played the brass horn in the German band that performed on the streets on Sundays. He would never have passed Miss Ryan's first grade, for he gargled his r's and said "oont" instead of "and." He and his roommate, another German, were inseparable. Sometimes they practiced for their Sunday concerts on the third floor landing, Mr. Hans on his horn and his partner on an accordion.

Mr. Howard, the walking delegate of a labor union, was short and rotund, always in a black derby hat and tight cutaway jacket. One leg was shorter than the other, which made him limp in spite of the high heel and thick sole he wore on that side. I always saw him with a book in the crook of his arm, and he never failed to notice me. I studied his limp because it looked to me like a dance step, the thick sole twisting sidewise as if he were grinding to powder a seed of corn at every step.

Mr. Chester and Big Ernie were the other two personalities I took note of. Mr. Chester was a huge young man who always appeared in an army uniform. He smiled continuously, spoke quietly, and moved slowly, as if he was afraid of bumping into something and demolishing it. After we became friends he taught me to stiffen my body while he rolled me around his shoulders and hoisted me by the ankles. The people on the porch who watched us said we could do a vaudeville act together.

Big Ernie, Mr. Chester's buddy, was Mrs. Dodson's grown-up son who had no trouble about his name until we moved into his mother's basement. Another Ernest in the house made it necessary to pair us as Big and Little Ernie, the name being about the only thing we had in common. Big Ernie, when he talked, always seemed to be chewing a sour pickle. He drove a new red automobile and let me watch while he polished it.

One thing that wasn't taught at the Lincoln School, but which I learned from experience, was that a place has to have somebody in charge to decide things and organize them. At 418 L that somebody was Mrs. Dodson and she organized matters from her apartment on the second floor rear. Running errands for her, I went in and out of the apartment often. I stepped softly on the rug, afraid to scuff it. There was a mahogany console with a record player and on the inside of the cover a picture of a white dog listening to the music coming from a tin horn. Above the victrola there was a picture of a naked lady standing ankle deep in a pool, which looked cold because the lady was holding her arms in front of her, her hands on her knees. In one corner of the parlor sat a huge brown teddy bear watching the glass bead curtain between the parlor and the kitchen that tinkled every time you went through it. The apartment was a decorated, cozy place I liked to visit except for Pinkey, Mrs. Dodson's pint-sized lap dog with toothpick legs and a nasty temper. He annoyed me with his squeaky bark which said plainly he didn't want me there.

Except for ourselves, the tenants of 418 L were far from being a family; they were more like a collection. There was something peculiar about each one; they were people who stayed out of each other's way but who didn't mind being noticed and who noticed you. I went for Mr. Howard's laundry and he loaned me a book called *Enoch Arden*. The Old Gentleman knocked on our wall when he was ready to put on his necktie and coat, a signal for me to go and help him. Every now and then he pressed a dime into my hand or bought me a chocolate bar when I walked with him to the corner and back. My mother helped the Indian lady with her wash, and she took me to the State Fair one summer where she bought me a whip and a cowboy belt. Tenants came and went but the familiar characters like us, stayed on. From them my circle of acquaintances and friends began to spread around the block.

One of the first of these was Big Singh, the brawny Hindu who ran a boarding house next door for his fellow countrymen. Big Singh with his thick black beard always wore a dark turban wound around his head and a white apron from his neck to his ankles. His side porch looked over our yard and Big Singh would lean on the railing chatting with us in the few English words he knew. I became Big Singh's tutor, for he often asked me how to say certain words in English, which I supplied with complete confidence. As a show of appreciation he hired me to work in his kitchen on Saturday afternoons to turn over the thick flour cakes he prepared for his boarders and which he called ruti. On weekends many of the Sikh laborers came there to eat and sleep. They were all enormous, like Big Singh, and all wore beards and turbans of different colors.

Up the street from us, toward Fourth, there was Miss Florence who lived in a second story flat and accompanied herself on the piano. She sang, very loudly, a song called "I want Sympathy," swooping up and down the bars melodiously like someone on a long, high swing. She beat rugs on her front porch and called out to me when she saw me pass by. Her rugged, unlovely face broke into smiles when I called back, as I always did, "Miss Florence, sing Sympathy."

Around the block, on the alley corner, there was Stacy's blacksmith shop, a small barn shaded by one of the soaring elms that made the street look like the inside of a cathedral. Stacy, a square-jawed strongman, allowed boys to stand in the wide doorway while he fitted iron shoes to the horses. When business was good, the customers lined up in the alley or the street, tied to the elm and the hitching posts. Stacy pumped the bellows of his forge with gusto, making the flames leap around the shoe he was shaping. He laid it red hot on the anvil and whammed it with his hammer, which he rested loosely so that it danced and tinkled after each blow. The hot shoe was dunked in a barrel of water and Stacy, rubbing one huge hand down the horse's withers pulled up the hoof, clamped it between his knees, and proceeded to secure it with the nails he held pressed between his lips. Stacy was a comedian and when we were watching he invented bits of funny business for us. One of these was to place an empty pail under a horse which decided to let go with his water while he was being shod. Stacy would offer us the bucket with a flourish and an invitation to "have a drink on the house." It was our cue to take the bucket and empty it in the gutter.

Behind Stacy's there was a Chinese hand laundry and above that a rickety loft where boxers trained. In all the years I did business with the laundryman as errand boy for some of his customers, we never said a word to each other; but when a boxer was tapping off a furious rhythm on the punching bag above us, shaking the building, the laundryman and I listened together. That, and a quick nod when he matched my ticket with a package of laundry, was the extent of our communication.

Halfway down the alley lived a Yugoslav who worked in the railroad shops and ran a bowling alley. It was a dirt strip, tamped down, with a border of planks. On Sundays the Slavs gathered to play bocce, and once a year the alley was covered with boards and turned into a winery. A large press was brought out of the cellar, and the men, chattering and drinking, pressed the grapes with their bare feet, their pants rolled up above the knees. They offered me nips of wine and lowered me into the press to tramp grapes myself.

At the Fourth Street end of the alley there was a fish shop run by a Japanese who sometimes bought from me the catfish I caught in the river. We never argued about the price. As with the laundryman, ours was a speechless acquaintance, my fish and his nickels crossing the counter in opposite directions, without a word being said.

This was our alley, along with the shanties, the barns, and the sagging cottages behind picket or plank fences. It was a refuge for sleeping drunks, and I often passed by them looking for gunnysacks, beer bottles, and scraps of tinfoil.

A different type altogether was Lettie, who lived next door in a rooming house very much like 418 L. She was petite, dark skinned, sculptured, and vivacious. She performed every night at a dancehall near Second Street. If I wasn't off on an errand I made it a point to sit on the flat-topped newel post of the front staircase of our house. When she passed on her way to work—with a red rose in her hair, lips rouged like her flower, eyelashes painted like coal, a tight velvet jacket with silver buttons, a flouncy mini-skirt, lace stockings and black slippers—she always mesmerized me. People on the second story porch followed Miss Lettie with their eyes as long as they could. I could see her until she turned into the dancehall. I ran errands for her and taught Albert, her son who was several years younger than I, to play marbles and whittle. When I was babysitting with Albert we played the victrola and looked at pictures of his mother in dancing poses tacked on the walls.

Less familiar to me were other characters of the lower part of town, people like Frisco, Speedy, and Shorty Lopez. Frisco played the piano in the saloon at the corner, always wearing a black vest and a straw hat. I couldn't watch him through the swinging doors of the saloon, but I often saw him walk in and out, and I could hear him banging out his tunes. Mr. Hans, who knew music, said that nobody could play "1912" and "Alexander's Ragtime Band" like Frisco. Speedy was a messenger boy who carried trays with dinners to hotels and rooming houses, balancing them on a flat cap with an upraised visor as he pedaled full speed on a bicycle.

But by far most of my admiration was for Lopez, a Mexican known to the gringos as Shorty and to us as Cho-ree. The nickname was unavoidable for he was several inches short of legs to match his barrel chest and the head and arms of a tall, powerful man. For that kind of a body Cho-ree had the perfect job. He drove a team of regal percherons harnessed to a beer truck with a platform that hung low over the street. Shorty delivered beer to the saloons, driving his team perched high on the truck, slapping them with the reins and himself jouncing from side to side like a prize rider at a horse show. He wrestled beer kegs on and off his truck all day long, but when he passed by 418 L, he was a charioteer master of two magnificent chargers.

Just as Cho-ree excited me to become a beer truck driver and Mr. Hans a horn player, Mr. Howard was affectionately trying to make me a scholar. He loved books and was always buying used ones on his travels. After *Enoch Arden* he gave me a Horatio Alger, reading paragraphs here and there to get me started. On the shelf of the wooden box that stood by my bunk I lined up Mr. Howard's gifts, which I read after I was sent to bed. Next to them stood the cloak-and-dagger novels in Spanish my mother handed on to me in which I read of noble ladies whose husbands were murdered and avenged, good guys and bad ones killing one another in moonlight duels; the adventures of Cacaseno, who saved himself from being hanged by getting a promise from the King of Spain that he could choose the tree from which to be strung up, and never finding one that was quite suitable.

To this select, bilingual library Mr. Howard one day added a frayed copy of Blackstone's *Commentaries on the Common Law of England*, a thick book with black covers, small print, broken corners, and no pictures except one of the formidable, bewigged Lord Justice himself.

Mr. Howard explained that he had bought it for me to read, if I should decide to become a lawyer. As I did with everything he gave me, I tried making sense of the *Commentaries*, finally leaving it on the bookshelf to read later, much later. I asked Mr. Howard to be on the lookout for a copy of Tio Tonche which we had lost somewhere between Mazatlán and Sacramento. He had never heard of the work and never turned one up.

Our block provided me with adventurers as well as scholars. Mr. Charley, who lived in a basement room with a dirt floor under Big Singh's boarding house, introduced me to history with a bang.

Mr. Charley was an elderly, slouching man who wore loose clothes and a cavalry hat slanted over his right ear. His moustache was enormous, twice as long as Mr. Brien's and a match for his thick eyebrows. On the Fourth of July we celebrated privately and secretly in his dark and stuffy little room. He invited me, Catfish, and Russell, two neighborhood boys of about my age, to what he called his own fireworks.

Mr. Charley sat us on the floor and told the story of his charge up San Juan Hill with Colonel Teddy Roosevelt. He dispatched, so he said, dozens of Spaniards with his two horse pistols. Pointing to the wall he exclaimed: "With them," and he took the two enormous irons carefully out of the holsters. Holding one in each hand he fired them by turns into the ground. The little room shook and filled with the smell of burnt powder. The explosions sounded like the torpedoes that people were setting off in the street above us so that no one could suspect that some real shooting was going on.

Choking delightfully from the gunsmoke and shaken wonderfully by the blasts, we sat and listened to Mr. Charley's glorious account of how he and Colonel Roosevelt won the war. When the pistols were back in the holsters he let us out with a caution not to tell anybody. "The pistols," he said, "make a hell of a bang. I can't shoot them except on the Fourth of July, when everybody thinks they are torpedoes." On the promise that he would show us more fireworks the next Fourth, we kept his secret.

Girolamo, who worked at the pasta factory three blocks from our place, had not read Blackstone or fought at San Juan, but he made macaroni. A barrel stood in the alley behind the factory into which "seconds" of macaroni, spaghetti, tagliarini, and vermicelli, were dropped. By sorting through these discards I could gather a bag of clean, fresh pasta, which my mother made into soup.

Whenever Girolamo saw me at my gleaning he came over with a fistful of whatever he was making at the moment and put it in my paper bag. We talked, he in Italian, I in Spanish. When he went back to his machines I could see him pouring flour dough into a metal tub high on an iron frame, squeezing it through a mold and cutting with a large knife the white threads of macaroni that came out below. Girolamo, who talked to me with waving arms and gentle pinches to make a point, shouting and making musical grunts all the while, made me think that perhaps the life of a macaroni maker was just as interesting as that of a lawyer or a Rough Rider.

The *barrio*, without particularly planning it that way, was providing me with an education out of school as well as in. I did not think of 418 L Street and the Lincoln School as in any way alike, but both had a principal, Miss Hopley and Mrs. Dodson. From Miss Hopley I learned that the man with the black beard and the sad eyes pictured on her wall was Abraham Lincoln, for whom our school was named. From Mrs. Dodson I found out that the picture of the nude lady was September Morn and that it was a famous painting. Miss Hopley conducted me firmly and methodically through the grades into the new world of books and manners she called America. Mrs. Dodson adopted us into the odd company of the rooming house, from which I found my way through the *barrio*.

When the Sumo wrestlers from Japan put on a match in a tent raised on a vacant lot, somebody in the house got me a job giving out handbills and a pass for my work. Wedged in a Japanese audience I saw two mountains of fat dressed in loincloths trying to kill each other. At 418 L with the help of my neighbors, I lined up business for a traveling photographer who took pictures of children sitting on a donkey that reminded me, joyfully, of our Relámpago in Jalcocotán. Mr. Hans gave us front porch lectures on the electric automobiles that passed by— stiff black boxes gliding by without a sound and without a smell with stiff ladies at the steering bar, also in black. There was an arrangement with the bartender on Fourth Street by which I could buy a pail of draught beer by signaling him from the alley door marked "Family Entrance." The cop on the beat objected mildly to this, as he did to Cho-ree's allowing me to nip rides on his truck. To please him we did it only when he was somewhere else in the *barrio*.

Once in a while, I also managed to get around the rule that I was not to run to skid row whenever a street fight was on. These fights were regular, especially on Saturday nights, and the news of a brawl spread fast. If they happened when I was on the waterfront my attendance at these bloody events was no problem. I simply joined the crowd. In one of these fights I saw Speedy and another American battle with their fists, both men streaming blood from their faces. The fight between two Mexicans was something memorable. I arrived in time to see the police loading the winner into the paddy wagon, and the loser lying in the alley in a bloody shirt. And there was the fire in our alley that burned down a shack and cremated an old man who lived there. A house was blown up on T Street, by the Black Hand, it was said. I walked by the place with Catfish stealthily. We thought we could see the smudged imprint of the Hand on the blasted chimney.

When there was a fight, a fire, or a murder the government paid a great deal of attention to the *barrio*. Police and firemen swarmed around for a while. We never called the police, they just came. José explained the wisdom of this to me. "When *los chotas* start asking questions," he said, "you never know what they will ask next." About one thing the entire *barrio* seemed to be in agreement: the dirtiest, most low-down human being was the stool pigeon, the sneak who turned you in to the Authorities.

Most of the time things were quiet in the lower part of town. The cop on our beat, with the half-moon palms and a double row of brass buttons on his uniform, walked by running his billy club along the pickets of our front fence and nodding at the porch sitters as he passed. The others, the ones that cruised in the paddy wagon, were less friendly.

The boys in our section of the *barrio* sorted themselves out by age, game skills of various kinds, and common causes against families, policemen, and other hazards. Russell, Sammie, Catfish, and I organized something that was neither a club nor a gang but could become either. Two people gave us a purpose for organizing—the floor walker of the basement store of Weinstock's, which faced our house; and Van, a *barrio* drifter who was much interested in younger boys.

The floor walker was a giant of a man who guarded the toys that Weinstock's displayed and which we had no money to buy. The vigilante seemed to be every-where, towering over the aisles of the store whenever we were wandering about, usually in pairs. In spite of him, Russell and Catfish had managed to lift a toy pistol and parts of an Erector set which they couldn't take home— for obvious reasons.

By a piece of luck Russell and I discovered a loose plank that hung by a single nail on the fence next to the Chinese laundry in the alley. The plank swung on the nail enough to allow us to squeeze through. Behind it there was a narrow passage enclosed on three sides by fencing, a no-man's-land that had been forgotten when the fences were built. There was room for five or six of us squatting, and no houses close enough for people to hear us if we talked in low voices.

The forgotten nook became our clubhouse which soon had a professional manager, Van himself.

He was twice our age and impressed us with a swag-ger we vaguely admired. He said he had been in the re-form school in a place called Pájaro Valley, had fooled the cops many times, and thought that floor walkers were stupid if you knew how to operate. Besides, he could teach us to smoke Fatimas and Cubebs.

Even though all the club members could not get to-gether at one time because of family interference, Van was always there to push our education. He brought cigarettes and passed the butts around. He demon-strated how we would get over the sour taste and the coughing once we learned to inhale. Van always carried a packet of pictures of naked ladies to show us. When he got back to the matter of Weinstock's he guaranteed that he could work out a plan to sneak a whole Erector set, box and all, in one swoop—if we listened to him.

Sammie, the nephew of the Jewish shoemaker up L Street; Catfish, the Japanese toughie; Russell the gringo, and I were plainly getting inside information on the lower part of town from Van. He knew a man who would buy copper wire, tools or anything else we could pilfer, all of which could be kept safely among the weeds of our hideout.

All this presented problems about what not to tell our families and Van swore us to secrecy.

Ours turned out to be the *barrio* club with the shortest history of any similar establishment in the United States. The loose plank which was our entrance to the underworld was in plain view of everyone who lived in the alley. Besides, we made a fatal mistake. I nominated Albert, Lettie's young son, for membership, and to try him out. I showed him our quarters one afternoon when his mother was not at home. We never found out whether it was Albert or the Chinese laundryman next door to our club or Stacey who turned us in, but soon after Albert's initiation it happened. Van was giving Catfish, Sammie, and me an illustrated lecture which had something to do with the naked ladies of his pictures, when the plank moved, wrenched loose by Doña Henriqueta and Lettie. Since there was no emergency exit to our clubhouse there was nothing for Van to do but to shut up, for Catfish to drop the butt, and for me to look as if I didn't understand English and knew nothing of what was going on. I was confined to my own back yard on Saturdays and Sundays. Sammie's uncle made him punch leather every day after school and watch the shop when he should have been playing with us. Catfish got a beating. Van disappeared.

It was not likely that I would have made as much pilfering at Weinstock's or selling stolen property as I did at my odd jobs. On the other hand, as Van had explained, you could learn to stick up a bank and live the rest of your life a rich man.

Whatever the case, when the raid blasted my chances of a successful gang career, the Lincoln School, 418 L and the *barrio* kept me busy enough, and straight.

Luckily, also, even though my gang was broken up, my friendships were not. Catfish and I continued to explore the waterfront together, bringing home our catch from the river and the pick-ups from the produce markets to show that we had been absent on legitimate business. My gang-busting mother became fond of Sammie, who was invited to supper occasionally and once to spend the night with us, sharing my bathroom bunk. We conversed in pig-Latin, at which he was an expert, and translated questions I asked him into Hebrew in exchange for questions he asked me which I translated into Spanish. What I told him about Mexicans struck him as odd or comical, but no more so than I thought some of the things he told me about Jews. His people, Sammie explained, cut pieces of skin off boy babies, and he showed me. Aghast, I told him Mexicans would never think of doing such a thing, and I showed him. Sammie could have been adopted at 418 L Street by way of our family, but one day his uncle was beaten up. He died, the shop was closed, and I never saw Sammie again.

Going to school did not prevent me from continuing my career as a working member of the family, which I had started as apprentice to La Pozolera. Whatever the surprising differences between Mazatlán and the *barrio* in Sacramento, in one thing they were powerfully the same—*trabajo*. If you didn't have it you spent the days looking for it. If you had it, you worried about how long it would last. You didn't spoil your chances of being hired by asking questions about wages or food or paydays. The thing to avoid was to pass the winter in the barrio without money, *de oquis*—without a job. New *chicanos* kept coming. They tramped the muddy alleys and the streets gathering in small groups on the sidewalks of skid row when it was sunny, inside the pool halls when it was hot. All this they found out, and other important things: that if you got to know a labor contractor well he would lend you money to carry you over the winter; that once you became a regular customer of the pawnbroker you could hock tools, musical instruments and even clothes; that there were Mexican families who would feed you on credit until spring; that in cold weather several men could sleep in a small room without heat.

Taking stock of the situation the family was already minus my mother's wages as a seamstress. The letters to the neighbor who had kept the Ajax for us in Mazatlán were never answered, and we at last realized we had lost it. Besides, nobody in the *barrio* had money to pay for sewing. Our apartment at 418 L became more of a base than a home for Gustavo and José. When they could they worked on the riverfront, in the railroad shops, the canneries, lumber yards, pipe plants, stables, and nearby rice mills. When they couldn't, they rolled their clothes and blankets into bindles, hobo style, and walked the railway tracks to Woodland, Roseville, Stockton, Marysville, or Folsom for fruit picking, building construction, wood chopping, or sand hogging. When river traffic was at the peak in the summer and fall, they loaded grain on the barges or shipped as deckhands on the sternwheelers that paddled between Colusa and San Francisco Bay. And one winter they walked to Truckee for a week's wages at a lumber mill.

We still called it *hacerle la lucha*, the daily match with the job givers, lay-offs, the rent, groceries, and the seasons. I was never told, and I never asked, about getting into the *lucha*. I simply asked permission to do the *trabajos* that I found, one by one, in the *burrio*.

Matti, my Italian buddy, coached me into selling the *Sacramento Union* on Sixth and K, where he made room on one corner for me. He showed me how to manage the small change. The rest I learned watching and listening to him yell the headlines and rush his customers. By school time I was through, had reported home, counted out my cash on the kitchen table, turned it over to my mother, and had breakfast. It was Matti also who pointed out that I could keep a copy of the *Union* to take home, the first regular newspaper we had in the house. At night I picked out words from the headlines and read them to whoever would listen. It was I who brought the headlines home that said an Austrian duke had been assassinated and that there was a war.

Lincoln School and the *barrio* cooperated to help me get further into *la lucha*. I never had any homework. I took my books home to show off but never to prepare lessons. This meant that Miss Campbell or Miss Delahunty or Mrs. Wood did not interfere with my free working time after school or on Saturdays.

I worked up a small income as a part-time bellhop and house boy in the rooming house. Nobody at 418 L could scamper up and down the three stories or relay a laundry package to the alley and back, as fast as I, or beat rugs with a stick on the laundry wire and hang blankets out to air. I wasn't paid in tips, but on Saturdays people flipped a nickel or a dime at me, and on holidays as much as a quarter. For me there was a smooth flow between these money-making employments and my tasks in our apartment—making my bed, sweeping the back yard, and checking the rat traps under the floor.

My services as a valet to the Old Gentleman next door brought ten cents a week, for nothing more than a fast hand when he dressed and undressed. After I noticed Big Singh cooking some round cakes on a grill in his kitchen, he offered me one through the window, saying "Ruti, ruti." I climbed the fence to the window, took the cake, examined it and said, "No, tortilla." Big Singh roared, asked me to come in and offered me a part-time job helping him with the baking. I checked with my mother, she checked with Mrs. Dodson, and permission was granted. I flipped the ruti on the griddle with my fingernails in a way that astounded the Sikh giant. On Saturdays I cooked ruti for him which the boarders ate by the basket, not unlike Mexicans ate tortillas.

After the Saturday morning chores and errands at the house I had almost the whole of Saturday to myself. With Matti, Catfish, and Russell as my instructors and guides, the entire *barrio* became my bonanza. With a gunnysack over my shoulder I collected empty beer bottles, tinfoil, discarded rags, bits of copper wire the linemen dropped around telephone poles, and pieces of scrap iron.

This was how I met the Negro lady who lived in the shanty on the alley behind our house. She was jet black, bigger sidewise than up and down, with eyes as bright as agates. Her back yard was noisy with laughter and loud talk, especially on Saturday nights, and the police sometimes came and took her away for a few days. One morning I asked for some empty beer bottles I spotted in the corner of her yard just inside the picket fence. I had to explain to her where I lived, why I wanted the bottles, and who my folks were. We turned out to be such close neighbors that she offered to pile all her empties in a box by the gate. The only condition was that I was not to come into the yard, but to call her. As long as she was allowed to live in the alley, I collected enough empties from her to give me a good start on my Saturday rounds. Next to her bottles I liked her musical, hooting laugh that seemed to explode merrily out of her whole body.

The alleys, I discovered, were the poorer part of my claim. The best payoff was along the riverfront, the railway tracks, the wharfs, the produce markets, and the warehouses. Sacks and crates were moved about on handtrucks over iron sheets placed between the freight cars and the loading platforms. When a sack ripped or a crate broke, potatoes, onions, beets and apples rolled about. The stevedores kicked them aside so they would spill to the ground, where I salvaged them. On the wharves where the company guards were friendly, we were allowed to scrounge in the unloaded box cars for specialties like cracked watermelons or bouquets of carrots. On a good Saturday, combing the waterfront all day, I could supply the family with all our needs of potatoes or onions for the week.

José taught me to fish, and I carried a line in my pants pocket on my rounds. If the pickings were light on the wharves I climbed down the bank of the river between the warehouses and threw my line close to where the cooks on the stern-wheelers threw the garbage into the water. Waiting for a bite, I sat on the rocks, listening to the lap of the river against the barges and the piles, and to the rumble of the handtrucks the stevedores pushed back and forth on the plank floors high above me. It was cool under the wharves. Through the tall black piles I could see framed pictures of tugboats straining their hawsers towing barges piled high with sacks of grain; the *Fort Sutter* or the *Capital City*, the floating palaces that sailed every night for San Francisco from their moorings at the M Street bridge; the struts and girders of the bridge above the muddy brown sweep of the Sacramento; and the wooded shore of Yolo beyond. There was a mile or so of riverfront like this, and I possessed it all.

Haciendole la lucha in my own way I found out how jobs are lost, and sometimes friends along with the jobs. One day the black lady was taken off by the police and never came back. Big Singh, during a Saturday carousal, threw one of his drunken guests over the railing of his porch to the sidewalk. My mother and Mrs. Dodson decided to end my employment as kitchen assistant, because of the danger of my being trapped under a falling Sikh.

Not long after that the Old Gentlemen left us. Late one afternoon he was sitting on the stuffed chair on our front porch, the walker by his side. I was sitting on the floor dangling my legs and watching people pass along the sidewalk, flickering between the pickets of the fence as they walked by. The Old Gentleman asked me to get him a drink of water. I got up and went down the dark corridor to our kitchen. When I came back the Old Gentleman was still sitting, his head lowered, his right hand in his lap. There was a small pistol on the floor. No one would tell me what happened to him, except that he would not come back to 418 L.

It was during these disturbing days that José got me a pass on the *Dover,* the stern-wheeler on which he was working as a deckhand. I sailed the Sacramento for the first time, working off my pass as an assistant mess boy. My principal job was to keep the big enameled tin cups filled with tea or coffee for the crew and to help clean up after the meal. I squeezed myself and my pots between the steel shoulders and sheet-iron backs of the black and brown men who were my shipmates. I passed their tin plates for seconds and thirds of meat and potatoes, and took some of their dirty jokes in stride. "Hey, Ernie, you got a woman down in Frisco?"

"No, sir, I never been to Frisco," I said, which wasn't quite true, but the crew put me down as a cool character, and polite besides.

It was a memorable trip. After supper one of the blacks, José, and a gringo and I played twenty-one on the fantail of the steamer, where the breeze threw the spray from the wheel paddles in our faces. I slept below decks next to the engine room in the bunk above José's, close under the deck above, scared by the chunking of the boiler and the pistons a few feet away. The second night I made my bed atop a pile of sacks on the cargo deck, from which I watched the blue and white navigation lights of the passing ships and the glow of cities on the rim of Suisuin Bay. Directly ahead of my perch was the forward mast and the low prow of the *Dover* over which I stared at the immense sheet of black water. Here the noise of the machinery was a soothing rumble. The boat glided and quivered through the night, and I listened to the halyard slap the mast and the water swish against the hull.

It was while we were tied up on the San Francisco waterfront that I became tangled in the First World War.

José was picked up by immigration police because he was not carrying his registration card. Carefully instructed by him, I ran to the Ferry Building to send a telegram home asking that the document be mailed at once.

Telegram writing was new to me. At the Western Union office I watched and learned the approach. On a pad of yellow sheets I wrote a long composition in Spanish, in the style I was used to from the family letters, addressed to my dear mother, and complete with greetings and salutations. I signed it "your son."

Western Union and I immediately had a misunderstanding. The clerk said my Spanish script was hard to read. Could I write it in English, and make it shorter? I explained that my mother could not read English. Was there anyone at 418 L who could read English? I said, yes, Mrs. Dodson. Would my mother understand her? I knew that by means of signs, gestures, and short words she could. The long letter was boiled down to telegram style, but there was one more problem, the signature. Since the message was going to Mrs. Dodson, I said write "Little Ernie." The clerk asked me if that was my real name to which I responded that it was Ernesto but that at 418 there was also a big Ernie. The clerk refused to destroy my Mexican cultural image, returned the sheet and told me to sign Ernesto and after it my address in San Francisco, the *Dover*. I handed him the dollar bill José had given me, picked up the change, and ran back to report. The papers came and we steamed back to Sacramento. Until I explained how it all happened, Mrs. Dodson and my mother were amazed at my English telegram. It was kept to show around the rooming house and to family friends. I copied it to make it, in fact, my own telegram.

At about this time my mother remarried. We made room for my stepfather, a *chicano* who had come to California not too long after us. His problems with the Americans were the same as ours, especially their language.

To begin with, we didn't hear one but many sorts of English. Mr. Chester, my soldier friend, and Big Ernie spoke as if they were tired and always arguing. The Old Gentleman nibbled his words, like a rabbit working on a carrot, perhaps because all his teeth weren't there. Mr. Brien's words came through in a deep voice from behind the hair screen of his moustache. Big Singh spoke English in his own way, brittle and choppy, hard to understand unless you watched his lips. These people sounded nothing like the Sicilian vegetable hawker or the Greek grocer at the corner or the black lady in the alley who saved beer bottles for me. And of course none of them sounded like Miss Hopley or Miss Campbell.

It took time to realize that when the Americans said "Sackmenna" they meant Sacra-men-to, or that

"Kellyphony" was their way of saying Cali-for-nia. Worse yet, the names of many of their towns could not be managed. I tried to teach Gustavo that Woodland was not pronounced "Boor-lan," and that Walnut Grove was not "Gualen-gro." A secondhand shop on our block that called itself The Cheap Store sounded to us like the Sheep Store, and the sign did not spell it like the school books.

There was no authority at 418 L who could tell us the one proper way to pronounce a word and it would not have done much good if there had been. Try as they did the adults in my family could see no difference between "wood" and "boor." Words spelled the same way or nearly so in Spanish and English and whose meanings we could guess accurately—words like *principal* and *tomato*—were too few to help us in daily usage. The grown-ups adapted the most necessary words and managed to make themselves understood, words like the *French loff, yelly-rol, eppel pai, tee-kett,* and *kenn meelk.* Miss Campbell and her colleagues lost no time in scrubbing out these spots in my own pronunciation. Partly to show off, partly to do my duty to the family, I tried their methods at home. It was hopeless. They listened hard but they couldn't hear me. Besides, *Boor-lan* was *Boor-lan* all over the *barrio.* Everyone knew what you meant even though you didn't say Woodland. I gave up giving English lessons at home.

The *barrio* invented its own versions of American talk. And my family, to my disgust, adopted them with no little delight. My mother could tell someone at the door asking for an absent one: "Ess gon." When some American tried to rush her into conversation she stopped him with: "Yo no pick een-glees." But at *pocho* talk my mother drew the line, although José and Gustavo fell into it easily. Such words as *yarda* for yard, *yonque* for junk, *donas* for doughnuts, *grocería* for grocery store, *raite* for ride, and *borde* for meals shocked her and I was drilled to avoid them. Woolworth's was *el fei-en-ten* to the *barrio* but it was *el baratillo* to her and by command to me also. Gustavo could say *droguería* because there wasn't anything she could do about it, but for me *botica* was required.

Prowling the alleys and gleaning along the waterfront I learned how *chicano* workingmen hammered the English language to their ways. On the docks I heard them bark over a slip or a spill: "Oh, Chet," imitating the American crew bosses with the familiar "Gar-demme-yoo." José and I privately compared notes in the matter of "San Afabeechee," who, he said, was a saint of the Americans but which, as I well knew, was what Americans called each other in a fist fight.

Our family conversations always occurred on our own kitchen porch, away from the gringos. One or the other of the adults would begin: *Se han fijado?* Had we noticed—that the Americans do not ask permission to leave the room; that they had no respectful way of addressing an elderly person; that they spit brown over the railing of the porch into the yard; that when they laughed they roared; that they never brought *saludos* to everyone in your family from everyone in their family when they visited; that *General Delibree* was only a clerk; that *zopilotes* were not allowed on the streets to collect garbage; that the policemen did not carry lanterns at night; that Americans didn't keep their feet on the floor when they were sitting; that there was a special automobile for going to jail; that a rancho was not a rancho at all but a very small hacienda; that the saloons served their customers free eggs, pickles, and sandwiches; that instead of bullfighting, the gringos for sport tried to kill each other with gloves?

I did not have nearly the strong feelings on these matters that Doña Henriqueta expressed. I felt a vague admiration for the way Mr. Brien could spit brown. Wayne, my classmate, laughed much better than the Mexicans, because he opened his big mouth wide and brayed like a donkey so he could be heard a block away. But it was the kind of laughter that made my mother tremble, and it was not permitted in our house.

Rules were laid down to keep me, as far as possible, *un muchacho bien educado*. If I had to spit I was to do it privately, or if in public, by the curb, with my head down and my back to people. I was never to wear my cap in the house and I was to take it off even on the porch if ladies or elderly gentlemen were sitting. If I wanted to scratch, under no circumstances was I to do it right then and there, in company, like the Americans, but I was to excuse myself. If Catfish or Russell yelled to me from across the street I was not to shout back. I was never to ask for tips for my errands or other services to the tenants of 418 L, for these were *atenciones* expected of me.

Above all I was never to fail in *respeto* to grownups, no matter who they were. It was an inflexible rule; I addressed myself to *Señor* Big Singh, *Señor* Big Ernie, *Señora* Dodson, *Señor* Cho-ree Lopez.

My standing in the family, but especially with my mother depended on my keeping these rules. I was not punished for breaking them. She simply reminded me that it gave her acute *vergüenza* to see me act thus, and that I would never grow up to be a correct *jefe de familia* if I did not know how to be a correct boy. I knew what *vergüenza* was from feeling it time and again; and the notion of growing up to keep a tight rein over a family of my own was somehow satisfying.

In our musty apartment in the basement of 418 L, ours remained a Mexican family. I never lost the sense that we were the same, from Jalco to Sacramento. There was the polished cedar box, taken out now and then from the closet to display our heirlooms. I had lost the rifle shells of the revolution, and Tio Tonche, too, was gone. But there was the butterfly sarape, the one I had worn through the Battle of Puebla; a black lace mantilla Doña Henriqueta modeled for us; bits of embroidery and lace she had made; the tin pictures of my grandparents; my report card signed by Señorita Bustamante and Don Salvador; letters from Aunt Esther; and the card with the address of the lady who had kept the Ajax for us. When our mementos were laid out on the bed I plunged my head into the empty box and took deep breaths of the aroma of *puro cedro*, pure Jalcocotán mixed with camphor.

We could have hung on the door of our apartment a sign like those we read in some store windows—*Aquí se habla español*. We not only spoke Spanish, we read it. From the *Librería Española*, two blocks up the street, Gustavo and I bought novels for my mother, like *Genoveva de Brabante*, a paperback with the poems of Amado Nervo and a handbook of the history of Mexico. The novels were never read aloud, the poems and the handbook were. Nervo was the famous poet from Tepic, close enough to Jalcocotán to make him our own. And in the history book I learned to read for myself, after many repetitions by my mother, about the deeds of the great Mexicans Don Salvador had recited so vividly to the class in Mazatlán. She refused to decide for me whether Abraham Lincoln was as great as Benito Juarez, or George Washington braver than the priest Don Miguel Hidalgo. At school there was no opportunity to settle these questions because nobody seemed to know about Juarez or Hidalgo; at least they were never mentioned and there were no pictures of them on the walls.

The family talk I listened to with the greatest interest was about Jalco. Wherever the conversation began it always turned to the pueblo, our neighbors, anecdotes that were funny or sad, the folk tales and the witchcraft, and our kinfolk, who were still there. I usually lay on the floor those winter evenings, with my feet toward the kerosene heater, watching on the ceiling the flickering patterns of the light filtered through the scrollwork of the chimney. As I listened once again I chased the *zopilote* away from Coronel, or watched José take Nerón into the forest in a sack. Certain things became clear about the *rurales* and why the young men were taken away to kill Yaqui Indians, and about the Germans, the Englishmen, the Frenchmen, the Spaniards, and the Americans who owned the haciendas, the railroads, the ships, the big stores, the breweries. They owned Mexico because President Porfirio Díaz had let them steal it, José explained as I listened. Now Don Francisco Madero had been assassinated for trying to get it back. On such threads of family talk I followed my own recollection of the years from Jalco—the attack on Mazatlán, the captain of Acaponeta, the camp at El Nanchi and the arrival at Nogales on the flatcar.

Only when we ventured uptown did we feel like aliens in a foreign land. Within the *barrio* we heard Spanish on the streets and in the alleys. On the railroad tracks, in the canneries, and along the riverfront there were more Mexicans than any other nationality. And except for the foremen, the work talk was in our language. In the secondhand shops, where the *barrio* people sold and bought furniture and clothing, there were Mexican clerks who knew the Mexican ways of making a sale. Families doubled up in decaying houses, cramping themselves so they could rent an extra room to *chicano* boarders, who accented the brown quality of our Mexican *colonia*.

It was at the family parties that the world of the Americans was completely shut off. Usually they were arranged by families from the same part of Mexico who considered themselves *paisanos*. The host family prepared the tamales or the enchiladas and everyone brought something for the feast. But these occasions were mainly for talking and not for eating. They were long parties, from late afternoon to midnight, the men in the front room, the mothers in the kitchen, the young women serving and whispering in the hall, the boys playing on the porch and the babies put to bed all over the house.

When the case of beer arrived the singing began. A guitar came down from a peg on the wall and those who could sing took turns with the ballads and the country love songs, the girls crowding the door to listen, the boys at the windows. As the singers warmed up there were duets and the fighting songs of the revolution, like "La Valentina" and "Adelita."

When the party was at the Duran's, a family from Sonora, the singing drifted into talk of the revolution. Duran had been a miner in Cananea, had taken part in the great strike there that was put down by gringo soldiers, and knew the Flores Magan brothers, who had stirred the miners to revolt. Duran's face was a burnt brown, the dark shade of an olive skin turned nearly charcoal by the sun. He had a slightly hawked nose and powerful black eyes. His talk turned into a passionate lecture on the sufferings of the Mexican people, with detailed accounts of great events, like the massacre of the mill workers of Rio Blanco. Duran had been crippled in an accident and he limped slightly, something about him suggesting a crippled man even when he fidgeted in his chair denouncing Porfirio Díaz and the rich despots who owned the country.

It was Duran, also, who brought us up to date on the revolution at our doors, for that was how he explained the Industrial Workers of the World, who were holding meetings on sandlots and in out-of-the way spots along the river. He snorted now and then as he talked, to clear his throat, and to bear down on his contempt for the capitalists who were breaking up meetings of the I.W.W. and sending them to jail. The circle of brown faces in the room caught some of the glow in Duran's face, and after we said good-bye and walked home across town I kept thinking of him.

We invited friends for New Year's supper, preparing for which I spent the day running to the store and in the kitchen grinding corn in the coffee mill, hammering cones of brown sugar into powder, and pounding herbs in the pestle. Somehow we crowded our guests into the living room where my mother served *atole* and the tissue-thin *buñuelos* dunked in syrup. We had no guitar so José, on his new mouth organ named *La Filarmónica*, provided the music.

In the family parties, the funerals, the baptisms, the weddings and the birthdays, our private lives continued to be Mexican. And there was a public affair that once a year brought the *colonia* together, the celebration of the Sixteenth of September.

The year José was chosen a member of the committee to arrange the program for the Sixteenth, I was drafted to assist as interpreter in obtaining from the American authorities permits of one kind or another. As José's aide-de-camp I also helped decorate the hall with streamers of green, white, and red crepe paper and the colored portrait of Don Miguel Hidalgo hung under a large Mexican flag.

The program went along smoothly. The hall was crowded, family style with whole clans in attendance from babies to grandparents. There was a short speech by the president of the Comisión Honorífica; the crowning of the queen, elected with votes paid for by her admirers; the singing of the national anthem; a poetic reading; and one hour before midnight *El Grito*, the call to arms in remembrance of the cry of the Illustrious Father of the Nation, the rebel Catholic priest, Don Miguel Hidalgo y Costilla.

For those between fifteen and thirty the real business of the Sixteenth was the dance. After *El Grito*, the floor was cleared, the mothers and elders sitting on chairs and benches along the walls, a stolid line of chaperones, the girls in a double row in front of them. Across from them the young men stood, like runners at the starting line of a hundred-yard dash. On the first downbeat of the band leader, they rushed across the floor, each man headed for his favorite girl who, according to the rules, accepted her partner on a first come first served basis.

During the early rounds of the dancing the rushes created no problems. I watched them from a back corner of the bandstand, my duty post as assistant to the floor manager. There were intermissions for soft drinks and beer.

But it wasn't the coca-cola or the brew that gradually enlivened the festival. It was the trips to the men's toilet for short nips from flasks of tequila and other fiery stuff.

By one o'clock in the morning a good deal of tequila had been consumed. Everybody knew, of course, that a Mexican's honor became more sensitive the more nips he had. In the presence of the choicest girls of the *colonia*, there are some things a man cannot tolerate. And in one of the rushes one of these things happened. Two young men collided within reach of the girl they both wanted for the dance. Like perfect gentlemen they picked themselves up from the floor paying no heed to the giggles of the girls and the owlish grins of the old folks. I saw them rush out of the ballroom, my uncle at their heels. When I caught up with him in the toilet it was too late. The two bantams were in a corner, squared off and slugging it out, my uncle taking cuffs from both as he tried to separate them.

Instantly, word of the fight reached the dance floor and the men rushed to see it, first as spectators and then as partisans of the fighters. With Mexican honor now running hot through their veins, they insulted one another until the free-for-all began in earnest. I watched the *chicanos* pair off, pushing each other against the walls and swinging wildly. Two of them were on the floor kicking and rolling, half hidden under the swinging door of a toilet. A beer bottle crashed through a window.

José slugged his way through the melee to my corner, yanked me by the arm, and we headed for the ballroom. A policeman was already at the door of the toilet looking in bewilderment for a way to take hold of a roomful of rioting Mexicans.

The ballroom was emptying fast. Mothers were herding their daughters through the hall and out into the street. The elders gathered on the sidewalk waiting to group their families and hasten away. My uncle ordered the band to play on, "to restore the calm," as he said. But it was the police and not the music that restored the calm. Someone with more experience than José had yelled in the hall, "La Julia," and before the paddy wagon appeared in the street and a pair of cops walked in, the hall was deserted, except for ourselves and the musicians.

It was nearly dawn before we finished taking down the decorations, mopping up the spilled beer, scrubbing the blood on the toilet floor, sweeping up broken glass, and heaping the cigarette butts in a pail. The colored portrait of Don Miguel was the last thing we took down.

With the intense, dark face of Duran, the celebrations of the Sixteenth and the *Cinco de Mayo*, the family get-togethers, the evening conversations at 418 L, the readings in *Cacaseno* and *Amado Nervo* and *Genoveva*, it was not easy for the Mexican images in my mind to bleach away. But over them new experiences were being laid, pleasant or interesting things the Americans did.

The collection of blue plates, bowls, and cups which came free with the Carnation cereal grew on the kitchen shelf and with it my mother's pride. We also began to collect wrappers of Octagon soap, which we exchanged for merchandise. Gustavo opened an account with the Eastern Outfitting Store, where they spoke Spanish and gave you an extra pair of pants with a new suit for a down payment of a few dollars. Mrs. Dodson introduced us to Mr. Fox, the teller of the bank, with whom thereafter I had many dealings, interpreting for my uncle and sometimes making deposits myself. Above the black marble counter of his cage, I could see nothing of Mr. Fox except his round beaming face, and his slicked-back hair. In a small book he wrote numbers for the money we passed over to him, and one day he gave me, free, a metal box with a black leather cover, a coin slot and a lock, which only Mr. Fox could open when I deposited our savings. We couldn't break it, as we did the clay pig.

We learned about hotcakes for Sunday breakfast from Mrs. Dodson, who served them floating in Karo, cheaper than honey and sweeter than *panocha*. It was she also who made me a fan of the Katzenjammer Kids and Mutt and Jeff, which she read aloud in the *Sacramento Bee* every evening and which I then hurried downstairs to translate for the family, even though the jokes did not seem funny in Spanish. At home I tried Spanish versions of *The Perils of Pauline* and *The Broken Coin*, the horror serials I saw on Saturdays in motion pictures, as one of a howling audience of children of all ages and races from the *barrio*. And it was I who drew the whole family under the spell of Charlie Chaplin's film stories which made my mother weep and José roll in the seat with belly pains of laughter. El *Chapooleen*, as José called him, came through to us from the screen, sad or hilarious, without words.

In the *barrio*, music seemed to be everywhere: the records I heard on Mrs. Dodson's victrola; the Sunday concerts of the German brass band; Pork Chops, the black minstrel who played his twelve-stringed guitar on our sidewalk, humping gently and shuffling as he sang; Frisco at his delirious piano; Miss Florence, pealing out her "Sympathy"; the Slavs, blowing wild melodies through the stops of an accordion that could be heard all over the block.

And there was the Salvation Army. They marched down from their headquarters on Sixth and L to Third Street or Second or some other corner where the lower part of town was lowest. In a half circle off the curb they blew their trumpets, pumped their organ, jiggled their tambourines and sang joyously and loudly about Jesus. The pretty girl in the blue dress and the red stripes passed the tambourine for the collection, and contributions were also received on the bass drum, which for the purpose was laid flat on the street.

It all led to the purchase of a violin for me so that I, too, could make and not just hear music. We bought it for five dollars at a pawnshop on Fifth Street, and José arranged with a fiddler who played in a saloon to give me two lessons a month for fifty cents.

Something remarkable came out of my becoming a violinist. The schools of the city were being requested to recommend candidates for the Sacramento Boys Band, then being organized. The band needed a piccolo player and Miss Hopley sent my name up as musically and physically equipped for the part.

I was accepted into the band, and in that way became the possessor of a short black tube made of hard wood, with holes covered by padded keys operated by tiny brass levers. When I blew on it shrieks came out of the far end. The bandmaster gave me a handbook for the piccolo from which I gradually learned to make my wooden tube trill and pipe above the rest of the band. We toured Davis, Woodland, Lodi, Galt, Marysville, and other towns near Sacramento, dedicating a new milk plant, serenading an important citizen on his birthday, rousing the citizens at rallies, and preparing ourselves to become boy's band champions of the State of California. In one of these contests at the State Fair I conducted the warming up march on a platform in front of the grandstand under a broiling sun. Taking the baton from the master with a bow, I swept the band into "Invercargill," which crashed into the finale several bars ahead of me. Sweating miserably I bowed to the thunder of applause from the grandstand, and sat down. My family were somewhere in the audience.

The Y.M.C.A., with the band, opened to me the rest of the wide world around Sacramento. On one side of the new brick building on 5th and J there were posters with boys popping into a swimming pool like frogs and playing ping-pong and handball. There was a conference at 418 L in which my mother, Gustavo, and José, Mrs. Dodson, and Mr. Howard took part. The conclusion was that the "Y" was a good thing, that we had the money, and that I could join. For a dollar I drew my membership pass to the games, the gym class, swimming lessons, and many hours of talk with Chief Wilson, the boy's secretary. In due time he obtained for me a five dollar scholarship for two weeks at summer camp in the

Sierras. As a part-time worker I helped clear the camp sites deep in the pine forest and worked my shift in the icy water of a mountain stream raising the dam for our swimming hole.

These experiences and new friendships about which my family knew so little and guessed a great deal became the other side of my double life. Gustavo and José were away much of the time but when they were home my education at their hands went on. Gustavo told me endless jokes, like the one about the green *chicano*, fresh from a village like Jalco, who tried to put out the electric light by puffing on it. José sorted out odds and ends of metal, wire, wood, and discards of all sorts, which we kept in a kind of you-never-can-tell box in the back yard. With a pocket knife, a pair of pliers, and a screwdriver we repaired furniture, shoes, clotheslines, iceboxes, and anything else around the house that needed maintenance. We collected useful things the Americans threw away, mechanical gadgets that showed how ingenious they were, and how wasteful, like a discarded alarm clock which we repaired and set up on the kitchen shelf. Watching my uncles test the edge of a sharpened tool, splice a rope, straighten out a nail, whittle a bottle stopper, or shape a leather sole I was apprenticed to craftsmen who invented as they worked.

Part Five

ON THE EDGE OF THE BARRIO

TO MAKE ROOM for a growing family it was decided that we should move, and a house was found in Oak Park, on the far side of town where the open country began. The men raised the first installment for the bungalow on Seventh Avenue even after Mrs. Dodson explained that if we did not keep up the monthly payments we would lose the deposit as well as the house.

The real estate broker brought the sale contract to the apartment one evening. Myself included, we sat around the table in the living room, the gringo explaining at great length the small print of the document in a torrent of words none of us could make out. Now and then he would pause and throw in the only word he knew in Spanish: "Sabee?" The men nodded slightly as if they had understood. Doña Henriqueta was holding firmly to the purse which contained the down payment, watching the broker's face, not listening to his words. She had only one question. Turning to me she said: "Ask him how long it will take to pay all of it." I translated, shocked by the answer: "Twenty years." There was a long pause around the table, broken by my stepfather: "What do you say?"

Around the table the heads nodded agreement. The broker passed his fountain pen to him. He signed the contract and after him Gustavo and José. Doña Henriqueta opened the purse and counted out the greenbacks. The broker pocketed the money, gave us a copy of the document, and left.

The last thing I did when we moved out of 418 L was to dig a hole in the corner of the backyard for a tall carton of Quaker Oats cereal, full to the brim with the marbles I had won playing for keeps around the *barrio*. I tamped the earth over my buried treasure and laid a curse on whoever removed it without my permission.

Our new bungalow had five rooms, and porches front and back. In the way of furniture, what friends did not lend or Mrs. Dodson gave us we bought in the secondhand shops. The only new item was an elegant gas range, with a high oven and long, slender legs finished in enamel. Like the house, we would be paying for it in installments.

It was a sunny, airy spot, with a family orchard to one side and a vacant lot on the other. Back of us there was a pasture. With chicken wire we fenced the back yard, turned over the soil, and planted our first vegetable garden and fruit trees. José and I built a palatial rabbit hutch of laths and two-by-fours he gathered day by day on the waterfront. A single row of geraniums and carnations separated the vegetable garden from the house. From the vacant lots and pastures around us my mother gathered herbs and weeds which she dried and boiled the way she had in the pueblo. A thick green fluid she distilled from the mallow that grew wild around us was bottled and used as a hair lotion. On every side our windows looked out on family orchards, platinum stretches of wild oats and quiet lanes, shady and unpaved.

We could not have moved to a neighborhood less like the *barrio*. All the families around us were Americans. The grumpy retired farmer next door viewed us with alarm and never gave us the time of day, but the Harrisons across the street were cordial. Mr. Harrison loaned us his tools, and Roy, just my age but twice my weight, teamed up with me at once for an exchange of visits to his mother's kitchen and ours. I astounded him with my Mexican rice, and Mrs. Harrison baked my first waffle. Roy and I also found a common bond in the matter of sisters. He had an older one and by now I had two younger ones. It was a question between us whether they were worse as little nuisances or as big bosses. The answer didn't make much difference but it was a relief to have another man to talk with.

Some Sundays we walked to Joyland, an amusement park where my mother sat on a bench to watch the children play on the lawn and I begged as many rides as I could on the roller coaster, which we called in elegant Spanish "the Russian Mountain." José liked best the free vaudeville because of the chorus girls who danced out from the stage on a platform and kicked their heels over his head.

Since Roy had a bicycle and could get away from his sister by pedaling off on long journeys I persuaded my family to match my savings for a used one. Together we pushed beyond the boundaries of Oak Park miles out, nearly to Perkins and the Slough House. It was open country, where we could lean our wheels against a fence post and walk endlessly through carpets of golden poppies and blue lupin. With a bike I was able to sign on as a carrier of the *Sacramento Bee*, learning in due course the art of slapping folded newspapers against people's porches instead of into the bushes or on their roofs. Roy and I also became assistants to a neighbor who operated a bakery in his basement, taking our pay partly in dimes and partly in broken cookies for our families.

For the three men of the household as well as for me the bicycle became the most important means for earning a living. Oak Park was miles away from the usual places where they worked and they pedaled off, in good weather and bad, in the early morning. It was a case of saving carfare.

I transferred to the Bret Harte School, a gingerbread two-story building in which there was a notable absence of Japanese, Filipinos, Koreans, Italians, and the other nationalities of the Lincoln School. It was at Bret Harte that I learned how an English sentence could be cut up on the blackboard and the pieces placed on different lines connected by what the teacher called a diagram. The idea of operating on a sentence and rearranging its members as a skeleton of verbs, modifiers, subject, and prepositions set me off diagraming whatever I read, in Spanish and English. Spiderwebs, my mother called them, when I tried to teach her the art.

My bilingual library had grown with some copies of old magazines from Mexico, a used speller Gustavo had bought for me in Stockton, and the novels my mother discarded when she had read them. Blackstone was still the anchor of my collection and I now had a paperback dictionary called *El Inglés sin Maestro*. By this time there was no problem of translating or interpreting for the family I could not tackle with confidence.

It was Gustavo, in fact, who began to give my books a vague significance. He pointed out to me that with diagrams and dictionaries I could have a choice of becoming a lawyer or a doctor or an engineer or a professor. These, he said, were far better careers than growing up to be a *camello*, as he and José always would be. *Camellos*,

I knew well enough, was what the *chicanos* called them-selves as the workers on every job who did the dirtiest work. And to give our home the professional touch he felt I should be acquiring, he had a telephone installed.

It came to the rest of us as a surprise. The company man arrived one day with our name and address on a card, a metal tool box and a stand-up telephone wound with a cord. It was connected and set on the counter between the dining room and the parlor. There the black marvel sat until we were gathered for dinner that evening. It was clearly explained by Gustavo that the instrument was to provide me with a quick means of reaching the important people I knew at the Y.M.C.A., the boy's band, or the various public offices where I interpreted for *chicanos* in distress. Sooner or later some of our friends in the *barrio* would also have telephones and we could talk with them.

"Call somebody," my mother urged me.

With the whole family watching I tried to think of some important person I could ring for a professional conversation. A name wouldn't come. I felt miserable and hardly like a budding engineer or lawyer or doctor or professor.

Gustavo understood my predicament and let me stew in it a moment. Then he said: "Mrs. Dodson." My pride saved by this ingenious suggestion, I thumbed through the directory, lifted the earpiece from the hook, and calmly asked central for the number. My sisters, one sitting on the floor and the other in my mother's arms, never looked less significant; but they, too, had their turn saying hello to the patient Señora Dodson on the other end of the line.

Every member of the family, in his own way, missed the *barrio*. José and Gustavo could no longer join the talk of the poolrooms and the street corners by walking two blocks down the street. The sign language and simple words my mother had devised to communicate with the Americans at 418 L didn't work with the housewives on 7th Avenue. The families we had known were now too far away to exchange visits. We knew no one in Oak Park who spoke Spanish. Our street was always quiet and often lonely with little to watch from our front porch other than boys riding bicycles or Mrs. Harrison hanging out her wash. Pork Chops and the Salvation Army never played there.

I, too, knew that things were different. There was no corner where I could sell the *Union* and my income from running errands and doing chores around the rooming house stopped. There were no alleys I could comb for beer bottles or docks where I could gather saleable or edible things. The closest to Big Singh I could find was a runty soothsayer in Joyland who sat on a rug with a feather in his turban and told your fortune.

We now had an infant boy in the family who with my two sisters made four of us. The baby was himself no inconvenience to me, but it meant that I had to mind the girls more, mostly chasing them home from the neighbors. If I had been the eldest girl in the family I would have stepped into my mother's place and taken over the management of all but the youngest. But being a boy, the female chores seemed outrageous and un-Mexican. Doña Henriqueta tried telling me that I was now the *jefe de familia* of all the juniors. But she was a gentle mother and the freedom of the house, the yard, and my personal property that she gave the two girls did nothing to make them understand that I was their *jefe*. When Nora, the oldest of the two, demolished my concertina with a hammer (no doubt to see where the notes came from) I asked for permission to strangle her. Permission was denied.

During the first year we lived at Oak Park we began to floor and partition the basement. Some day, we knew, the Lopez's would come through and we would have a temporary home ready for them. With three-and-a-half men in the house earning wages, if work was steady, we were keeping up with the installments and saving for the reunion.

An epidemic erased the quiet life on 7th Avenue and the hopes we had brought with us.

I had been reading to the family stories in the *Bee* of the Spanish influenza. At first it was far off, like the war, in places such as New York and Texas. Then the stories told of people dying in California towns we knew, and finally the *Bee* began reporting the spread of the "flu" in our city.

One Sunday morning we saw Gustavo coming down the street with a suitcase in his hand, walking slowly. I ran out to meet him. By the front gate, he dropped the suitcase, leaned on the fence, and fainted. He had been working as a sandhog on the American River, and had come home weak from fever.

Gustavo was put to bed in one of the front rooms. José set out to look for a doctor, who came the next day, weary and nearly sick himself. He ordered Gustavo to the hospital. Three days later I answered the telephone call from the hospital telling us he was dead. Only José went to Gustavo's funeral. The rest of us, except my step father, were sick in bed with the fever.

In the dining room, near the windows where the sunlight would warm her, my mother lay on a cot, a kerosene stove at her feet. The day Gustavo died she was delirious. José bicycled all over the city, looking for oranges, which the doctor said were the best medicine we could give her. I sweated out the fever, nursed by José, who brought me glasses of steaming lemonade and told me my mother was getting better. The children were quarantined in another room, lightly touched by the fever, more restless than sick.

Late one afternoon José came into my room, wrapped me in blankets, pulled a cap over my ears, and carried me to my mother's bedside. My stepfather was holding a hand mirror to her lips. It didn't fog. She had stopped breathing. In the next room my sister was singing to the other children, "A birdie with a yellow bill/ hopped upon my windowsill/ cocked a shiny eye and said/ Shame on you you sleepy head."

The day we buried Doña Henriqueta, Mrs. Dodson took the oldest sister home with her. The younger children were sent to a neighbor. That night José went to the *barrio*, got drunk, borrowed a pistol, and was arrested for shooting up Second Street.

We did not find out what had happened until I bicycled the next morning to Mrs. Dodson's to report that José had not come home. By this time our friends in the *barrio* knew of José's arrest and a telephone call to a bartender who knew us supplied the details. Nothing serious, Mrs. Dodson repeated to me. Nobody had been hurt. She left me in charge of my sister and went to bail out my uncle.

They returned together. Gently, Mrs. Dodson scolded José, who sat dejectedly, his eyes closed so he would not have to look her in the eye, cracking the joints of his fingers, chewing on his tight lips, a young man compressing years of hard times and the grief of the past days in a show of manhood.

When the lecture was nearly over, Mrs. Dodson was not talking of drunkenness and gunplay, but of the future, mostly of mine, and of José's responsibility for it. She walked with us down the front stairway. Pushing my bicycle I followed him on foot the miles back to Oak

Park, keeping my distance, for I knew he did not want me to see his face. As he had often told me, "Men never cry, no matter what."

A month later I made a bundle of the family keepsakes my stepfather allowed me to have, including the butterfly sarape, my books, and some family pictures. With the bundle tied to the bars of my bicycle, I pedaled to the basement room José had rented for the two of us on O Street near the corner of Fifth, on the edge of the *barrio*.

José was now working the riverboats and, in the slack season, following the round of odd jobs about the city. In our basement room, with a kitchen closet, bathroom, and laundry tub on the back porch and a woodshed for storage, I kept house. We bought two cots, one for me and the other for José when he was home.

Our landlords lived upstairs, a middle-aged brother and sister who worked and rented rooms. As part payment on our rent I kept the yard trim. They were friends of Doña Tránsito, the grandmother of a Mexican family that lived in a weather-beaten cottage on the corner. Doña Tránsito was in her sixties, round as a barrel, and she wore her gray hair in braids and smoked hand-rolled cigarettes on her rickety front porch. To her tiny parlor *chicanos* in trouble came for advice, and the firm old lady with the rasping voice and commanding ways often asked me to interpret or translate for them in their encounters with the *Autoridades*. Since her services were free, so were mine. I soon became a regular visitor and made friends with her son, Kid Felix, a prizefighter who gave free boxing lessons to the boys in the neighborhood.

Living only three houses from Doña Tránsito, saying my *saludos* to her every time I passed the corner, noticing how even the Kid was afraid to break her personal code of *barrio* manners, I lived inside a circle of security when José was away. On her front porch, summer evenings, the old Mexican dame talked about people such as I had known in the pueblo and asked how I was doing in school and where I was working.

It was Doña Tránsito who called in the *curandera* once when the child of a neighbor was dying. I had brought a doctor to the house and was in the sick room when he told the family there was nothing more he could do. Doña Tránsito ordered me at once to fetch the old crone who lived on the other side of the railroad tracks towards the river and who practiced as a healer.

With Doña Tránsito I watched the ritual from a corner of the sick room. The healer laid on a side table an assortment of bundled weeds, small glass jars, candles, and paper bags tied with strings. On the floor next to her she placed a canvas satchel. A bowl and some cups were brought to her from the kitchen. She crumpled stems of herbs into one of the cups and mixed them with oil from one of her jars. She hooked her finger into another jar and pulled out a dab of lard which she worked into a powder in another cup to make a dark paste. Two candles were lighted and placed at the head of the bed. The electric light was turned off. She opened the satchel and took out a framed picture of the Virgin of Guadalupe, which was hung on the wall over the sick child's head. The window blind was pulled down.

The little girl was uncovered. She lay naked, pale, and thin on the sheet, her arms straight down her sides. Around her the healer arranged a border of cactus leaves, which she took out of her satchel one by one, cutting them open around the edge. She warmed the cup with the powdered herbs and rubbed the concoction on the soles of the child's bare feet. With the paste, which she also warmed over the candle, the healer made a cross on the forehead of the patient and another on her chest. A blanket was then laid over her, leaving only the head uncovered.

The healer knelt before the picture of the Virgin and began to pray. The parents of the child, some relatives who were there, Doña Tránsito and I formed a circle around the room, on our knees.

We had been praying a long while when the healer arose and bent over the bed, looking intently at the wasted face. To nobody in particular she said the child was not sweating. She wrapped her black shawl around her head and shoulders, left the room, and closed the street door quietly behind her. In the morning the child died.

Through Doña Tránsito I met other characters of the *barrio*. One of them was Don Crescencio, stooped and bony, who often stopped to chat with my neighbor. He told us stories of how he had found buried treasure with two twigs cut from a weeping willow, and how he could locate an underground spring in the same way, holding the twigs just so, feeling his way on bare feet over the ground, watching until the twigs, by themselves, crossed and dipped. There were the Ortegas, who raised vegetables on a sandlot they had bought by the levee, and explained to Doña Tránsito, who knew a great deal about such matters herself, what vegetables did better when planted according to different shapes of the moon. The Kid gave us lectures and exhibitions explaining jabs and left hooks and how he planned to become the world's Mexican champion. In our basement José gathered his friends to listen to songs of love, revenge, and valor, warmed with beer and tequila.

When troubles made it necessary for the *barrio* people to deal with the Americans uptown, the *Autoridades*, I went with them to the police court, the industrial accident office, the county hospital, the draft board, the county clerk. We got lost together in the rigamarole of functionaries who sat, like *patrones*, behind desks and who demanded licenses, certificates, documents, affidavits, signatures, and witnesses. And we celebrated our successes, as when the worker for whom I interpreted in interviews that lasted many months, was awarded a thousand dollars for a disabled arm. Don Crescencio congratulated me, saying that in Mexico for a thousand American dollars you could buy the lives of many peons.

José had chosen our new home in the basement on O Street because it was close to the Hearkness Junior High School, to which I transferred from Bret Harte. As the *jefe de familia* he explained that I could help earn our living but that I was to study for a high school diploma. That being settled, my routine was clearly divided into schooltime and worktime, the second depending on when I was free from the first.

Few Mexicans of my age from the *barrio* were enrolled at the junior high school when I went there. At least, there were no other Mexican boys or girls in Mr. Everett's class in civics, or Miss Crowley's English composition, or Mrs. Stevenson's Spanish course. Mrs. Stevenson assigned me to read to the class and to recite poems by Amado Nervo, because the poet was from Tepic and I was, too. Miss Crowley accepted my compositions about Jalcocotán and the buried treasure of Acaponeta while the others in the class were writing about Sir Patrick Spence and the Beautiful Lady without Mercy, whom they had never met. For Mr. Everett's class, the last of the day, I clipped pieces from the *Sacramento Bee* about important events in Sacramento. From him I learned to use the ring binder in which I kept clippings to prepare oral reports. Occasionally he kept me after school to talk. He sat on his desk, one leg dangling over a corner, behind him the frame of a large window and the arching elms of the school yard, telling me he thought I could easily make the debating team at the high school next year, that Stanford University might be the place to go after graduation, and making other by-the-way comments that began to shape themselves into my future.

Afternoons, Saturdays, and summers allowed me many hours of worktime I did not need for study. José explained how things now stood. There were two funerals to pay for. More urgently than ever, Doña Esther and her family must be brought to live with us. He would pay the rent and buy the food. My clothes, books, and school expenses would be up to me.

On my vacations, and when he was not on the river-boats, he found me a job as water boy on a track gang. We chopped wood together near Woodland and stacked empty lug boxes in a cannery yard. Cleaning vacant houses and chopping weeds were jobs we could do as a team when better ones were not to be had. As the apprentice, I learned from him how to brace myself for a heavy lift, to lock my knee under a loaded handtruck, to dance rather than lift a ladder, and to find the weakest grain in a log. Like him I spit into my palms to get the feel of the axe handle and grunted as the blade bit into the wood. Imitating him I circled a tree several times, sizing it up, *tanteando*, as he said, before pruning or felling it.

Part of one summer my uncle worked on the river while I hired out as a farmhand on a small ranch south of Sacramento. My senior on the place was Roy, a husky Oklahoman who was a part-time taxi driver and a full-time drinker of hard whiskey. He was heavy-chested, heavy-lipped and jowly, a grumbler rather than a talker and a man of great ingenuity with tools and automobile engines. Under him I learned to drive the Fordson tractor on the place, man the gasoline pump, feed the calves, check an irrigation ditch, make lug boxes for grapes and many other tasks on a small farm. Roy used Bull Durham tobacco which he rolled into the same droopy cigarettes that Doña Eduvijes smoked in Jalco and Doña Tránsito on her front porch.

Roy and I sat under the willow tree in front of the ranch house after work, I on the grass, he on a creaky wicker chair, a hulking, sour man glad for the company of a boy. He counseled me on how to avoid the indulgences he was so fond of, beginning his sentences with a phrase he repeated over and over, "as the feller says." "Don't aim to tell you your business," he explained, "but, as the feller says, get yourself a good woman, don't be no farmhand for a livin', be a lawyer or a doctor, and don't get to drinkin' nohow. And there's another thing, Ernie. If nobody won't listen to you, go on and talk to yourself and hear what a smart man has to say."

And Roy knew how to handle boys, which he showed in an episode that could have cost me my life or my self-confidence. He had taught me to drive the tractor, walking alongside during the lessons as I maneuvered it, shifting gears, stopping and starting, turning and backing, raising a cloud of dust wherever we went. Between drives Roy told me about the different working parts of the machine, giving me instructions on oiling and greasing and filling the radiator. "She needs to be took care of, Ernie," he admonished me, "like a horse. And another thing, she's like to buck. She can turn clear over on you if you let 'er. If she starts to lift from the front even a mite, you turn her off. You hear?"

"Yes, sir," I said, meaning to keep his confidence in me as a good tractor man.

It was a few days after my first solo drive that it happened. I was rounding a telephone pole on the slightly sloping bank of the irrigation ditch. I swung around too fast for one of rear tracks to keep its footing. It spun and the front began to lift. Forgetting Roy's emphatic instructions I gunned the engine, trying to right us to the level ground above the ditch. The tractor's nose kept climbing in front of me. We slipped against the pole, the tractor, bucking, as Roy said it would.

Roy's warning broke through to me in my panic, and I reached up to turn off the ignition. My bronco's engine sputtered out and it settled on the ground with a thump.

I sat for a moment in my sweat. Roy was coming down the ditch in a hurry. He walked up to me and with a quick look saw that neither I nor the tractor was damaged.

"Git off" he said.

I did, feeling that I was about to be demoted, stripped of my rank, bawled out, and fired.

Roy mounted the machine, started it, and worked it off the slope to flat ground. Leaving the engine running, he said: "Git on."

I did.

"Now finish the discing." he said. Above the clatter of the machine, he said: "Like I said, she can buck. If she does, cut 'er. You hear?" And he waved me off to my work.

Except for food and a place to live, with which José provided me, I was on my own. Between farm jobs I worked in town, adding to my experience as well as to my income. As a clerk in a drug store on Second and J, in the heart of the lower part of town, I waited on *chicanos* who spoke no English and who came in search of remedies with no prescription other than a recital of their pains. I dispensed capsules, pills, liniments, and emulsions as instructed by the pharmacist, who glanced at our customers from the back of the shop and diagnosed their ills as I translated them. When I went on my shift, I placed a card in the window that said "Se habla

Español." So far as my *chicano* patients were concerned it might as well have said "Dr. Ernesto Galarza."

From drugs I moved to office supplies and stationery sundries, working as delivery boy for Wahl's, several blocks uptown from skid row. Between deliveries I had no time to idle. I helped the stock clerk, took inventory, polished desks, and hopped when a clerk bawled an order down the basement steps. Mr. Wahl, our boss, a stocky man with a slight paunch, strutted a little as he constantly checked on the smallest details of his establishment, including myself. He was always pleasant and courteous, a man in whose footsteps I might possibly walk into the business world of Sacramento.

But like my uncles, I was looking for a better *chanza*, which I thought I found with Western Union, as a messenger, where I could earn tips as well as wages. Since I knew the lower part of town thoroughly, whenever the telegrams were addressed to that quarter the dispatcher gave them to me. Deliveries to the suites on the second floor of saloons paid especially well, with tips of a quarter from the ladies who worked there. My most generous customer was tall and beautiful Miss Irene, who always asked how I was doing in school. It was she who gave me an English dictionary, the first I ever possessed, a black bound volume with remarkable little scallops on the pages that made it easy to find words. Half smiling, half commanding, Miss Irene said to me more than once : "Don't you stop school without letting me know." I meant to take her advice as earnestly as I took her twenty-five cent tip.

It was in the lower town also that I nearly became a performing artist. My instructor on the violin had stopped giving me lessons after we moved to Oak Park. When we were back on O Street he sent word through José that I could work as second fiddler on Saturday nights in the dancehall where he played with a mariachi. Besides, I could resume my lessons with him. A dollar a night for two hours as a substitute was the best wages I had ever made. Coached by my teacher, I second-fiddled for sporting *chicanos* who swung their ladies on the dance floor and sang to our music. Unfortunately I mentioned my new calling to Miss Crowley when I proposed it to her as a subject for a composition. She kept me after school and persuaded me to give it up, on the ground that I could earn more decorating Christmas cards during the vacation than at the dancehall. She gave me the first order for fifty cards and got subscriptions for me from the other teachers. I spent my Christmas vacation as an illustrator, with enough money saved to quit playing in the saloon.

It was during the summer vacation that school did not interfere with making a living, the time of the year when I went with other *barrio* people to the ranches to look for work. Still too young to shape up with the day-haul gangs, I loitered on skid row, picking up conversation and reading the chalk signs about work that was being offered. For a few days of picking fruit or pulling hops I bicycled to Folsom, Lodi, Woodland, Freeport, Walnut Grove, Marysville, Slough House, Florin, and places that had no name. Looking for work, I pedaled through a countryside blocked off, mile after mile, into orchards, vineyards, and vegetable farms. Along the ditchbanks, where the grass, the morning glory, and the wild oats made a soft mattress I unrolled my bindle and slept.

In the labor camps I shared the summertime of the lives of the *barrio* people. They gathered from barrios of faraway places like Imperial Valley, Los Angeles, Phoenix, and San Antonio. Each family traveling on its own, they came in trucks piled with household goods or packed in their secondhand *fotingos* and *chevees*. The trucks and cars were ancient models, fresh out of a used-car lot, with license tags of many states. It was into these jalopies that much of the care and a good part of the family's earnings went. In camp they were constantly being fixed, so close to scrap that when we needed a part for repairs, we first went to the nearest junkyard.

It was a world different in so many ways from the lower part of Sacramento and the residences surrounded by trim lawns and cool canopies of elms to which I had delivered packages for Wahl's. Our main street was usually an irrigation ditch, the water supply for cooking, drinking, laundering, and bathing. In the better camps there was a faucet or a hydrant, from which water was carried in buckets, pails and washtubs. If the camp belonged to a contractor, and it was used from year to year, there were permanent buildings—a shack for his office, the privies, weatherworn and sagging, and a few cabins made of secondhand lumber, patched and unpainted.

If the farmer provided housing himself, it was in tents pitched on the bare baked earth or on the rough ground of newly plowed land on the edge of a field. Those who arrived late for the work season camped under trees or raised lean-to's along a creek, roofing their trucks with canvas to make bedrooms. Such camps were always well away from the house of the ranchero, screened from the main road by an orchard or a grove of eucalyptus. I helped to pitch and take down such camps, on some spot that seemed lonely when we arrived, desolate when we left.

If they could help it, the workers with families avoided the more permanent camps, where the seasonal hired hands from skid row were more likely to be found. I lived a few days in such a camp and found out why families avoided them. On Saturday nights when the crews had a week's wages in their pockets, strangers appeared, men and women, carrying suitcases with liquor and other contraband. The police were called by the contractor only when the carousing threatened to break into fighting. Otherwise, the weekly bouts were a part of the regular business of the camp.

Like all the others, I often went to work without knowing how much I was going to be paid. I was never hired by a rancher, but by a contractor or a straw boss who picked up crews in town and handled the payroll. The important questions that were in my mind—the wages per hour or per lug box, whether the beds would have mattresses and blankets, the price of meals, how often we would be paid—were never discussed, much less answered, beforehand. Once we were in camp, owing the employer for the ride to the job, having no means to get back to town except by walking and no money for the next meal, arguments over working conditions were settled in favor of the boss. I learned firsthand the chiseling techniques of the contractors and their pushers—how they knocked off two or three lugs of grapes from the daily record for each member of the crew, or the way they had of turning the face of the scales away from you when you weighed your work in.

There was never any doubt about the contractor and his power over us. He could fire a man and his family on the spot and make them wait days for their wages. A man could be forced to quit by assigning him regularly to the thinnest pickings in the field. The worst thing one could do was to ask for fresh water on the job, regardless of the heat of the day; instead of iced water, given freely, the crews were expected to buy sodas at twice the price in town, sold by the contractor himself. He usually had a pistol—to protect the payroll, so it was said. Through the ranchers for whom he worked, we were certain that he had connections with the *Autoridades*, for they never showed up in camp to settle wage disputes or listen to our complaints or to go for a doctor when one was needed. Lord of a rag-tag labor camp of Mexicans, the contractor, a Mexican himself, knew that few men would let their anger blow, even when he stung them with curses like, "Orale, San Afabeeches huevones."

As a single worker, I usually ate with some household, paying for my board. I did more work than a child but less than a man, neither the head nor the tail of a family. Unless the camp was a large one I became acquainted with most of the families. Those who could not write asked me to chalk their payroll numbers on the boxes they picked. I counted matches for a man who transferred them from the right pocket of his pants to the left as he tallied the lugs he filled throughout the day. It was his only check on the record the contractor kept of his work. As we worked the rows or the tree blocks during the day, or talked in the evenings where the men gathered in small groups to smoke and rest, I heard about *barrios* I had never seen but that must have been much like ours in Sacramento.

The only way to complain or protest was to leave, but now and then a camp would stand instead of run, and for a few hours or a few days work would slow down or stop. I saw it happen in a pear orchard in Yolo when pay rates were cut without notice to the crew. The contractor said the market for pears had dropped and the rancher could not afford to pay more. The fruit stayed on the trees, while we, a committee drafted by the camp, argued with the contractor first and then with the rancher. The talks gave them time to round up other pickers. A carload of police in plain clothes drove into the camp. We were lined up for our pay, taking whatever the contractor said was on his books. That afternoon we were ordered off the ranch.

In a camp near Folsom, during hop picking, it was not wages but death that pulled the people together. Several children in the camp were sick with diarrhea; one had been taken to the hospital in town and the word came back that he had died. It was the women who guessed that the cause of the epidemic was the water. For cooking and drinking and washing it came from a ditch that went by the ranch stables upstream.

I was appointed by a camp committee to go to Sacramento to find some *Autoridad* who would send an inspector. Pedaling my bicycle, mulling over where to go and what to say, I remembered some clippings from the *Sacramento Bee* that Mr. Everett had discussed in class, and I decided the man to look for was Mr. Simon Lubin, who was in some way a state *Autoridad*.

He received me in his office at Weinstock and Lubin's. He sat, square-shouldered and natty, behind a desk with a glass top. He was half-bald, with a strong nose and a dimple in the center of his chin. To his right was a box with small levers into which Mr. Lubin talked and out of which came voices.

He heard me out, asked me questions and made notes on a pad. He promised that an inspector would come to the camp. I thanked him and thought the business of my visit was over; but Mr. Lubin did not break the handshake until he had said to tell the people in the camp to organize. Only by organizing, he told me, will they ever have decent places to live.

I reported the interview with Mr. Lubin to the camp. The part about the inspector they understood and it was voted not to go back to work until he came. The part about organizing was received in silence and I knew they understood it as little as I did. Remembering Duran in that camp meeting, I made my first organizing speech.

The inspector came and a water tank pulled by mules was parked by the irrigation ditch. At the same time the contractor began to fire some of the pickers. I was one of them. I finished that summer nailing boxes on a grape ranch near Florin.

When my job ended I pedaled back to Sacramento, detouring over country lanes I knew well. Here and there I walked the bicycle over dirt roads rutted by wagons. The pastures were sunburned and the grain fields had been cut to stubble. Riding by a thicket of reeds where an irrigation ditch swamped I stopped and looked at the red-winged blackbirds riding gracefully on the tips of the canes. Now and then they streaked out of the green clump, spraying the pale sky with crimson dots in all directions.

Crossing the Y Street levee by Southside Park I rode through the *barrio* to Doña Tránsito's, leaving my bike hooked on the picket fence by the handlebar.

I knocked on the screen door that always hung tired, like the sagging porch coming unnailed. No one was at home.

It was two hours before time to cook supper. From the stoop I looked up and down the cross streets. The *barrio* seemed empty.

I unhooked the bicycle, mounted it, and headed for the main high school, twenty blocks away where I would be going in a week. Pumping slowly, I wondered about the debating team and the other things Mr. Everett had mentioned.

Glossary

abuelitos: one's grandparents, from *abuelos*, or an elderly couple; *ito* at the end of a word means "little" or "dear."

aficionados: sport fans; enthusiastic ones are *fanáticos*.

aguardiente: brandy or rum, literally burning water; the cheapest brands are in the American class of rotgut.

alboroto: excitement in a crowd; usually starts as a hubbub and sometimes ends in a riot.

alcancía: a container for saving money, coins in a piggy bank.

arañas: two-wheeled public taxis drawn by a nag; nicknamed "spiders" on account of their high, spindly wheels.

arriero: a driver of pack animals—mules, burros, or horses.

arrimados: poor relatives or friends who stayed with a family temporarily when they had no place of their own; from *arrimarse*, "to get close to."

arroyo: a stream, creek.

asistencia: meals provided in camps and lodging houses or to persons who are not members of the family.

asqueroso: a most filthy person, a person so untidy or of such unhygienic habits as to make one's skin creep.

atajo: a small herd of cattle, a mule or burro pack train.

atole: corn gruel, about the consistency of thin mush; best when served too hot to drink.

autoridades: the authorities, the police; persons who enforce or administer the law and who generally behave so as to be held in awe.

avenidas: freshets or flash floods, usually following a cloudburst; not to be confused with city *avenidas* or avenues, passable thoroughfares, which country *avenidas* are not.

barrio: a neighborhood within a city containing an underground society of young males who regarded the area as their exclusive territory.

bola: any group of persons who got together to overthrow the establishment or to inflict upon it anguish or alarm; when armed and operating in the mountains, they were more accurately called "guerillas."

bolillo: a small French loaf, or an American; a name for both on account of the strong resemblance between them in complexion and crustiness.

brecha: a path through the forest, a trail.

bule: a gourd hollowed out and polished for use as a water flask or canteen; when empty and dry and turned upside down also a percussion instrument amusing to children.

calabozo: a small room about the size of a telephone booth in which schoolboys were locked while waiting punishment; preferably located in a stuffy, dark corner of the building.

calzones: pants for a man, or a boy soon to become one; made of unbleached cotton with bell bottoms and a wraparound waistband that made buttons and zippers in front unnecessary; a word on which some virile folk sayings are based such as, *fajarse muy bien los calzones,* translatable as "to show them who is the boss."

camello: a manual laborer who drudged at the hardest tasks and like a camel humped to make a living.

campesino: peasant or country dweller, a man of the *campos* or fields.

candil: if an ordinary beer can were cut in thirds, the bottom part capped, a wick inserted and the drum filled with kerosene, the result would be a candil.

cántaro: any clay jar with two ears and a wide mouth for bringing water from the arroyo.

capataz: a field foreman, an overseer of farm workers who was more inclined to behave like an overlord.

casa de vecindad: living quarters for various families arranged around a patio or courtyard, with common facilities for washing clothes, personal hygiene, drinking water and keeping an eye on one another.

casa redonda: roundhouse in a railway terminal where locomotives were serviced between runs ; more accurately, a half-round house because of its semi-circular construction.

centavos: pennies, small change, money on hand.

cerro: a hill, somewhat more than a *loma* and somewhat less than a *montaña.*

cervecería: brewery.

chanza: a job, or the chance of finding one.

charro: horseman bedecked in tight pants, bolero jacket, wide-brimmed hat, spurred boots, sarape, cartridge belt and holster, most of it trimmed with silver ornaments and gold braid.

chicano: a Mexican recently arrived in the United States and definitely a working-class type; a term of sympathy and identity among persons of this class.

chicote: a whip, used on mules to make them run faster, and on children to make them learn *vergüenza* and *respeto* (see below).

chiquihuite: a wicker basket with a looped handle, used for shopping in the *mercado.*

chota: the police, a policeman; also called a *cuico.*

chueco: the exchange or sale of goods stolen or acquired freely.

colegio: a private school for families who could afford one, different from *escuela,* for families who could not.

colonia: that part of a city where foreigners lived, more or less apart and according to nationality; the members of such a nationality; for instance, the *colonia americana de Mazatlán.*

comadre: a lady's relationship to parents whose baby she has presented for baptism, of whom she is the *madrina; comadres* frequently became intimate to the point of not being on speaking terms.

compadre: a gentleman's relationship to the parents of a baby he has presented for baptism, of whom he is the *padrino;* two adult males may bestow the honorary title of *compadre* on each other in an excess of fondness, especially when drunk.

consultorio: a doctor's office.

correo: the mail, or the post office.

corrida de toros: bullfight.

corrido: a dramatic or heroic story sung to the accompaniment of guitars; a sort of Mexican folk opera on subjects such as The Disobedient Son, The Great Flood of Papasquiaro, Juan Charrasqueado the Valiant One; a form of art of which every Mexican is capable.

curandera: a woman who practices folk medicine with herbs, unguents, brews, compresses, poultices, a little prayer, and much faith on the part of the patient.

diligencia: stagecoach; a more or less diligent vehicle, depending on the condition of the mules, the roads, and the rivers and on the absence of bandits.

director: the principal of a school, always addressed as *Señor Director.*

enganchador: an agent who went about the country recruiting workers for railway construction with promises of high wages, comfortable quarters, and steady promotion; the process being known as the *enganche* or hooking, which produced the *enganchado* or hooked one.

escribano: a public letter writer, a penman.

filarmónica: a town or village orchestra culturally a peg or two above the *mariachi* (see below).

fotingo: any jalopy, but especially a travel-worn Ford.

gachupín: a Spaniard; the only thing more disagreeable to a Mexican were two *gachupines.*

gallo: rooster; *muy gallo* meaning "cocky," "daring."

gasto: the amount of money set aside for buying food, the allowance for the family's groceries.

gente decente: persons who set themselves off as a better class on account of their delicacy of language, refined manners, wholesome thoughts, carriages and footmen and book learning; the opposite of decent people being the indecent.

gringo: a white-skinned foreigner but especially an American.

hacerle la lucha: to make one's living, to try hard.

huacal: a boxlike container for transporting chickens, pottery, and all manner of products to market; an openwork crate made of sticks tied together with thongs or rope, giving the appearance of a cage.

huaraches: sandals made of thongs laced to a heavy sole.

jalcocotecano: a native or resident of Jalcocotán; also *jalcocoteco.*

jarro: a jug, being a *jarrito* if small and *jarrón* if large.

jefe de familia: the head of the family, called *el jefe* for short; by whichever name now rapidly becoming extinct.

kiosko: in the center of the main plaza of a town, a raised construction of iron grilles, roofed and enclosed by railings, where concerts were given and patriotic speeches were made.

La Julia: police paddy wagon, also called *El Pullman Mexicano* and *La Chirona.*

larga: a candy bar made of brown sugar, designed for licking as it was very soluble in saliva.

lianas: a tropical ivy which twisted itself around trees, also known as bush rope.

lista de correo: general delivery.

loma: a hill somewhat smaller than a *cerro* (see above).

los ricos: the rich, never said by the rich about themselves.

machete: a heavy steel blade about thirty inches long, with a single edge, a grip, and a rounded tip; an all-purpose work tool and weapon.

machetero: one who worked with a machete.

maderistas: supporters and partisans of Don Francisco Madero, who ran for President of Mexico and thus started the Revolution of 1910.

maestro: master craftsman, teacher, a highly skilled artisan or artist.

mandado: the food staples bought and carried home for the meals of one family for the day.

manta: coarse cotton yardage for making clothing such as *calzones.*

marchante: customer, shopper; could be made into a very chummy greeting by adding *ito* or *ita*, thus, *marchantita*.

mariachis: ensembles of musicians who walked from place to place playing guitars, violins, trumpets, marimbas and harps, singing *corridos*, serenades, and laments of love; when serenading at four o'clock in the morning they were called *gallos*.

masa: cornmeal ground to a rough dough from which tortillas are made; people caught red-handed are said to be caught with their fingers in the *masa*.

mercado: marketplace.

merolico: a pitchman who hawked patent medicines, cure-alls, and fakeries of various kinds in *mercados* and street fairs.

mesón: a sort of rough motel for *arrieros* and their *atajos*; a caravansary entered by a *zaguán* consisting of a large open patio where men and beasts rested overnight.

metate: a three-legged slab of stone, about nine by fourteen inches, slanted forward, on which *masa* for tortillas is ground by hand.

milpa: corn field.

mixto: train composed of passenger and freight cars.

mochila: knapsack, bedroll, or bindle containing mostly rations surrounded by a blanket.

monte: the woods, a forest; any terrain with cover of trees or brush.

muy gallo: tough guy, fond of crowing about himself and apt to be touchy.

nayarita: a native or resident of the State of Nayarit.

nieve: snow; abbreviation for *nieve de leche*, meaning "ice cream."

niños decentes: the sons of the *gente decente*, scrubbed little prigs who went to school to learn how to become upper class.

ocate: pine kindling, highly combustible and aromatic; used for starting fires on the *pretil*.

olla: a large, deep pot made of clay used for boiling, steaming, and pressure cooking.

palacio de gobierno: the state capitol, where the important *autoridades* spent most of their time.

palacio municipal: city hall, where the not-so-important *autoridades* did likewise.

palo: tree or stick; a piece of wood.

palomilla: a group of persons, usually boys, who hung around together, practicing unseen the vices of their elders.

panocho: unrefined brown sugar molded in a flat-topped cone quite hard to crunch but extremely easy to lick.

patio: inner court of a house or public building; a yard enclosed by walls.

patrón: proprietor, landlord, employer, boss, the master; one who provides protection in exchange for hard work.

pelado: at the opposite pole from the *gente decente*, the *pelado* had no possessions, no income, no education, no refinement, no culture; literally, "one who has been peeled."

pendejo: fool, idiot, stupid fellow.

peón: unskilled laborer in agriculture, building trades, railway maintenance, highway construction, and the like; a *pelado* with a temporary job, whose employment was part of the process of being skinned.

pésame: condolences offered to a family on the death of kin.

peseta: one quarter of a peso.

peso: a unit of money once worth fifty cents of the American dollar, now devaluated to slightly more than eight cents; formerly a silver coin, the peso most commonly seen now is a scruffy piece of paper money called *lana* by *pelados* because it feels like worn-out flannel.

petaca: a small trunk or foot locker.

petate: straw mat used as a mattress when placed on the floor.

pilón: a bonus given to children by grocerymen, such as a chip of *panocha* or a jelly bean.

piñata: a paper pig, burro, chicken, or other animal, decorated with colored tissue paper and ribbons, stuffed with candy or peanuts and hung from the ceiling for the purpose of being demolished by a blindfolded person, armed with a stick, following which there is a scramble for the goodies; *piñata*-bashing is the climax of a party.

pizarra: a small slate used by schoolchildren instead of paper and pencil; could be wiped clean with a wet rag, a sponge, or with the tongue.

pizarrín: slate pencil, wrapped like a barber's pole.

plática: conversation between friends and neighbors; at its best a duet to no purpose other than matching wits, news, and gossip.

plaza de armas: the main plaza of a town.

poncho: a heavy blanket with a slit in the middle for the head to pass through, and worn like a cloak or cape.

porfiristas: supporters of President Porfirio Díaz, the dictator who was overthrown by the *maderistas.*

por mientras: temporary, until something better comes along.

portales: arcades around the *plaza de armas* occupied by shops and sidewalk displays of merchandise.

posada: an inn, hostelry.

postigo: a small door framed within a larger one through which vehicles entered the patio of a house by the *zaguán.*

pretil: adobe bricks mortared and banked against a kitchen wall to form a waist-high counter which served as a stove.

puestos: sidewalk shops laid out under the *portales* and around the *mercados;* also stalls in such places.

puros: cigars.

rancho: a rural homestead, a small piece of ground on which a family subsisted; the dwelling on such a place.

reata: rope or lasso.

respeto: consideration and esteem for one's elders, and all the ways in which such esteem was shown.

revolucionario: one who fought with or supported or sympathized strongly with Francisco Madero, Emiliano Zapata and other *jefes revolucionarios;* a believer in the need for drastic changes in Mexican society.

rurales: the special mounted police of the Díaz dictatorship that kept law and order in the countryside by means of violence and terror approved by the *autoridades.*

sarape: a colorful blanket with fringes at both ends, folded and worn over one shoulder jauntily.

segunda: secondhand store.

sentimiento: an emotional disturbance brought on by a real or imagined offense, injured pride, grief, homesickness, or the like.

Sierra Madre: the coast range of western Mexico.

soldadera: wife or companion of a Mexican soldier, or a freelance female who fought in the revolution; a combination helpmate, nomad housekeeper, mother, and front-line fighter.

sota: whip boy on a stagecoach.

tapanco: loft inside a cottage reached by a notched pole and serving as storage space or as a bedroom.

tequila: strong alcoholic beverage distilled from the century plant, sometimes pronounced "t' kill ya" by gringos unfamiliar with Spanish.

tienda de raya: company store on large plantations by which the *patrón* took back the wages he paid the *peones* through high prices and hanky-panky bookkeeping.

tortillera: a woman who made tortillas for sale.

tostón: half-dollar.

trabajo: work.

tranca: wooden bar inside a cottage to secure doors at night; a pole or timber so used.

vámonos: all aboard, when bawled by a conductor to alert train passengers.

varillero: an ambulant peddler who traveled from village to village selling notions, gimcracks, and knickknacks; also peddled gossip.

veredas. trails, foot paths.

vergüenza: a sense of shame, of personal dignity; conscience; doing right; modesty; responsible behavior; trustworthiness not based on the fear of being caught.

víbora: a poisonous snake, a money belt.

viva: hurrah; long live so-and-so!

zaguán: the hall or vestibule leading to a patio.

zopilote: turkey vulture.